CONFLICT AND CRISIS COMMUNICATION

Conflict and crisis communication is the management of a critical incident which has the potential for resolution through successful negotiations. This can include negotiating with individuals in crisis, such as those threatening self-harm or taking individuals hostage as part of emotional expression, and also critical incidents such as kidnapping and terrorist activities.

By focusing on the empirical and strong theoretical underpinnings of critical incident management, and including clear demonstrations of the practical application of conflict and crisis communication by experts in the field, this book proves to be a practical, comprehensive and up-to-date resource. Discussion of relevant past incidents – such as the 1993 WACO siege in the United States – is used to enhance learning, whilst an examination of the application of critical incident management to individuals with mental disorders offers groundbreaking insight from clinicians working in this area.

Conflict and Crisis Communication is an excellent source of reference for national and international law enforcement agencies, professionals working in forensic settings, and also postgraduate students with an interest in forensic psychology and forensic mental health.

Carol A. Ireland is a chartered psychologist, forensic psychologist and chartered scientist. She works for Mersey Care NHS Trust, where she is lead for sex offender therapies and crisis (hostage) negotiation, and acts as an advisor in crisis/conflict situations. She is also Director of Studies for the MSc in Forensic Psychology at the University of Central Lancashire, and Vice-Chair of the British Psychological Societies Division of Forensic Psychology.

Martin J. Fisher is a forensic psychologist, chartered psychologist and chartered scientist. Until June 2009 he was the area psychologist for the south central area of NOMS, and with responsibility for specialist services including drugs strategy, safer custody, and mental and physical health service provision. He is now the consultant psychologist in the HMPS Public Sector Bids Unit, as well as being a visiting lecturer in forensic psychology at the University of Portsmouth.

Gregory M. Vecchi is the unit chief of the Behavioral Science Unit (BSU), Federal Bureau of Investigation (FBI). Dr Vecchi conducts research, training and consultation activities in behaviour-based conflict analysis and resolution, crisis management, crisis communication and global hostage-taking. He has conducted extensive research and is published in the areas of conflict and crisis management and communication and he teaches, trains and consults executive law enforcement officers on the topic.

CONFLICT AND CRISIS COMMUNICATION
Principles and practice

Edited by Carol A. Ireland, Martin J. Fisher and Gregory M. Vecchi

Routledge
Taylor & Francis Group
LONDON AND NEW YORK

First published 2011 by Routledge
4 Park Square, Milton Park, Abingdon, Oxon OX14 4RN
605 Third Avenue, New York, NY 10017

Routledge is an imprint of the Taylor & Francis Group, an informa business

Typeset in Bembo
by GCS, Leighton Buzzard, Bedfordshire

British Library Cataloguing in Publication Data
A catalogue record for this book is available from the British Library

Library of Congress Cataloguing in Publication Data
Conflict and crisis communication: principles and practices/edited by Carol A. Ireland,
Martin J. Fisher and Gregory M. Vecchi.
p. cm.
1. Conflict management. 2. Interpersonal communication. 3. Negotiation. I. Ireland, Carol A. II. Fisher, Martin. III. Vecchi, Gregory M.
HM1126.C616 2011
363.2′3–dc22
2010034979

ISBN 978-0-415-61511-2 (hbk)
ISBN 978-0-415-61512-9 (pbk)
ISBN 978-0-203-33040-6 (ebk)

To my mum: for her guidance and continued inspiration. She never doubted me. You are my closest friend.

(Carol A. Ireland)

To Michele.

(Martin J. Fisher)

For Monica, my wife and best friend.

(Gregory M. Vecchi)

CONTENTS

LIST OF FIGURES AND TABLES

Figures

Tables

LIST OF ABBREVIATIONS

ALS	active listening skills
APA	American Psychological Association
ASAP	Assaulted Staff Action Program
BCM	Barriers to Change Model
BCSM	Behavioral Change Stairway Model
BISM	Behavioral Influence Stairway Model
BPS	British Psychological Society
BSU	Behavioral Science Unit
CCT	Crisis in Context Theory
CEOP	Child Exploitation Online Protection Agency
CID	Criminal Investigation Division
CIRG	Critical Incident Response Group
CISD	Critical Incident Stress Debriefing
CISM	Critical Incident Stress Management
CNT	crisis negotiation team
CNU	Crisis Negotiation Unit
CPR	cardiopulmonary resuscitation
CRIP	content/relational/identity/process [needs]
EFPA	European Federation of Psychologists' Associations
EPI	Early Psychological Intervention Subcommittee
ESC	Emotional and Spiritual Care team (Salvation Army)
FBI	Federal Bureau of Investigation
FIRE	Face, Instrumental demands, Relationship and Emotion
GAD	Generalised Anxiety and Depression Scale
HMPS	Her Majesty's Prison Service (UK)
HNCU	Hostage and Crisis Negotiation Unit
HOBAS	Hostage Barricade Database System

HPC	Health Professions Council
ICISF	International Critical Incident Stress Foundation
ICS	incident command system
IESE	Impact of Events Scale: Extended Version
IOM	Institute of Medicine
LEO	law enforcement officer
LEOSS	Law Enforcement Officer Stress Survey
MMPI	Minnesota Multiphasic Personality Inventory
NCNC	National Crisis Negotiation Course
NICE	National Institute for Health and Clinical Excellence
NIMH	National Institute of Mental Health
NIMS	National Incident Management System
NRM	Negotiated Resolution Model
NVOAD	National Volunteer Organizations Active in Disaster
OHSA	Occupational Health & Safety Administration
OIG	Office of the Inspector General
OPSI	Office of Public Sector Information
PBL	problem-based learning
PTSD	post-traumatic stress disorder
RDLU	Rapid Deployment/Logistics Unit
RCF	Readiness to Change Framework
RPG	rocket-propelled grenade
RPT	role-play test
SAFE	Substantive demands, Attunement, Face and Emotion
SDT	Self-Determination Theory
STEPS	Structured Tactical Engagement Process
SWAT	special weapons and tactics
TADMUS	Tactical Decision Making Under Stress
16-PF	16-Personality Factor Questionnaire

NOTES ON CONTRIBUTORS

Andrea M. Brockman, MS, is a clinical psychology doctoral candidate at Nova Southeastern University, Center for Psychological Studies, Florida. Ms Brockman has published and presented research in the areas of Internet crime, corrections and crisis negotiations. Her clinical and research interests are in the areas of police psychology, correctional psychology and crisis negotiations.

Samuel L. Browning, MS, is a clinical psychology doctoral candidate at Nova Southeastern University, Center for Psychological Studies, Florida. He was a certified police officer in the state of Georgia before beginning his doctoral programme. He has published and/or presented on topics including role playing as a measure of programme effectiveness, crisis negotiations and crisis intervention teams in law enforcement.

Joanna Capelin is a Chartered Psychologist and Forensic Psychologist and has worked for HM Prison Service for the last sixteen years. Currently Head of Psychology at HM Prison Kingston, Surrey, she has extensive experience of working with life sentence prisoners and has also managed an investigation team within the Service. She is a trained critical incident debriefer and is also involved in incident management through her work as a negotiation advisor and negotiator trainer. She holds a BSc in Psychology with English, an MA in Psychoanalysis and an MSc in Applied Criminological Psychology.

Martin J. Fisher is a Chartered Psychologist, Forensic Psychologist and Chartered Scientist. Until June 2009 he was the Area Psychologist for the South Central Area of NOMS with responsibility for specialist services including Drugs Strategy, Safer Custody, and Mental and Physical Health Service provision. He is now a Consultant Forensic Psychologist in the National Offender Management Service

(England and Wales) and continues to have input on clients in secure and mental health settings as well as being a visiting lecturer in Forensic Psychology at the University of Portsmouth. He has published work in the areas of risk assessment and hostage negotiation. He is currently CPD lead for the Division of Forensic Psychology of the British Psychological Society, as well as leading a working group for the Division on psychological testing in forensic settings. He is on the editorial board of the *British Journal of Forensic Practice* and is a certified expert witness.

Neil Gredecki is a Forensic Psychologist working in a secure forensic mental health setting. He has input into the assessment and treatment of forensic psychiatric patients both upon admission and during their period of hospitalisation. Neil has over seven years' experience working in secure forensic settings having worked for the National Probation Service, Her Majesty's Prison Service and the National Health Service. Throughout his career Neil has been directly involved in the assessment and treatment of offenders, including those with mental health and/or personality disorder diagnoses. In addition to being the lead first author on the internationally reviewed *Thinking Minds* group-based therapy, Neil is trained in the delivery of a number of accredited group therapies and has engaged in group-based therapies with violent and sexual offenders. Neil has experience in the selection and training of crisis negotiators and has delivered further training in the area to a range of professionals including the police, psychologists and prison-based staff. He has also acted as a Hostage Negotiation Advisor and has experience of being involved in the management of such incidents.

Carol A. Ireland is a Chartered Psychologist, Forensic Psychologist and Chartered Scientist. She works for Mersey Care NHS Trust at Ashworth Hospital, where she is the lead for sex offender therapies and crisis (hostage) negotiation, and acts as an advisor in crisis/conflict situations. She also works at the University of Central Lancashire, where she is the Director of Studies for the MSc in Forensic Psychology. At the university, as Director of Studies, she also leads on the postgraduate qualifications for the Child Exploitation Online Protection Agency (CEOP) and postgraduate qualifications in crisis communications. Dr Ireland manages her own consultancy firm, Bowland Psychological Services, delivering expert witness reports, training and consultancy. She has authored over 40 publications, including journal articles, books and book chapters, mainly on offending, consultancy and crisis (hostage) negotiation. Dr Ireland is currently Vice-Chair of the British Psychological Society's Division of Forensic Psychology.

Debbie Marsh is a Forensic Psychologist and Chartered Psychologist. She has worked for HM Prison Service for ten years, and in the field of negotiations for the past seven years. This work has included developing and delivering a negotiator training package to officers in HM Prison Service, providing specialist advice at critical incidents in HM Prison Service and providing specialist input to the Metropolitan Police Negotiator Training Course.

Abigail S. Tucker, PsyD, is a licensed psychologist in Denver, Colorado. She is the Program Manager of Forensics at Community Reach Center in Thornton, Colorado. Born and raised in Lehigh Valley, Pennsylvania, Dr Tucker completed her BA in psychology at Loyola College, Maryland, and her MS and PsyD in Clinical Psychology from the Center for Psychological Studies, Nova Southeastern University, Florida. After completing her internship at the Community Reach Center, Denver, Colorado, she relocated to the East Coast and completed her post-doctoral training at Eastern Shores Psychological Services as the Director of Forensics. The focus of her ongoing research includes forensics, community mental health and emergency services mental health.

Vincent B. Van Hasselt, PhD, is Professor of Psychology and Director of the Family Violence Program at Nova Southeastern University, Florida. He is also a certified police officer in the State of Florida. Dr Van Hasselt has published nearly 200 journal articles, books and book chapters including many on the assessment and treatment of family violence, substance abuse, and police stress and mental health. A licensed practising Clinical Psychologist, Dr Van Hasselt maintains a private practice specialising in the problems of emergency first responders.

Gregory M. Vecchi, PhD, is the Unit Chief of the Behavioral Science Unit (BSU) of the Federal Bureau of Investigation (FBI). Dr Vecchi conducts research, training and consultation activities in behaviour-based conflict analysis and resolution, crisis management, crisis communication and global hostage-taking. Dr Vecchi began his service with the FBI in Miami, Florida, in 1996, where he worked on a variety of organised crime and drug matters, both domestically and internationally. Dr Vecchi became an auxiliary crisis (hostage) negotiator in 1998 and was formally certified by the FBI in 2002 and later by the London Metropolitan Police Department in 2005. In his capacity as a field negotiator, Dr Vecchi responded to numerous warrant and barricade situations, co-managed the Miami Crisis Negotiation Team and trained local, state and federal law enforcement officers on a variety of crisis management and negotiation topics. In 2003, Dr Vecchi was promoted and transferred to the FBI's Critical Incident Response Group (CIRG), where he was assigned to the Rapid Deployment/Logistics Unit (RDLU) and subsequently to the Crisis Negotiation Unit (CNU) as a programme manager. During his time at RDLU, Dr Vecchi deployed to Iraq in support of counter-terrorism operations and while assigned to CNU he responded to and conducted research on international kidnapping matters. Prior to joining the FBI, Dr Vecchi was a special agent/criminal investigator with the US Department of Justice – Office of the Inspector General (OIG), US Department of Agriculture (OIG), and the US Army Criminal Investigation Division (CID). Dr Vecchi earned a PhD in Conflict Analysis and Resolution from Nova Southeastern University, Fort Lauderdale, Florida, in 2006, an MS in Criminal Justice from the University of Alabama, Tuscaloosa, Alabama, in 1999, and a BS in Human Resource Management from Park College, Parkville,

Missouri, in 1991. Dr Vecchi has conducted extensive research and is published in the areas of conflict and crisis management and communication. He also teaches, trains and consults executive law enforcement officers on the topic.

FOREWORD

Conflict can't be eliminated but it can be mitigated and managed. The more tools a conflict resolution practitioner is able to accumulate in his or her toolbox the greater the likelihood of success. Effective communication is the linchpin skill necessary to peacefully address conflict and crises.

Negotiation remains an art form that can be learned and improved upon through training and, practice. The hallmark trait of a professional is the never-ending quest for knowledge: knowledge that easily translates to practical application. *Conflict and Crisis Communication: Principles and Practice* achieves the invaluable and essential balance between theory and application. The talented and experienced authors who have contributed to this seminal work understand the importance of providing the reader with a strong theoretical foundation combined with application strategies and techniques deftly illustrated by case studies. Individual facts and circumstances, context and the totality of circumstances are recurrent themes in their situational approach.

Regardless of whether the operational milieu is a correctional institution, mental healthcare facility or a hostage/barricade situation, the ability to assess an individual's emotional stability, personality and motivation is paramount. Emotionally disturbed persons and subjects suffering from some form of mental disorder account for approximately half the crisis situations encountered by crisis negotiators. The authors strongly advocate the sound practice of negotiating with regard to the observable behaviour while staying clear of trying to diagnose and/or label a subject. A flexible approach to viewing personality disorders is suggested. Despite what a clinical diagnosis may suggest, each individual may present traits, characteristics and behaviours to different degrees along a continuum. Understanding how various personality disorders may derail a negotiation is a major factor in arriving at the most effective strategies, themes and techniques. Crisis negotiators must collect all available intelligence, plan and then actively manage the interaction. These best-practice approaches are clearly demonstrated throughout the work.

Negotiator selection and training are also highlighted. At a minimum, crisis negotiators should have maturity, resilience and patience. The most effective training to develop the essential skill sets is also discussed. Well structured role-playing scenarios are invaluable to a crisis negotiator's development. Emotion will always trump reason. Crisis negotiators must fully appreciate that strong emotions need to be addressed and have time to be vented before any meaningful attempts can be made at problem-solving. The authors illustrate the process necessary to influence and eventually modify a subject's behaviour. Active listening remains the baseline skill for crisis communicators to use in order to demonstrate empathy, build a working rapport and positively influence a subject. The behavioural influence stairway is fully explained and depicted by case examples of subjects who display both expressive and instrumental needs.

The management of crisis situations is crucial to the ultimate outcome. The authors remind us that when incident management falters, the costs are highly visible and many times result in the loss of life. Incident management is a complex process that relies on objective evidence and special input to maximise the chances for a positive resolution. Case studies of the Waco siege, the Moscow State Theatre siege and the Beslan school siege clearly depict how the pitfalls of over-confidence, selective exposure and confirmation bias can negatively impact on rational decision-making. Despite the professional agility and best efforts of crisis managers, not all critical incidents have a successful conclusion. At the end of the day, the subject has a free will and they may decide to exercise it in a counterproductive manner. In addition to the complexities of incident management, ethics must also be factored into the equation. A meaningful discussion is presented on the considerations necessary to effectively navigate a way through decision-making and the actions taken while maintaining one's professional integrity.

The book also considers the physiological, psychological and behavioural responses that may result from critical incidents. Trauma is a subjective experience and many times results in a discernible ripple effect. This issue is examined from the perspectives of both the victim and emergency responders. A thorough review of the history and evolution of critical incident stress debriefing and management is provided that accentuates the challenges, controversies and best practices. Additionally, the authors clearly distinguish the differences between an operational debrief and an emotional one. Both briefings are necessary but the goals and objectives are very different.

The behavioural dynamics experienced by victims of critical incidents is also an area of focus. Captivity is an important subject area for negotiators but many times receives scant attention or is overlooked completely. The authors look at this phenomenon from pre-incident to post-incident reintegration. The values and beliefs that a victim takes into captivity combined with their resiliency can determine the degree of the ordeal's impact and the length of recovery. The

Stockholm syndrome, an often misunderstood topic, is also clearly defined and illustrated through anecdotes.

The FBI provided me with the opportunity and privilege to steer their flagship crisis negotiation programme. I experienced first-hand the critical need for patience, flexibility and creativity when addressing conflicts and critical incidents. A former FBI executive once opined that crisis negotiation is law enforcement's most effective non-lethal weapon. I continue to share that opinion. The ability to peacefully resolve conflict has never been more in demand or relevant than in contemporary society. Virtually every week there seems to be another horrific incident of workplace violence taking place somewhere in our countries. Experts in the field of workplace violence prevention identify frustration as a result of communication breakdowns or a lack of communication as significant contributors to a number of active shooter incidents. The active shooter circumstance can easily morph into a hostage/barricade situation. Effective crisis communication skills can peacefully resolve conflict and save lives. That is why *Conflict and Crisis Communication: Principles and Practice* should become a 'go to' tool in every crisis negotiator's toolbox.

Stephen J. Romano
FBI's Chief Negotiator (retired)

Note: The views expressed in this book do not necessarily represent the views of the FBI.

1

CONFLICT AND CRISIS NEGOTIATION

The negotiated resolution model

Gregory M. Vecchi

This opening chapter bridges the gap between theory and practice by presenting a model for the attainment of desired negotiated outcomes. The negotiated resolution model (NRM) works in all aspects of negotiation but it is especially effective in high-conflict (instrumental) situations such as barricaded hostage or kidnapping events, as well as in crisis (expressive) situations such as barricaded crisis, suicide and psychopathological-related events. The NRM proposes a method for attaining a specified negotiated outcome based on the assessment (initial and continuous) of the subject's needs, conflict behavioural patterns and state of mind in order to determine the appropriate verbal skill sets to be employed. Embedded in the model is the continuous application of the Behavioral Influence Stairway Model (BISM: Van Hasselt *et al.* 2008), which is used to develop and maintain a relationship and credibility between the negotiator and the subject (individual in crisis/conflict) during problem-solving and crisis intervention processes, as well as dealing effectively with emotions during crisis intervention. Also embedded in the NRM are interaction manipulation techniques aimed at reframing the situation and influencing the perspective of the subject in order to obtain the desired outcomes of the negotiator. The chapter also focuses on when and how to use conflict and crisis negotiation techniques.

Negotiated resolution model

The NRM is a methodology by which to obtain desired negotiated outcomes through the assessment of the subject's needs and conflict behavioural patterns in order to determine instrumental or expressive states of mind. Once the type of mindset is determined, the negotiator is then able to select the most effective verbal skill sets to bring about the desired outcome: problem-solving for instrumental behaviour or crisis intervention for expressive behaviour (see Figure 1.1).

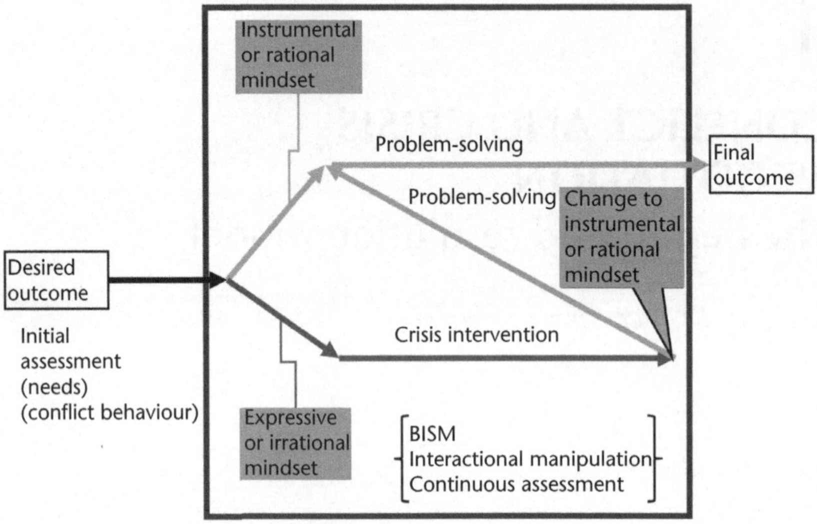

FIGURE 1.1 Negotiated resolution model

The NRM begins with the negotiator determining his or her *desired outcome* or end-game. For example, a law enforcement negotiator's desired end-game may be the surrender of the offender, whereas an investigator's desired end-game may be an admission or confession of guilt. In any event, it is critical to keep focused on the end-game throughout the negotiation even though it may be necessary to adjust it as a result of information obtained during the negotiation or because of circumstances outside the control of the negotiator. Once the negotiator determines the desired outcome, an *initial assessment* of the subject's needs (i.e. desires, objectives, values, etc.) and conflict behaviour (accommodating, avoiding, collaborating, competing or compromising) are used to determine instrumental or expressive mindsets. If it is determined that the subject has an *instrumental* or *rational mindset*, the negotiator would use *problem-solving* or *conflict negotiation* techniques to obtain the desired outcome. On the contrary, if it is determined that the subject has an *expressive* or *irrational mindset*, the negotiator would use *crisis intervention* or *crisis negotiation* techniques aimed at bringing the subject to a more instrumental or rational state of mind, at which point the negotiator would initiate problem-solving techniques to arrive at the final outcome. Throughout the process, the negotiator uses the *BISM* to develop and maintain a relationship and credibility between the negotiator and the subject during problem-solving and crisis intervention, as well as dealing effectively with emotions during crisis intervention in furtherance of moving the subject to a rational mindset. Moreover, the negotiator also uses *interactional manipulation* techniques aimed at reframing the situation and influencing the perspective of the subject in furtherance of obtaining the negotiator's desired outcomes. Throughout the negotiation process, *continuous assessment* is used by the negotiator to determine changes in mindset that signal adjustments regarding negotiation tactics in order to bring about the *final outcome*.

Determining outcomes

It is critical that the negotiator determine the *desired outcome* of the negotiation before interacting with the subject and keep the outcome in mind as the basis for the selection of the various strategies and tactics to be used during the negotiation. Ideally, the *final outcome* should match the *desired outcome*, such as surrender in a barricaded hostage situation or a confession during an interrogation; however, this may not be possible as a result of new information obtained during the negotiation, the behaviour of the subject or because of circumstances outside the control of the negotiator. For example, in 1999, Cuban prisoners took the warden and several correctional officers hostage at a correctional institution in St Martin Parish, Louisiana (Associated Press, 1999). The prisoners, who had finished their sentences, demanded that they be set free or they would kill the staff. As the negotiation progressed, it was determined that the prisoners had indeed completed their sentences but could not be released because they were Cuban citizens without legal status in the United States and Cuba refused to take them back. This situation resulted in them being in a 'legal limbo' which prevented their release into the United States or being deported abroad. Ultimately, a country agreed to take them, which resulted in the release of the hostages and their deportation out of the United States. In this example, the *desired outcome* of the negotiation was the release of the hostages without concessions; however, the *final outcome* had to be adjusted due to new information, legal considerations and decisions outside the control of the negotiators. Adjusted outcomes can also be based on the behaviour of the subject. For example, a commonly *desired outcome* of negotiation is the surrender of the offender without violence. This of course is dependent on the actions or inactions of the offender. If the offender kills a hostage on a deadline or if an individual who has symptoms of paranoid schizophrenia begins to shoot at police, then the *desired outcome* of no violence must be adjusted to a *final outcome* of deadly force. In this case, the negotiators might assist the tactical operators by persuading the offender to move near a window so the tactical team has the opportunity to use force via sniping, for example.

Assessing the subject

Assessing the subject involves evaluating his or her needs and conflict behavioural patterns. This step is critical to determining the mindset of the subject and choosing the most effective negotiation strategy and tactics for obtaining the negotiator's desired outcome.

Subject needs assessment

People communicate for the purpose of satisfying needs, whether they are substantive or expressive (Vecchi, 2002, 2003, 2004, 2009a, 2009b). Conflict occurs when there is a perceived blocking of important goals, needs or interests of one person or group by another person or group (Wilmot and Hocker, 1998). When this occurs, people tend to respond with the intention to remove the block in order to satisfy the need. For example, in a child custody battle, the losing parent (whose need to have her children is blocked by her former husband via a court order) could respond constructively by taking her ex-husband back to court or destructively by taking her children by force. Depending on the action taken, the behaviour can be adaptive or maladaptive (Rosenbluh, 2001). For instance, the wife could take an adaptive approach by returning the children and seeking counselling, or she could take a maladaptive approach by taking the children hostage, barricading herself and threatening to kill them if she is not awarded custody. In both approaches, the wife is attempting to resolve her conflict; however, the manner used to resolve the conflict in order to satisfy the need is a function of the wife's perception, previous experiences, level of resiliency and coping skills, which need to be accurately assessed by the negotiator.

Wilmot and Hocker (1998) see needs as falling into one of four general categories: (1) content, (2) relational, (3) identity and (4) process (CRIP). Content needs are external and tangible, such as food, money or transportation. These needs are fairly easy to ascertain because they are easily communicated by the subject to the negotiator. For example, robbing a bank in order to support a lavish lifestyle would be an example of a content need (money). Some common perceptions of conflict relating to content needs assessment include:

- People want different things.
- People want the same things.
- Perception of scarce resources.

Sometimes it is necessary for the negotiator to reframe these perceptions in a manner that makes the subject rethink his or her position, such as in the example of the orange (Vecchi, 2009a: 37).

> Monica and Janice are roommates. In their refrigerator is one orange, which they both need. Both Monica and Janice state that they want the orange, and they refuse to split it, therefore either Monica or Janice will get the orange or no one will. On the surface, it appears that they want the same thing and there are not enough resources (oranges) to satisfy their needs; however, through further inquiry, the negotiator determines that Monica wants to eat the meat of the orange and Janice wants to use the peel of the orange to bake a cake. The situation can now be reframed and described as Monica and Janice wanting different things with sufficient

resources rather than them wanting the same thing with scarce resources. This changes the perception of Monica and Janice from one of conflict to one of collaboration allowing for the needs of both parties to be satisfied: Monica gets to eat the fruit and Janice gets the peel for cooking.

Relational needs have to do with the way people treat each other with regard to respect and interdependence. Everyone has different expectations as to how they expect to be treated and these expectations differ based on social status and roles. For example, a person has different expectations with regard to interactions with their children versus parents versus peers versus supervisors, etc. If these expectations are not met, then negative feelings of disrespect and over-control will prevail (Vecchi, 2009a, 2009b).

Identity needs have to do with self-esteem issues with regard to saving face and protecting the self-image from the threat of feelings of humiliation, embarrassment, exclusion, unimportance and being demeaned. More importantly, identity needs translate directly to the need for physical and emotional security, recognition, control, dignity and accomplishment. These needs are the most personal of the CRIP needs, thus they are the hardest to disclose by the subject to the negotiator (Vecchi, 2009a, 2009b).

Process needs relate to the structure or forum of the dialogue such as the degree of creativity, participation and formal/informal and public/private contexts. Process needs are a matter of preference and are connected to personality. For example, in the case of a contested divorce, a married couple often has the option of choosing to resolve the divorce through court or mediation.[1] If the couple each differed in their preferences regarding court and mediation (formal versus informal), then the person who did not obtain their preference would experience a conflict with regard to process needs (Vecchi, 2009a, 2009b).

It can be difficult for the negotiator to accurately assess CRIP needs, especially relational and identity needs, simply because these needs are often of a very personal nature and emotion-based and the subject will hide or not reveal these needs until he or she is comfortable and trusts the negotiator. In these cases the negotiator must listen carefully to the context of the situation in order to gauge the accuracy of the needs assessment. Some people may initially be hesitant to reveal conflict associated with relational and identity needs but, in the interest of cooperation, may instead reveal a content need that is in conflict, which is only a symptom of the problem. For example, in a divorce mediation, a wife complains that her spouse is a 'bad husband' because he does not make enough money for them to raise their son in the manner which he deserves (content need conflict). Based only on that information, the mediator suggests three options: (1) the husband could find another job; (2) the wife could get a job; or (3) they could remove their son from private school and buy his clothes at discount stores. All of these suggestions serve to increase the amount of money available to the family; however, it turns out that lack of money is only a symptom of a bigger problem. When examined further, it is determined that the husband never lets his wife have any say in the way their son is raised; he dictates what he wears, where he goes to school and what sports he plays, which makes her feel excluded and demeaned (identity need conflict), as well as disrespected and controlled (relational need conflict). This overlap of CRIP needs is common early on in a negotiation, especially when it relates to identity and relational needs conflict. Negotiators should be aware that conflict in the context of interpersonal relationships oftentimes has identity and relational needs at its core, even though the subject may indicate content and process needs as being the primary issue. In other words, content need conflict solutions rarely succeed in interpersonal disputes (Vecchi, 2009a, 2009b).

Subject conflict behaviour assessment

When a person's needs, values, objectives, goals or desires are perceived to be blocked or delayed, conflict ensues, which causes certain behavioural tendencies or 'knee-jerk' reactions to the conflict. These reactions are subject to a person's personality make-up, which usually remains consistent throughout their lifetime with the exception of substance abuse, certain brain injuries and some mental disorders such as psychosis. In other words, a person's conflict behaviour or reactions to conflict are somewhat 'hardwired' and remain stable although these characteristics may mellow with age. Of course, this does not mean that a person automatically becomes a slave to his or her reactions; with effort, these unconscious tendencies can be managed and new behaviours learned (Vecchi, 2009a, 2009b).

Thomas (2002) posited that conflict is 'the condition in which people's concerns – the things they care about – appear to be incompatible' (p. 3). This view of conflict allows recognition that people have choices in how they deal with conflict and how the conflict process can be controlled through constructive choices. Thomas and Kilmann (1997) posit that assertiveness and cooperativeness are the most basic dimensions for describing choices in a conflict situation. Assertiveness is the degree to which a person tries to satisfy his or her own concerns and cooperativeness is the degree to which a person tries to satisfy the other person's concerns. Along these two dimensions fall five conflict handling modes: competing, collaborating, compromising, avoiding and accommodating. Figure 1.2 graphically depicts the assertive and cooperativeness dimensions along the x (cooperativeness) and y (assertiveness) axes. The five conflict modes are grouped along various dimensions in relationship to assertiveness and cooperativeness. When reading this figure, it is important to note where on the assertiveness/cooperativeness continuum a specified conflict mode falls.

When a competing mode is used, the person is both assertive and uncooperative, and satisfies his or her own needs at the expense of another. Collaborating is both assertive and cooperative, where a person tries to find a win-win solution that completely satisfies the concerns of both persons. Compromising is intermediate in both assertiveness and cooperativeness, where the person tries to find an acceptable solution that only partially meets both people's concerns. Avoiding

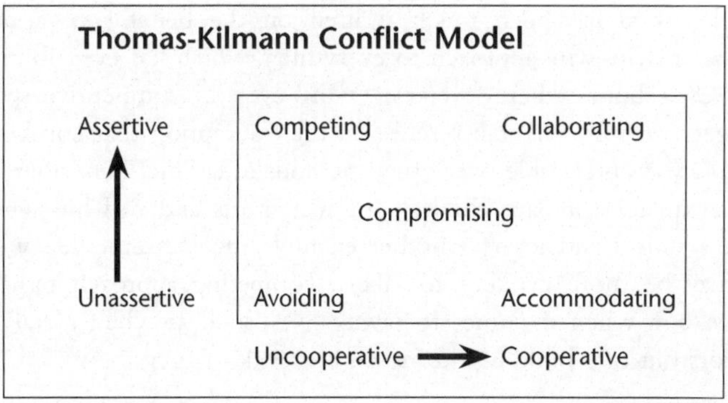

FIGURE 1.2 TKI Conflict Model (Thomas and Kilmann, 1997).

is both unassertive and uncooperative, where a person sidesteps the conflict without trying to satisfy either person's concerns. Accommodating is unassertive and cooperative, where a person tries to satisfy the other person's concerns at the expense of his or her own. It should be noted that these conflict-handling modes are aims or goals in a conflict situation rather than specific behaviours (Vecchi, 2006, 2009a, 2009b).

It is important to remember that none of these behaviours, by themselves or in a vacuum, are inherently good or bad. They all have costs and benefits and should be judged entirely within context; the success in handling conflict lies in knowing when to use each mode and having the skills to perform each mode effectively (see Table 1.1).

TABLE 1.1 Costs and benefits of conflict behaviours

Conflict behaviour	*Costs*	*Benefits*
Accommodating	Sacrifices needs	Helps other party
	Loss of respect	Restores harmony
	Loss of motivation	Builds relationships
Avoiding	No relationship	Reduces stress
	Delays	Steers clear of danger
	Resentment	Buys time
Collaborating	Time and energy	High-quality decisions
	Psychologically demanding	Resolution and commitment
	Vulnerable disclosures	Strong relationship
Competing	Strained relationships	Asserting position
	Decreased motivation	Possibility of quick victory
	Escalation of deadlock	Fast decision-making
Compromising	Partially sacrificed needs	Pragmatic and fair
	Superficial understandings	Speed and expediency
	Conflict not resolved	Maintaining relationships

For example, there has been much written on the benefits of a universally collaborative or 'win–win' approach to everything, which has even found its way into some US schools where 'everyone wins' even in competitive sports. This 'everyone gets a trophy' mentality relies on the assumption that collaboration or 'win–win' is always preferable over other methods of conflict behaviour; however, it fails to adequately prepare children for real sports and real life where there actually are winners and losers. Another example involves emergency situations where it may be more prudent to take a competing approach rather than a collaborative one when it comes to saving lives, such as when a staff member orders visitors out of a building during an outbreak of fire.

Outcome and relationship variables

The previous discussion of the importance of properly assessing and understanding subject needs conflict and conflict behaviour provides a baseline from which to engage in effective negotiation. This baseline provides a starting point for determining the *outcome* and *relationship* variables between the negotiator and the subject, and that provides the strategic basis from which to determine the most effective negotiation tactics aimed toward obtaining the negotiator's desired outcome (see Figure 1.3).

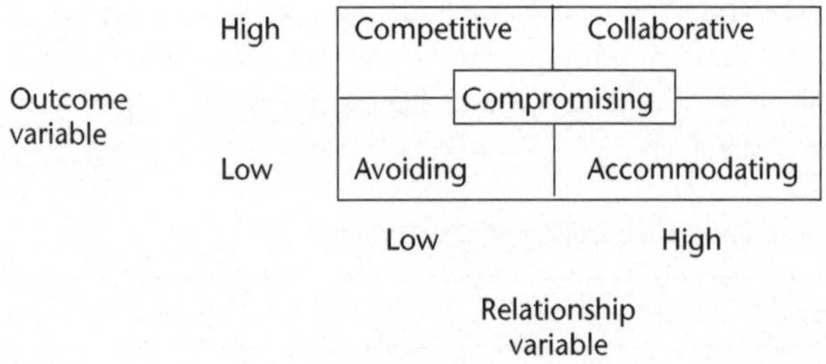

FIGURE 1.3 Conflict behavioural spectrum.

This process starts with the negotiator making a judgment as to the degree of importance placed on the desired outcome compared to the degree of importance placed on the relationship with the subject (Vecchi, 2006, 2009a, 2009b):

- If the negotiator places high importance on both the outcome of the negotiation and the relationship with the subject then the negotiator should engage in collaborating behaviour.
- If the negotiator places low importance on both the outcome of the negotiation and the relationship with the subject then the negotiator should engage in avoiding behaviour.
- If the negotiator places high importance on the outcome of the negotiation and low importance on the relationship with the subject then the negotiator should engage in competing behaviour.

- If the negotiator places low importance on the outcome of the negotiation and high importance on the relationship with the subject then the negotiator should engage in accommodating behaviour.

Typically, compromising behaviour should not be pursued as a desired outcome by the negotiator because it tends to only postpone the conflict for another time and can provide mixed signals to the subject. Of course, there are times when the outcome of the negotiation ends up becoming a compromise due to factors beyond the control of the negotiator (e.g. forced time limits, political interference, etc.).

Interactional manipulation

Sometimes there are situations that require the negotiator to obtain a specific outcome without regard to the relationship with the subject, such as in certain life-threatening situations. Barricaded hostage situations are one example. In these situations, the police cannot force the offender to surrender because there is a barricade or obstruction between the police and the offender (e.g., a wall, door, vehicle, etc.) so the only avenue of resolution is to convince the offender to surrender through negotiation. Normally in situations where the *desired outcome* of the negotiator overrides the importance of the relationship with the subject, the negotiator will engage in competing behaviour; however, in a barricaded hostage situation, engaging in competing behaviour would place the hostage in danger. These situations require the negotiator to engage in *interactional manipulation*, where the subject perceives that the negotiator is being collaborative when in reality the negotiator is actually engaging in competing behaviour.

Interactional manipulation is used to facilitate the desired outcome of the negotiator in instances where overt competing behavioural patterns would impede obtaining the negotiator's desired outcome. It is a subtle form of manipulation that works on affecting the perception of the subject by making it appear that the negotiator is being collaborative when s/he is not. The process begins by obtaining an agreement between the negotiator and the subject on the outcome of the situation which is cloaked in abstractness on the part of the negotiator. For example:

> A man addicted to prescription drugs uses forged scripts that he stole from a doctor to obtain Oxycontin and Valium from a local pharmacy. On his third attempt to obtain the drugs, the pharmacist, who realises the script is forged, refuses to provide the drugs to the man, who is experiencing severe withdrawal symptoms. In a fit of desperation, the man jumps over the counter and takes the pharmacist hostage while holding a knife to his throat. The police arrive and begin to negotiate with the man.

In this situation the negotiator must obtain the surrender or neutralisation of the offender or the pharmacist may die. To directly articulate this outcome to the offender would only serve to increase the danger to the hostage, so the negotiator must reframe the outcome in terms of 'helping' the offender and getting agreement with the offender on his (offender's) desire to be 'helped'. The negotiator does this by informing the offender that he knows the offender has a drug addiction problem and that he is not a criminal, just someone who made a mistake. The negotiator frames his 'help' in terms of the offender possibly going to a rehabilitation centre rather than jail in order to get help. As time passes, the offender's high emotional level will dissipate and he will most likely want help in getting out of the situation without painful consequences and he will look to the negotiator to assist him, as long as the negotiator is perceived as being collaborative.

In high-risk and dangerous situations, it is important to cement or freeze the *outcome* and *relationship* variables as high for both the negotiator and subject. This is accomplished by the negotiator obtaining an agreement with the subject on a specific outcome. In the above example, both the negotiator and the offender had different desired outcomes that were at odds with each other, which created a stalemate, in which the negotiator needed the offender to surrender and the offender needed his drugs and escape. In order for the negotiator to prevail, he had to define the outcome in a more abstract manner that was both palatable and agreeable to the offender. Once there was agreement on the part of the offender to be 'helped' (high outcome variable) and the negotiator was perceived by the offender as an ally in getting that 'help' (high relationship variable) then the offender exhibited collaborating conflict behaviour (see Figure 1.3). In analysing this situation, the negotiator actually maintained a competing conflict behaviour throughout the negotiation; however, by framing both variables in terms of 'helping,' the negotiator manipulated the offender's perception of the negotiator's conflict behaviour as collaborating, which influenced the offender to also collaborate, resulting in the offender ultimately surrendering.

A key point to this process is the purposeful absence of clarity on exactly what the negotiator means by 'help.' To the negotiator, 'help' simply means the surrender or neutralisation of the subject; exactly how this occurs is ultimately dependent on the action or inaction of the subject. For example, the offender in the above example agreed to surrender after rehabilitation became a believable option; however, if the offender had killed the pharmacist, the negotiator may have assisted the SWAT team in a tactical resolution such as influencing the offender to move towards a window so a sniper could apply deadly force. Regardless of the manner of the resolution, the negotiator obtains his or her objective, which is the surrender or neutralisation of the subject. Although both negotiated and tactical outcomes are legitimate depending on the actions or inactions of the offender, it is always preferable to resolve high-risk or dangerous situations in a peaceful manner by influencing the subject to engage in collaborating conflict behaviour.

Assessing instrumental and expressive behaviour in conflict and crisis situations

The ability to accurately assess instrumental and expressive behaviour in conflict and crisis situations is critical to successfully employing the most effective *conflict* and *crisis negotiation techniques*. To do this, the negotiator needs to carefully observe verbal and non-verbal cues that indicate whether the subject is rational (instrumental) or not (expressive). For example, people communicate on two levels: content and emotion (NCNC, 2003; Vecchi, 2009a, 2009b; Vecchi, *et al.*, 2005). These levels vary depending on the degree of conflict or crisis that a person is experiencing. For example, someone can say, 'I hate you' or 'I HATE YOU!' In both instances, the content is the same, but the emotional component is different; the former indicates content with no emotion or *instrumental behaviour* whereas the latter indicates content with emotion (in the form of anger) or *expressive behaviour* (Vecchi, 2009b) (see Figure 1.4).

Instrumental behaviour is prevalent in *conflict situations*, which are characterised by parties who are rational and goal-directed, produce substantive demands and require an outside party (law enforcement, negotiators, mediators, etc.) to assist in order to meet their needs (Vecchi *et al.*, 2005; Vecchi, 2002, 2006, 2009a. 2009b, 2009e). Examples of conflict situations include barricaded hostage situations, kidnapping, divorce mediation and political terrorism. In instrumental situations the focus is on *content* or *process* needs, such as trading hostages for ransom. Instrumental situations are rational and require problem-solving approaches (Fisher *et al.*, 2001; Vecchi, 2009a, 2009b, 2009e; Vecchi *et al.*, 2005). Expressive behaviour is prevalent in *crisis situations*, which are characterised by parties who are irrational, have no clear goals, produce non-substantive demands and are resistant to the

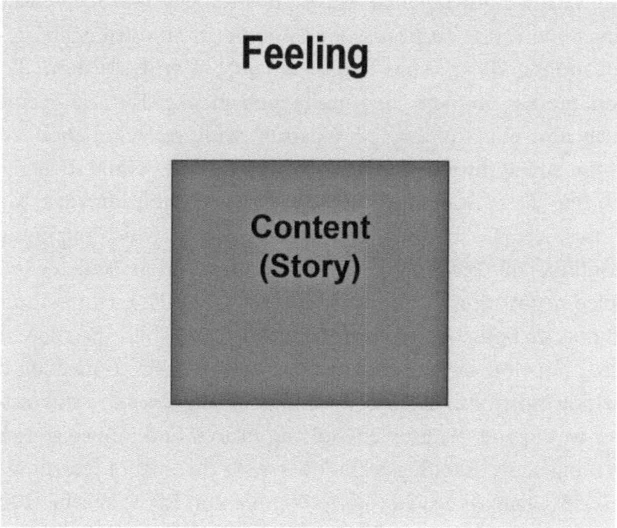

FIGURE 1.4 Content feeling levels (Vecchi, 2009b).

effort by others to resolve the situation (NCNC, 2003; Strentz, 2006). Examples of crisis situations include suicidal individuals, people with mental illness and grief/bereavement situations (Vecchi, 2009b, 2009c, 2009e). In expressive situations the focus is on *relational* or *identity* needs, such as ventilating emotion, saving face or earning recognition (Lanceley, 2003; McMains and Mullins, 2006; Rogan *et al.*, 1997; Slatkin, 2005; Strentz, 2006; Vecchi, 2009a, 2009b, 2009e; Vecchi *et al.*, 2005). In addition, expressive situations have the additional element of the subject having exceeded his or her ability to cope. Expressive situations are irrational and require crisis intervention approaches.

If the subject is displaying seemingly rational behaviour, then the negotiator would use problem-solving or *conflict negotiation techniques* (principled negotiation, bargaining); however, if the offender is displaying seemingly irrational behaviour, then the negotiator would use *crisis negotiation techniques* (crisis intervention) (Fisher *et al.*, 2001; Strentz, 2006; Vecchi, 2003, 2004, 2009a, 2009b, 2009e; Vecchi, *et al.*, 2005). Although this distinction seems clean, it is much harder to put into actual practice because sometimes instrumental and expressive behaviour can be difficult to accurately assess. For example, some cultures express rational behaviour as highly emotional and animated. To the uninitiated, it would seem the person was being irrational and in crisis, where in reality he or she was totally rational. Likewise, some cultures may not place an emphasis on emotion, which could be viewed as being rational even though a person is in crisis and has exceeded his or her ability to cope. In both of these situations, if the negotiator applies the wrong strategy and tactics, then the situation will only get worse and possibly result in violence. This is precisely why conflict and crisis negotiation is both an art and a science that requires both study and practice to be effective (Fisher, Chapter 7 this volume).

It is not unusual for instrumental and expressive behaviour to oscillate back and forth in conflict and crisis situations, such as going from instrumental-to-expressive in conflict situations and expressive-to-instrumental in crisis situations. For example, the mediation process employs an outside person (e.g. law enforcement officer, mediator, facilitator, etc.) to assist the parties with resolving their conflict and obtaining an agreement through problem-solving techniques and strategies; however, sometimes during these sessions, emotions flare and impediments to resolution occur. When this occurs, a 'high conflict' situation arises, which requires the outside person to continue the process (albeit in a more cautious and focused manner) using principled negotiation techniques (Fisher, *et al.*, 2001; Ury, 1991). If a situation arises where one or both of the parties exceed their ability to cope, usually as a result of feeling hopeless, helpless or powerless with respect to meeting their needs, then the situation turns into a crisis event. This changeover to crisis status requires the negotiator to suspend the problem-solving process and immediately begin crisis intervention using active listening techniques with the goal of returning the parties to their pre-crisis state (Rogan *et al.*, 1997; Slatkin, 2005; Vecchi, 2009a, 2009b, 2009e; Vecchi *et al.*, 2005). Once this state is reached, the problem-solving process can resume (Vecchi, 2009a, 2009b; Vecchi *et al.*, 2005).

Hostage-taking and victim-taking situations

The concept of instrumental and expressive situations, and their respective problem-solving and crisis intervention approaches, can be directly applied to specific conflict and crisis situations (Vecchi, 2009e). For example, hostage-taking (conflict) situations involve the involuntary holding of a person captive for 'instrumental' or tangible reasons; the individual needs the police or other authorities to meet specific demands (e.g. ransom, transportation, money) (Vecchi, 2002, 2003, 2009a, 2009b, 2009e). In these events, the captive is used as leverage to obtain other substantive goals (Vecchi, 2009a, 2009b; Vecchi *et al.*, 2005), such as when foreign nationals hold prison guards captive in exchange for the release of political prisoners, money and transportation. The Russian hostage situation that occurred in September 2004 (see Marsh, Chapter 8 this volume), involving the holding of children by Chechnya terrorists in exchange for releasing political prisoners (Mcevers, 2006) is an example of instrumental behaviour where problem-solving (*conflict negotiation*) techniques would be best applied.

In contrast, victim-taking (crisis) situations involve the involuntary holding of a person captive for 'expressive' or intangible reasons (Vecchi, 2009a, 2009b, 2009c, 2009d, 2009e; Vecchi *et al.*, 2005). Unlike hostage situations, the individual does not need the police or other authorities at the location. In these situations, the captive is held by a person who is in a highly emotional state (e.g. anger, jealousy, frustration), usually as a victim or 'homicide-to-be' (NCNC, 2003; Strentz, 2006), such as holding one's spouse captive as a result of an extra-marital affair or rejection due to an impending separation or divorce. In crisis situations not involving a captive, a person holds up for 'expressive' or intangible reasons; again, he or she does not need or want the authorities. In these situations, the person is oftentimes depressed or suicidal because of a real or perceived loss and the inability to cope with that loss (Strentz, 2006), such as being fired from a job or rejection by peers or loved ones. In crisis (captive and lone) situations, crisis intervention (*crisis negotiation*) techniques would be best applied (Vecchi, 2009a, 2009b).

Conflict negotiation (problem-solving)

Problem-solving is the process by which the negotiator helps the subject explore other alternatives and solutions to the conflict. McMains and Mullins (2006) identify the following problem-solving steps:

- Defining the problem
- Brainstorming all possible solutions
- Eliminating unacceptable solutions
- Choosing a solution that both the negotiator and subject can live with
- Planning the implementation
- Implementing the plan.

Part of effective problem-solving involves listening for distorted thinking on the part of the subject. As a result of life experiences, individuals develop different patterns of thinking. These thinking patterns influence how an individual perceives himself and how others perceive the individual. This can be viewed as a 'filter' through which the world is viewed, which may influence the subject's reaction to events and lead to emotional distress and crisis. Sometimes these distortions affect the potential for problem-solving and must be addressed by the negotiator (Vecchi, 2009a, 2009b).

Another factor in problem-solving involves the concept of problem ownership (NCNC, 2003). Although it is the duty of the negotiator to assist the person with problem-solving, the problem belongs to the person, not the negotiator. Each person 'owns' their own problems, thus they also 'own' their own emotional reaction to the problem and subsequent actions. It is important that the negotiator should never accept responsibility for another person's problem or actions because the final responsibility belongs to them. This sets an important social boundary that must be established and remain between the negotiator and the subject. For example, if the subject says, 'If I kill these people, you will be responsible for their deaths!' the negotiator should reject taking responsibility for the subject's proposed actions by saying, 'You will be responsible for their deaths because of your decision to do so' (Vecchi, 2009a, 2009b).

Principled negotiation

In conflict situations, rational, problem-solving strategies and techniques work best in most cases, especially approaches that provide the perception of the most collaborative gain for all parties and one which gives all stakeholders the perception of ownership throughout the process. Principled negotiation is the name given to the interest-based approach championed by Fisher *et al.* (2001). Principled negotiation is a problem-solving approach that advocates four fundamental principles to negotiation: (1) separating the people from the problem; (2) focusing on interests, not positions; (3) inventing options for mutual gain; and (4) insisting on objective criteria. Unlike positional bargaining, principled negotiation gives the perception of ownership of the outcome of the negotiation to all the stakeholders. This approach to negotiation addresses *content* and *process* need issues in conflict situations, such as barricaded hostage situations, kidnappings and high-stakes mediation where the parties are rational and focused on the outcome (Vecchi, 2009a, 2009b).

Separating the people from the problem refers to the emphasis of the negotiation whereby the negotiator focuses on the behaviour of the person, not the person as a whole. This assists in guarding against the perception that the negotiator is stereotyping the subject as being a 'bad person'. Instead, the negotiator should focus only on the subject's 'bad' behaviour so it can be isolated, thus providing the opportunity for the person to talk about it in the context of mitigation without fear of losing face (Fisher *et al.*, 2001; Vecchi, 2009a, 2009b).

Negotiating interests means negotiating about things that people really want and need, not what they say they want or need (Vecchi, 2002, 2003). People tend to take extreme positions designed to counter their opponent's positions; however, if asked why they are taking those positions, it often turns out that the underlying reasons – their true interests and needs – are actually compatible with and not mutually exclusive of the other's interests, as previously believed (Fisher *et al.*, 2001; Ury, 1991; Vecchi, 2009a, 2009b).

By focusing on interests, disputing parties can more easily fulfil the third principle – inventing options for mutual gain. This means negotiators should look for new solutions to the problem that will allow both sides to win, not just fight over the original positions, which assume that for one side to win the other side must lose (Fisher *et al.*, 2001; Vecchi, 2009a, 2009b).

Insisting on objective criteria for decision-making is paramount. While not always available, if some outside, objective criteria for fairness can be found, this can greatly simplify the negotiation process. This gives both sides more guidance as to what is 'fair' and makes it hard to oppose offers within this range (Fisher *et al.*, 2001; Vecchi, 2009a, 2009b). Negotiators also need to know what alternatives are available, as prematurely accepting or rejecting an agreement may be worse than the one that might otherwise have been achieved if other alternatives had been explored (Fisher *et al.*, 2001; Ury, 1991; Vecchi, 2009a, 2009b).

As an example of principled negotiation, let's look at the previously mentioned scenario regarding the drug addict who took the pharmacist captive:

- *Separating the people from the problem.* Throughout the negotiation, the negotiator focuses on the behaviour of the offender and separates his 'bad' behaviour (taking the pharmacist captive) from the fact that the offender is suffering from a drug addiction and has no criminal record.
- *Focus on interests, not positions.* As the negotiation progresses, the man becomes depressed and demands to be set free or he will kill himself. The negotiator focuses on the fact that the man needs help and the negotiator is there to help him via social support and coping suggestions.
- *Inventing options for mutual gain.* The man becomes focused on going to jail, which is not an option in his mind. The man's distorted thinking leads him to the assumption that there are only two options to resolving the situation: going free or going to jail, and he insists on going free. In response, the negotiator helps the man to articulate and discuss the 'universe' of possibilities (being killed, being set free, escaping, jail and rehabilitation). In the end, the idea of rehabilitation moves the negotiation out of stalemate, as the man gets 'help' and doesn't go to jail and the negotiator ends the situation with the apprehension of the man.
- *Insisting on objective criteria.* Once the negotiator and the man agree on the outcome (rehabilitation) the man is still concerned about being 'arrested' because he equates being arrested with going to jail. To overcome this fear, the negotiator 'paints the picture' of how the man is to surrender by telling

him that he will need to disarm himself and walk out of the pharmacy to police officers who will place handcuffs on him and take him to the office to be 'processed,' prior to seeing a medical doctor for rehabilitation options. The 'processing' is described to the man in terms of being 'booked', which is a universally accepted objective criterion that everyone has to endure regardless of whether they go to jail or rehabilitation.

Conflict negotiation techniques in law enforcement applications

By definition, conflict situations are rational and substantive and involve the perception that action is required in order to obtain the stated goals, needs or interests (Lanceley, 2003; McMains and Mullins, 2006; Rogan *et al.*, 1997; Slatkin, 2005; Strentz, 2006; Vecchi, 2009a, 2009b, 2009e; Vecchi *et al.*, 2005). For example, in barricaded hostage and kidnapping situations, this action manifests itself as the taking of people against their will and threatening their lives in order to leverage specific action or obtain something tangible from someone else (the authorities in barricaded hostage situations or the family in kidnapping situations). Actions may include the release of political prisoners, transportation, escape or ransom. In other words, there is an understanding that there is something for trade. In this context, the hostage-taker is the seller, the negotiator is the buyer and the hostage is the capital used by the hostage-taker in exchange for a desired outcome (Cooper, 2004; Vecchi, 2009a, 2009b).

Historically, the most successful traders are those who can best understand the other party's needs and desires and who are capable of developing and operating the means to take advantage of them. In these situations, the best deals are those that provide the highest measure of perceived satisfaction to both parties (Cooper, 2004; Vecchi, 2009a, 2009b). In most cases, the negotiator is faced with demands that he or she cannot meet (releasing political prisoners, changing foreign policy, escape, promise of no prosecution, etc.). Due to the high stakes involved, the negotiator cannot simply walk away or immediately reply that the terms are impossible, but must find an alternative that will appeal to the hostage-taker and secure the safe release of the hostage(s). This is where the process of selling begins, where the negotiator persuades the hostage-taker to release the hostage for a much more realistic price than what was previously demanded (Cooper, 2004; Vecchi, 2009a, 2009b). For example, an initial demand of '$1 million dollars and a helicopter' can be reframed as 'you want money and transportation' (NCNC, 2003; Vecchi, 2009a, 2009b). This reframed demand can be downgraded further to releasing the hostages in exchange for surrendering out of view of the media or even a pizza. The process of selling also relates to the negotiator, in that the hostage-taker has to perceive that the negotiator is trustworthy and acting in good faith or simply 'trying'. Cooper (2004) summed up this process:

> Hostage taking is, in essence, a defensive action. The hostage taker must be sold on the idea that, with each passing moment, his precious merchandise

> is becoming less and less valuable, that his power, and the protection the hostage affords him, is ebbing away. He must not be forced into desperate action but gently persuaded to see, sensibly, the realities of his position and the advantages in any bargain that might be offered to him. (p. 102)

Simply stated, a good negotiator will create the illusion that there is no better deal possible and that what is currently on the table is the best deal going under the circumstances (Vecchi, 2009a, 2009b).

Advanced conflict negotiation techniques in law enforcement applications

The focus of any negotiation is to obtain the best deal for yourself or for the entity you are representing. If possible, it is desired that the negotiation also meets the needs of the other party; however, in barricaded hostage and crisis situations, the focus is on obtaining rapid compliance and surrender of the hostile party, which requires the negotiator to move beyond standard communication techniques. Mullins (2002) used a five-step model developed by Ury (1991) and applied it to law enforcement negotiations (Vecchi, 2009a, 2009b):

1. Don't react – go to the balcony
2. Step to their side
3. Change the game
4. Build a golden bridge
5. Make it hard to say no.

The first step: *Don't react – go to the balcony*, relates to the very common practice of verbal attacks on the negotiator (Mullins, 2002; Ury, 1991). It is natural for the negotiator to want to verbally retaliate against the subject, but this serves only to make the situation worse and risk failure (Vecchi, 2009a, 2009b). This technique requires that the negotiator step back and become an observer to the communication process, akin to watching a play from a balcony (Mullins, 2002; Ury, 1991). In this way, the risk of emotional outbursts by the negotiator is reduced. The key is for the negotiator to keep his or her eye on the target of obtaining compliance. Mullins (2002) provides some approaches:

- Use pauses instead of responding immediately.
- Slow the pace of the conversation to reduce emotions. ('I'm trying to write down what you are saying so I don't forget. Could you slow down a little?')
- Rephrase what the subject just said in non-emotional terms.
- Take a time-out.

The second step, *Step to their side*, refers to developing the perception that the negotiator is an ally to the subject (Mullins, 2002; Ury, 1991). This is accomplished through the perception of the subject that the subject and the negotiator are partners and that, to a degree, the subject and negotiator are working against the rest of the police (Mullins, 2002; Ury, 1991). This is an 'us against the world' approach that is based on the assumption that the rest of the police do not care to solve the situation peacefully or meet the needs of the subject and which requires the subject and negotiator to work together to find a solution that the rest of the police. will accept (Vecchi, 2003, 2004, 2009a, 2009b). Mullins (2002) provides some approaches:

- Demonstrate to the subject that the negotiator is concerned and cares.
- Treat the subject as a real person and acknowledge his or her concerns or views.
- Search for areas of agreement beyond the instant situation (sports, movies, etc.).
- Use words of familiarity (subject's first name, insisting the subject use the negotiator's first name, slang, contractions, etc.).
- Obtain compliance without being forceful or confronting.

The third step, *Change the game*, pertains to reframing rather than rejecting outright the demands of the subject (Mullins, 2002; Ury, 1991). Subjects naturally expect that their demands will be rejected by the police and they can be taken off guard when the negotiator replies that he/she will see what can be done or attempts to reframe in a manner that is not inflammatory, such as reframing a request by the subject for 'a car and $100,000' to 'you need transportation and money … I'll see what I can do' (Vecchi, 2009a, 2009b). Mullins (2002) further suggests:

- Focus on problem-solving and ignore personal attacks; ask the subject: 'How can we work together?'
- Use open-ended questions to make the subject think about his/her position and force a reality check.
- Reframe personal attacks into future solutions.

The fourth step, *Build a golden bridge*, is the process by which the negotiator makes it easier for the subject to say 'yes' than 'no' (Mullins, 2002). This is accomplished by soliciting ideas from the subject and then showing the flaws in some of those ideas, such as saying, 'If you really want to get legal custody of your kids, what do you think might be a better way to do this? What if they accidentally get hurt in this situation; how will that play with the judge?' (Vecchi, 2009a, 2009b). Mullins (2002) describes the 'go slow to go fast' process:

> The negotiator should slow down the negotiation process and get the hostage taker in a 'yes-saying' frame of mind. The negotiator who opens initial conversations with an attempt to get the hostage taker to release

all the hostages and surrender is doomed to failure. Instead, the negotiator should begin the process by getting the hostage taker to agree to several small requests. Not shouting, staying on the telephone or sitting in a chair are all small requests a negotiator could make to begin getting compliance from the hostage taker. Once the hostage taker begins saying 'yes,' the negotiator can then escalate the requests into larger requests designed to resolve the situation'. (p. 70)

The fifth step, *Make it hard to say no*, pertains to the ability of the negotiator to couch solutions that are perceived to be a win–win situation by the subject (Vecchi, 2009a, 2009b). The ability of the negotiator to work out an agreeable solution where the subject perceives surrender as the most advantageous resolution is important to a peaceful resolution (Mullins, 2002). The use of power by the negotiator in a subtle manner is also a key to resolving the situation. For example, instead of the negotiator saying, 'If you don't come out, I'm sending in the SWAT team,' the negotiator might say, 'The command staff is getting frustrated at our lack of progress here, and they are thinking of calling in the SWAT team. Let's come to an agreement so they won't have to do this' (Vecchi, 2009a, 2009b).

Crisis intervention

A crisis is the result of a conflict gone awry. Caplan (1961) and Carkhuff and Berenson (1977) described a crisis as that which a person perceives as presenting insurmountable obstacles to achieve desired goals or outcomes. Greenstone and Leviton (2002) and James and Gilliland (2001) further stated that in a crisis there is the sense that these goal and outcome impediments cannot be managed through the usual problem-solving methods. As discussed earlier, Wilmot and Hocker (1998) defined conflict as the perceived blocking of important goals, needs or interests of one person or group by another person or group. A person's response to conflict can be constructive or destructive. For example, in a child custody battle, the losing parent (whose need to have her children is blocked by her former husband via a court order) could respond constructively by taking her ex-husband back to court or destructively by taking her children by force. In the event of the latter, a crisis may result if she is unable to cope with the problem (Vecchi, 2009a, 2009b).

Crisis situations place demands on the subject to act in furtherance of resolving the crisis. Depending on the action taken, the behaviour can be adaptive or maladaptive (Rosenbluh, 2001). In the previous example, the wife could take an adaptive approach by returning the children and seeking counselling. Or, she could take a maladaptive approach by taking the children hostage, barricading herself, and threatening to kill them if she is not awarded custody (Vecchi, 2009a, 2009b).

Adaptive behaviour results in positive crisis resolution and maladaptive behaviour results in negative resolution. For example, a situation involving a man discovering that his wife has cheated on him has the potential to incite a crisis. How the man deals with the situation can be either adaptive or maladaptive, depending on his coping and social skills. An example of an adaptive strategy would be for the man to gather all information possible and constructively confront his wife about the situation and pursue marital counselling. An example of maladaptive behaviour would be for the husband to take his wife captive with the intent to kill her for cheating on him. In both examples, the man is attempting to resolve the crisis; however, in the former example, the negotiator would encourage the adaptive behaviour, whereas in the latter example, the negotiator would discourage the maladaptive behaviour by implementing the strategies and tactics of crisis intervention to assist in ending the crisis in a more adaptive manner (Vecchi, 2009a, 2009b).

Whether or not a situation is viewed as a crisis depends on current perception, previous experiences, level of resiliency and coping skills. This explains why a particularly horrific event will result in crisis for some but not others. For example, a police investigation involving a murder may have minimal impact on the seasoned homicide detective who has become desensitised to even the most gruesome crime scenes. By contrast, the murder scene could be a crisis-triggering event for the victim's neighbour who discovered the body (Vecchi, 2009a, 2009b).

Most expressive situations requiring negotiator intervention are due to a significant loss or rejection, termination from employment, a decline in health status, financial reversal or loss of freedom. Two or more losses within a short period of time (often referred to by police negotiators as a 'double whammy') are often the 'final straw' or antecedent that sends a person into crisis (McMains and Mullins, 2006; NCNC, 2003; Vecchi, 2009a, 2009b).

Once coping and social support mechanisms fail and a person falls into a crisis state, normal functioning is disrupted. What is normally resolved at a rational or cognitive level (as in conflict situations) is now dealt with at an emotional or affective level, which further enhances the volatility of the crisis, much in the same manner as throwing fuel on a fire (Vecchi, 2009a, 2009b; Vecchi *et al.*, 2005). Therefore, providing social support by restoring the ability of a person to cope through the re-establishment of baseline functioning levels is the primary purpose of crisis intervention (Hendricks and Byers, 2002; James and Gilliland, 2001; McMains and Lanceley, 2003; Roberts, 2000; Vecchi, 2009a, 2009b, 2009c, 2009d; Wiger and Harowski, 2003).

Crisis intervention process

For the negotiator, the key to implementing crisis intervention techniques towards adaptive resolution is to focus on understanding the needs of the subject, which is oftentimes hidden behind more seemingly substantive concerns (Vecchi, 2009a, 2009b, 2009d). For example, an elderly man who takes his daughter captive and threatens to harm her may appear to be mentally ill, but in reality he doesn't want her to place him in a nursing home because he feels he will lose control of his life (Vecchi, 2009a, 2009b). In this example, the negotiator would attempt to unveil this 'hidden' need and use it as a 'hook' to develop a theme in furtherance of resolving the crisis in an adaptive manner (NCNC, 2003). Therefore it is important to note that people don't always say what they mean, so it is important to attempt to listen for the meaning behind the words in order to reveal the needs of the subject (Vecchi, 2009a, 2009b; Vecchi *et al.*, 2005). Remember, negotiators don't meet demands, but they do satisfy needs (NCNC, 2003).

The crisis intervention process comprises six steps: (1) establishing and maintaining effective communication; (2) buying time; (3) defusing intense emotions; (4) identifying the precipitating event; (5) gaining intelligence; and (6) transition to problem-solving (Vecchi, 2009a, 2009b; Vecchi *et al.*, 2005; McMains and Mullins, 2006).

Step 1: Establishing and maintaining effective communication

Establishing communication is the vehicle for the delivery of crisis intervention strategies and tactics. Thus, in crisis intervention, it is important that the negotiator establish effective communication and actively listen to what the person is saying. When speaking to the person, it is important to speak slowly and calmly and to choose your words, tone and manner with care. How the negotiator says something is much more important than what is said; content can be easily adjusted by telling the subject that you simply are trying to understand; however, it is much more difficult to fix an attitude that is perceived by the subject as being 'bad.' In addition, the communication delivery should be deliberate, methodical and, most importantly, non-judgmental (Vecchi, 2009a, 2009b).

Step 2: Buying time

Time can be one of the negotiator's best tools simply because it is difficult for most people to maintain high emotional levels for extended periods. The passage of time tends to decrease stress levels and sets the stage for obtaining some semblance of rational behaviour on the part of the subject. Buying time is sometimes known as 'verbal containment', which is the process of keeping the person 'occupied' in discussions with the negotiator (Vecchi, 2009a, 2009b).

Step 3: Defusing intense emotions

People who make clear statements of feeling are in a better position to solve their problems. When a negotiator is able to reflect the subject's feelings, the negotiator is perceived as being understanding, which is the basis of developing a relationship in which the subject is ready to accept and act upon the suggestions of the negotiator, thus ending the crisis. The emotional reaction to a crisis situation and subsequent behaviour based on that reaction is what makes a situation a crisis, not the facts or content of the situation. How a person feels about a situation will strongly influence their behaviour; therefore listening for and addressing the intense emotions behind the content will help control the subject's behaviour. Dealing with emotions is a baseline skill that every negotiator must learn because intense emotions are a hallmark of crisis situations (Lanceley, 2003; McMains and Mullins, 2006; Rogan *et al.*, 1997; Slatkin, 2005; Strentz, 2006; Vecchi, 2009a, 2009b; Vecchi *et al.*, 2005).

Step 4: Identifying the precipitating event

A precipitating event is the 'last straw' or 'trigger' that puts a person into crisis. The precipitating event is usually associated with some sort of loss, which could be the result of losing a job, losing a significant other or losing money. Identifying the precipitating event is crucial in laying the groundwork for problem-solving because it identifies the problem that needs solving (NCNC, 2003; Vecchi, 2009a, 2009b).

Sometimes, the subject is unaware or confused about the nature of the precipitating event, as the conflict or crisis may involve a conflict of values. Values are what people believe are important and cherish, and they are the 'hooks' used by negotiators to assist in alleviating the crisis (NCNC, 2003; Vecchi, 2009a, 2009b). For example, a religious person who values non-violence is robbed and defends himself, resulting in the death of the robber. This results in conflict between his convictions of non-violence and his violent actions (even though justified), which triggers a crisis. In this situation, it is necessary for the negotiator to assist the person in clarifying his values. For instance, the negotiator could point out that the death of the robber was unintended and in blind reaction to the actions of the robber. Through the attachment of 'intent' as a requirement to defining something as violent, the action of the person can be reframed as not violating the value of non-violence, thus alleviating the internal conflict and setting the stage for problem-solving (Vecchi, 2009a, 2009b).

Step 5: Gaining intelligence

Gaining intelligence concerns the ongoing assessment of the crisis situation. This goal strives to determine the lethality or potential harm to the subject and others, formulating proposed courses of action and options to be considered after the crisis is over, such as referral for therapy, medical follow-up, or incarceration (Vecchi, 2009a, 2009b).

Step 6: Transition to problem-solving

Once the negotiator has moved the subject to a more instrumental or rational state of mind, the negotiator can then transition to problem-solving (see previous section) in order to arrive at the final outcome. This is a critical point because crisis intervention alone will not resolve anything; resolution can only be brought about through problem-solving, which requires the subject to be in a rational mindset and view the negotiator as credible (Vecchi, 2009a, 2009b).

Behavioral Influence Stairway Model

The Behavioral Influence Stairway Model (BISM) (see Figure 1.5) is used throughout the conflict and crisis negotiation process by the negotiator to develop a relationship and maintain credibility with the subject and is a key component of the *interactional manipulation* process with regard to keeping the relationship variable high (see Figure 1.3). The BISM is also used to move a subject from an expressive to an instrumental mindset so the negotiator's *desired outcome* can be achieved through problem-solving. Law enforcement negotiators have honed this process over the past 30 years to be effective even in the most volatile of situations and this model has proved to be highly effective in resolving crises without injury and within a relatively short period of time (NCNC, 2003; Vecchi, 2009a; 2009b; Vecchi *et al.*, 2005).

The BISM graphically depicts and explains the process of establishing a positive relationship between the negotiator and the subject and moving the mindset of the subject from *expressive behaviour* to *instrumental behaviour*, which allows for the negotiator to influence and ultimately persuade the subject to do as the negotiator suggests with the goal of obtaining the negotiator's *desired outcome*. This is accomplished in four stages as a product of time that includes active listening, empathy, rapport and influence. The upward arrow depicts the movement from *no relationship/expressive behaviour* to *relationship/instrumental behaviour* and the downward arrow represents mistakes made by the negotiator ('falling down the

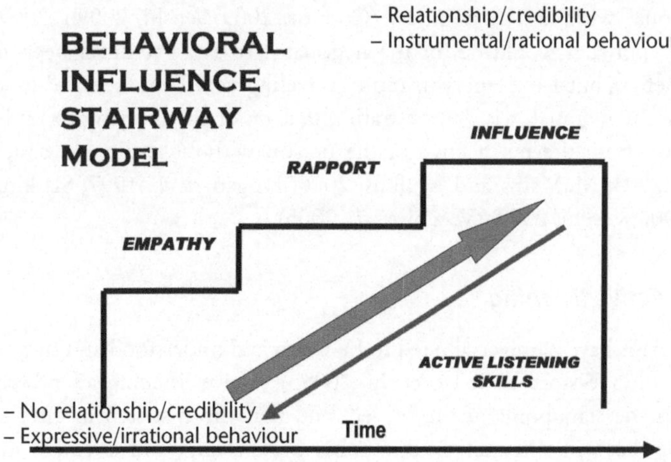

FIGURE 1.5 Behavioral Influence Stairway Model.

stairs') that require the negotiator to return to the active listening stage and begin again.

The BISM is comprised of four stages which occur in a specified order (Vecchi, 2009b):

- Active listening
- Empathy
- Rapport
- Influence.

It is important to note that these stages occur in order and one stage cannot be skipped in order to get to the next stage faster (Vecchi, 2009b). For example, a negotiator cannot skip from Stage 1 (active listening) to Stage 4 (influence) without first having developed empathy and rapport (Stage 2 and Stage 3) with the subject (Vecchi, 2009b).

The most important thing to remember is that if the negotiator is not making progress or makes a mistake, it is best to go back to the foundation (Stage 1) and start over again and to stay focused on the process of developing a relationship with the subject rather than on the outcome of ending the crisis (NCNC, 2003; Vecchi, 2003, 2004, 2009a, 2009b; Vecchi *et al.*, 2005). For example, although emotions are universal, experiences are not. Making assumptions about a subject's emotions based upon the circumstances can stall crisis intervention. For instance, during a situation where a man is threatening to commit suicide, the negotiator attempts to demonstrate empathy by saying, 'I know how you feel.' The man responds, 'You don't know how I feel … just go away.' In this case, the negotiator's attempt at empathy is counterproductive because the man does not believe the negotiator has ever tried to commit suicide before and, regardless of whether or not this is true, the perception of the man is his reality; therefore arguing or trying to be rational with him is pointless (Connor, 2009; Vecchi, 2009b, 2009d). An alternative approach would be for the negotiator to say, 'I've never been in your situation before, but I imagine you must be feeling very depressed and lonely.' By saying this, the negotiator is demonstrating that he or she is trying to understand the situation from the perspective of the person without leaping to conclusions (Lanceley, 2003; McMains and Mullins, 2006; Rogan *et al.*, 1997; Slatkin, 2005; Strentz, 2006; Vecchi, 2009b; Vecchi *et al.*, 2005).

Stage 1: Active listening

People in crisis have a universal need to be heard and understood and they all have their own unique story to tell (Vecchi, 2009b). Active listening attends to these needs from the standpoint of the subject and it is the first step in developing a relationship that will ultimately lead to behavioural change and an end to the crisis (Booth *et al.*, 2009; Daniels *et al.*, 2007; Greenstone and Leviton, 2002; McMains and Lanceley, 2003; Rogan *et al.*, 1997; Rosenbluh, 2001; Slatkin, 2005; Van Hasselt *et al.*, 2005; Vecchi, 2009b). Active listening skills (ALS) form the foundation of the BISM and are comprised of core and supplemental groupings. The core group elements are mirroring, paraphrasing, emotion labelling and summarising. The supplemental group consists of effective pauses (silence), minimal encouragers, open-ended questions and 'I' messages. Although there are no hard or fast rules, supplemental ALS should be used when necessary to enhance the effectiveness of core ALS (NCNC, 2003; Vecchi, 2003, 2004, 2009a, 2009b; Vecchi *et al.*, 2005).

Core active listening skills

Mirroring refers to repeating the last few words or gist of the subject. It demonstrates to the subject that the negotiator is attentive and it also serves as a method by which to draw out specific concerns and problems for use in furthering the interaction. In this way, the negotiator ensures that the discussion content is provided solely by the subject rather than by the negotiator, thereby remaining in the subject's frame of reference (Vecchi, 2009b). It is also a good way to get 'new' material to talk and gain intelligence about that is relevant to the subject for use when transitioning to problem-solving (NCNC, 2003; Vecchi, 2003, 2004, 2009a, 2009b; Vecchi *et al.*, 2005). An example of mirroring would be:

> *Negotiator* (*N*): 'Are you okay?'
> *Subject* (*O*): 'I don't want to talk about it.'
> *N*: 'You don't want to talk about it?'
> *O*: 'No, I had a bad day.'
> *N*: 'Bad day?'
> *O*: 'Yeah, I lost my job.'
> *N*: 'You lost your job?'
> *O*: 'Yeah, for no apparent reason.'

Paraphrasing refers to putting the content of what the subject said into the negotiator's own words (Vecchi, 2009b). This demonstrates to the subject that the negotiator is trying to understand his or her specific situation from a cognitive or content perspective (NCNC, 2003; Vecchi, 2003, 2004, 2009a, 2009b; Vecchi *et al.*, 2005). An example of summarising would be: 'Let me make sure I understand what you're saying, you lost your job for no apparent reason and you're having a bad day' (Vecchi, 2009b).

Emotion labelling refers to identifying the emotion(s) that the subject is feeling. This gets at the heart of what the subject is experiencing because most content is surrounded by emotion(s) (NCNC, 2003; Vecchi, 2003, 2004, 2009a, 2009b; Vecchi *et al.*, 2005) (see Figure 1.4). Even if the negotiator misidentifies the emotion, it still demonstrates to the subject that the negotiator is trying to understand the situation, which demonstrates empathy and tends to de-escalate highly volatile emotions. An example of emotion labelling would be: 'you sound angry', 'you seem frustrated' or 'I hear disgust in your voice' (Vecchi, 2009b).

Summarising combines the content of the paraphrase with the emotion identified by emotion labelling into the negotiator's own words (Vecchi, 2009b). This process is a final clarification to the negotiator of what the subject is experiencing and it assures the subject that the negotiator either understands or is trying to understand the situation from the perspective of the subject (NCNC, 2003; Vecchi, 2003, 2004, 2009a, 2009b; Vecchi *et al.*, 2005). An example of summarising would be: 'Let me make sure I understand what you're saying, you lost your job for no apparent reason [paraphrase] and this makes you angry [labelled emotion]' (Vecchi, 2009b).

Supplemental active listening skills

Effective pauses equate to deliberate silence before or after meaningful comments by the negotiator (Vecchi, 2009b). This provides the subject with the ability to focus on what the negotiator is saying. Pausing just before or after saying something important tends to cause the subject to listen to the content of the message because the pause breeds anticipation (if done before the meaningful comment) and reflection (if done after the meaningful comment) (NCNC, 2003; Vecchi, 2003, 2004, 2009a, 2009b; Vecchi *et al.*, 2005). For example, the negotiator could use an effective pause in this way: 'Tell me if I have this right …[pause] … you are angry with your mother because she never showed you love' or 'you sound angry about the loss of your father … [pause] … tell me more about that' (Vecchi, 2009b).

Minimal encouragers are verbal and non-verbal cues to the subject that the negotiator is being attentive to what he or she is saying and experiencing (Vecchi, 2009b). Minimal encouragers also demonstrate that the negotiator is psychologically present and 'in the moment' with the subject and that he or she is genuinely trying to understand the subject's perspective (NCNC, 2003; Vecchi, 2003, 2004, 2009a, 2009b; Vecchi *et al.*, 2005). Minimal encouragers are used while the negotiator is listening. Verbal encouragers are comments such as 'uh-huh', 'yes', 'right', and 'okay'. Non-verbal encouragers are actions such as nodding the head, tilting the head, leaning forward, watching the person's eyes or mouth as they speak or mirroring the non-verbal behaviour of the subject (Vecchi, 2009b).

Open-ended questions prompt the subject to expand on his or her concerns and perspective and encourages clarification which is used by the negotiator in employing more primary active listening strategies (mirroring, paraphrasing, emotion labelling, and summarising), all in an effort to bring the person to a more rational state of mind (NCNC, 2003; Vecchi, 2003, 2004, 2009a, 2009b; Vecchi *et al.*, 2005). Open-ended questions do not limit the responses to either-or or yes-no answers, but require elaboration and detail on the part of the subject. Open-ended questions may include those that start with 'what' or 'when' or statements such as 'tell me more about …' (Vecchi, 2009b).

'I' messages are used sparingly by the negotiator when it is appropriate to make a personal disclosure in furtherance of developing the relationship or when the subject is verbally attacking the negotiator (Vecchi, 2009b). A negotiator uses a personal disclosure to connect an emotion or experience within the context of what the subject is describing (NCNC, 2003; Vecchi, 2003, 2004, 2009a, 2009b; Vecchi *et al.*, 2005). For example, the negotiator may say: 'I am a father too, but I can only imagine what it must be like to lose a son. It must be terrible.' When being verbally attacked, the negotiator can use the 'I' message in this way: 'When you say that I don't care, it frustrates me because I really am trying to understand your situation and I really want to help you. I am here because I want to be, not because I have to be' (Vecchi, 2009b).

In many cases, the negotiator is the only person in the life of the subject who has expended effort to understand and respond to the crisis situation in *their* frame of reference (Vecchi, 2009b). Active listening is the starting point of effective crisis intervention and the first stage towards influencing behavioural change (NCNC, 2003; Vecchi, 2003, 2004, 2009a, 2009b; Vecchi *et al.*, 2005). In addition, active listening is always the fallback position when communication begins to deteriorate.

Stage 2: Empathy

Empathy is a natural by-product of effective active listening. Empathy implies an identification with and understanding of another's situation, feelings and motives (Vecchi, 2009a, 2009b). The negotiator uses empathy to see through the eyes of the subject and to absorb tension. Being right is not the issue; making the attempt to get it right on the part of the negotiator is what counts (NCNC, 2003). An example of an empathetic statement would be: 'It is understandable how you would be angry over that' (Vecchi, 2009b).

Empathy should not be confused with sympathy, which indicates pity (NCNC, 2003). In crisis intervention, the goal is not to feel sorry for the subject, but to establish a relationship and credibility through effective communication in which positive steps can be taken towards resolving the crisis in a collaborative fashion from the standpoint of the subject (Vecchi, 2009a, 2009b). A crucial consideration with regard to developing empathy is the importance of tone (Vecchi, 2009a, 2009b). Tone influences how the subject perceives the meaning of what the negotiator is saying and it is this perception of meaning that counts the most in effective crisis intervention, whether or not the perception is based in reality; therefore all strategies and tactics must be based on their impact upon the subject. Tone indicates attitude and genuineness through inflection and pitch and it expresses emotion, demeanour and projected sincerity. Remember that the way a negotiator says something is far more important than the content alone (NCNC, 2003). Empathy seeks first to understand and then to be understood on the part of the negotiator, which forms the building blocks of rapport (Vecchi, 2009a, 2009b).

Stage 3: Rapport

Up to this point on the BISM, the relationship has been one-sided in that the subject has been talking and the negotiator has been actively listening and empathetic (NCNC, 2003; Vecchi, 2003, 2004, 2009a, 2009b; Vecchi *et al.*, 2005). Once empathy has been established from the standpoint of the subject, rapport develops, which is a relationship characterised by trust and mutual affinity (Vecchi, 2009a). Once rapport has been developed, the subject is poised and ready to listen to what the negotiator has to say. At this stage, the negotiator, in collaboration with the subject, begins to build themes, defence mechanisms, minimisations or blending concepts that serve as precursors to ending the crisis (Dattilio and Freeman, 2000; Fisher *et al.*, 2001; Mullins, 2002; Rogan *et al.*, 1997; Slatkin, 2005; Ury, 1991). Themes comprise reasons that would explain, justify, mitigate or excuse the behaviour of the subject and address distorted thinking by putting a 'different spin' on the situation. Defence mechanisms use rationalisation and projection of blame to reduce volatile emotions, whereas minimisation downplays any negative behaviour exhibited by the subject. Blending is where the negotiator and the subject agree where they can without conceding, reduce real or perceived differences and find common ground. At this point, the subject is ready to be influenced by the negotiator and be persuaded to act (Vecchi, 2009b).

Stage 4: Influence

Influence is the act or power of producing an effect without apparent force or direct authority (Vecchi, 2009a, 2009b). At this stage, the relationship has now grown to the point where the subject is ready to accept the suggestions of the negotiator as a prelude to behavioural change (Vecchi, 2003, 2004, 2009a, 2009b; Vecchi *et al.*, 2005). In other words, the negotiator has earned the right to suggest a course of action to the subject as a result of collaborative problem-solving (NCNC, 2003). At this point, the negotiator and subject work together to identify solutions and alternatives that are suitable to both (Vecchi, 2009a, 2009b).

Behavioural change

The difficulty of successfully influencing behavioural change is oftentimes the result of the negotiator moving too quickly through the stages or skipping stages in a misguided effort to solve the crisis through premature problem-solving (NCNC, 2003; Vecchi, 2003, 2004, 2009a, 2009b; Vecchi *et al.*, 2005). Behavioural change will occur only if the previous four stages have been successfully completed, resulting in the forming of a positive relationship between the negotiator and the subject, as well as the negotiator moving the subject into a rational mindset, which sets the stage for problem-solving and resolution of the crisis. At this point, the subject will do as the negotiator suggests for no other reason than the fact that the negotiator asked the person to do so (Vecchi, 2009a, 2009b).

Points to remember

It is important to note that for any type of negotiation to work there must be three enablers present. The first enabler requires that all parties be willing and able to communicate (Fisher *et al.*, 2001; Vecchi, 2009b; Vecchi *et al.*, 2005; Wilmot and Hocker, 1998). Some issues to consider are language barriers, motivation to negotiate and the ability to be heard and understood (Vecchi, 2009b). The second enabler requires that all parties listen attentively to one another (Fisher *et al.*, 2001; Vecchi, 2009b; Vecchi *et al.*, 2005). This requires each party to actively listen to what all the stakeholders are saying rather than planning their own next response. The third enabler requires that all parties be attuned to clarifying misunderstandings and misinterpretations, as many nuances of language can be perceived differently from what was intended (Fisher *et al.*, 2001; Rogan *et al,*, 1997; Vecchi, 2009b). It should be noted that cultural differences and tone are oftentimes the basis for misunderstandings and misinterpretations.

It is also important for the negotiator not to inject his or her own values into the situation; however, this does not mean that the negotiator has to agree with the values or morals (or lack of values or morals) of the subject (Vecchi, 2009b). This disagreement can be relayed to the subject by saying something like: 'From what you're saying, I can imagine how your wife could have made you angry … that would have made me angry too, but I don't think I could have done what you did' (Vecchi, 2009b).

When dealing with a subject, the negotiator gives the person a 'hearing' (Vecchi, 2009b). This is because people want their needs and values to be understood; thus listening is the cheapest yet most effective concession a negotiator can make and it demonstrates respect (Lanceley, 2003; McMains and Mullins, 2006; Rogan *et al.*, 1997; Slatkin, 2005; Strentz, 2006; Vecchi, 2009b; Vecchi *et al.*, 2005). Being right is not the issue; making the attempt to get it right is what counts. Tone speaks louder than words and indicates the negotiator's attitude; a calm, controlled demeanour is always more effective than a brilliant argument (Vecchi, 2009b). The following are some points to keep in mind during the negotiation process (McMains and Mullins, 2006; Lanceley, 2003; Strentz, 2006; Vecchi, 2003, 2004, 2009b):

- Listen to the person.
- Acknowledge his or her point of view.
- Agree wherever you can without conceding your own values or morals (find common ground).
- Create a positive atmosphere for problem-solving.
- Don't argue.

When negotiation seems to be failing, it is important to look at possible obstacles to agreement that may include (Vecchi *et al.*, 2005):

- unsatisfied needs (fear of losing face);
- not being vested in the solution;
- not yet ready for agreement;
- inclination to resist perceived aggression;
- sense of being misunderstood or mistreated;
- feeling aggrieved or maligned.

Conclusion

Conflict and crisis situations occur oftentimes with little or no notice and many of them can be volatile with a high potential for violence. These situations require the ability of the negotiator to quickly assess the behaviour of the subject and select the negotiation strategies and tactics that are most likely to be successful, all in a very compressed timeframe. The NRM provides a process with which a negotiator can bridge the desired outcome with the final outcome through the continuous assessment of the subject's needs and conflict behaviour in light of instrumental or expressive mindsets. With this information, and the application of the BISM and interactional manipulation techniques, the negotiator is able to select the appropriate problem-solving or crisis intervention tactics to succeed in the negotiation.

Note

1. Court is a formal mechanism where the judge makes the final decision and the parties are represented by legal professionals. Moreover, the content of the testimony must be based on facts as articulated by the parties. On the contrary, mediation is a much more informal mechanism where the parties make the final decision and they represent themselves. In addition, feelings and information that would not be allowed under the formal rules of the court are allowed in mediation.

References

Associated Press (1999) 'Hostage stand-off ends in Louisiana jail'. Retrieved on 20 December 2009, from http://www.nytimes.com/1999/12/19/us/hostage-standoff-ends-at-louisiana-jail.html.

Booth, B., Vecchi, G. M., Finney, E. J., Van Hasselt, V. B. and Romano, S. J. (2009) 'Captive-taking in the context of workplace violence: descriptive analysis and case examples', *Victims and Offenders*, 4: 76–92.

Caplan, G. (1961) *An Approach to Community Mental Health*. New York: Grune & Stratton.

Carkhuff, R. R. and Berenson, B. G. (1977) *Beyond Counseling and Therapy* (2nd edn). New York: Holt, Rinehart & Winston.

Connor, M. G. (2009) *Suicide*. Retrieved 7 May, 2009 from: http://www.crisiscounseling.com.

Cooper, H. H. A. (2004) 'Police hostage negotiations: an exercise in salesmanship. *Journal of Police Crisis Negotiations: An International Journal*, (4) 1: 97–109.

Daniels, J. A., Royster, T. E. and Vecchi, G. M. (2007), 'Barricaded hostage and crisis situations in schools: a review of recent incidents', in D. L. White, B. C. Glenn, and

A. Wimes (eds), *Proceedings of Persistently Safe Schools: The 2007 National Conference on Safe Schools*. Washington, DC: Hamilton Fish Institute, George Washington University, pp. 61–7.

Dattilio, F. M. and Freeman, A. (eds) (2000) *Cognitive-behavioral strategies in crisis intervention* (2nd edn). New York: Guilford Press.

Fisher, R., Ury, W. and Patton, B. (2001) *Getting to Yes: Negotiating Agreement Without Giving In* (2nd edn). New York: Penguin.

Greenstone, J. L. and Leviton, S. C. (2002) *Crisis Intervention: Crises and How to Respond to Them* (2nd edn). Pacific Grove, CA: Brooks/Cole.

Hendricks, J. E. and Byers, B. D. (eds) (2002) *Crisis Intervention in Criminal Justice/Social Service* (3rd edn). Springfield, IL: Hendricks & Byers.

James, R. K. and Gilliland, B. E. (2001) *Crisis Intervention Strategies* (4th edn). Stamford, CT: Brooks/Cole.

Lanceley, F. J. (2003) *On-scene Guide for Crisis Negotiators* (2nd edn). Boca Raton, FL: CRC Press.

Mcevers, K. (2006) *Beslan Timeline: How the School Siege Unfolded*. Retrieved on 28 May 2010, from http://www.npr.org/templates/story/story.php?storyId=5740009.

McMains, M. J. and Lanceley, F. J. (2003) 'The use of crisis intervention principles by police negotiators', *Journal of Police Crisis Negotiations*, 3 (1): 3-30.

McMains, M. J., and Mullins, W. C. (2006) *Crisis Negotiations: Managing Critical Incidents and Hostage Situations in Law Enforcement and Corrections* (3rd edn). Cincinnati, OH: Anderson.

Mullins, W. C. (2002) 'Advanced communication techniques for hostage negotiators', *Journal of Police Crisis Negotiations: An International Journal*, 2 (1): 63-81.

National Crisis Negotiation Course (NCNC) (2003) Quantico, VA: FBI Academy.

Roberts, A. R. (2000). 'An overview of crisis theory and crisis intervention', In A. R. Roberts (ed.), *Crisis Intervention Handbook* (2nd edn). New York: Oxford University Press, pp. 3–30.

Rogan, R. G., Hammer, M. R. and Van Zandt, C. R. (eds) (1997) *Dynamic Processes of Crisis Negotiation: Theory, Research, and Practice*. Westport, CT: Praeger.

Rosenbluh, E. S. (2001) 'Police crisis intervention: a dilemma in the aftermath of Columbine High School', *Journal of Police Crisis Negotiations*, 1 (1): 35-46.

Slatkin, A. A. (2005). *Communication in Crisis and Hostage Negotiation: Practical Communication Techniques, Stratagems, and Strategies for Law Enforcement, Corrections and Emergency Service Personnel in Managing Critical Incidents*. Springfield, IL: Charles C. Thomas.

Strentz, T. (2006) *Psychological Aspects of Crisis Negotiation*. Boca Raton, FL: CRC Press.

Thomas, K. W. (2002) *Introduction to Conflict Management: Improving Performance Using the TKI*. Palo Alto, CA: CPP.

Thomas, K. W. and Kilmann, R. H. (1997) *Thomas-Kilmann Conflict Mode Instrument*. Tuxedo, NY: Xicom.

Ury, W. (1991) *Getting Past No: Negotiating with Difficult People*. New York: Bantum Books.

Van Hasselt, V. B., Romano, S. J. and Vecchi, G. M. (2008) 'Role playing: applications in hostage and crisis negotiation skills training', *Behavior Modification*, 32 (2): 248–63.

Van Hasselt, V. B., Flood, J. J., Romano, S. J., Vecchi, G. M., de Fabrique, N. and Regini, C. (2005) 'Hostage-taking in the context of domestic violence: some case examples', *Journal of Family Violence*, 20 (1): 21-7.

Vecchi, G. M. (2002) 'Hostage/barricade management: a hidden conflict within law enforcement', *FBI Law Enforcement Bulletin*, 71 (5): 1-7.

Vecchi, G. M. (2003) 'Active listening: the key to effective crisis negotiation', *ACR Crisis Negotiation News*, 1: 4-6.

Vecchi, G. M. (2004) 'Active listening and communication skills for crisis negotiation mediators', *ACResolution*, (3) 2: 18-23.

Vecchi, G. M. (2006) *Assessing Organizational Group Conflict in Law Enforcement Hostage/Barricade Management*. Ann Arbor, MI: Proquest.

Vecchi, G. M. (2009a) 'Conflict and crisis communication: a methodology for influencing and persuading behavioral change', *Annals of American Psychotherapy*, 12 (1): 34–42.
Vecchi, G. M. (2009b) 'Conflict and crisis communication: the behavioral influence stairway model and suicide intervention', *Annals of American Psychotherapy*, 12 (2): 32–39.
Vecchi, G. M. (2009c) 'Conflict and crisis communication: workplace and school violence, Stockholm Syndrome, and abnormal psychology', *Annals of American Psychotherapy*, 12 (3): 30–9.
Vecchi, G. M. (2009d) 'Conflict and crisis communication: methods of crisis intervention and stress management', *Annals of American Psychotherapy*, 12 (4): 54–63.
Vecchi, G. M. (2009e) 'Critical incident response, management, and resolution: structure and interaction in barricaded hostage, barricaded crisis, and kidnapping situations', *Inside Homeland Security*, 7 (2): 7–16.
Vecchi, G. M., Van Hasselt, V. B. and Romano, S. J. (2005) 'Crisis (hostage) negotiation: current strategies and issues in high-risk conflict resolution', *Aggression and Violent Behavior: A Review Journal*, 10: 533–51.
Wiger, D. E. and Harowski, K. J. (2003) *Essentials of crisis counseling and intervention*. Hoboken, NJ: John Wiley & Sons.
Wilmot, W. W. and Hocker, J. L. (1998) *Interpersonal Conflict* (5th edn). Boston: McGraw-Hill.

Note: The views expressed in this chapter do not necessarily represent the views of the FBI.

2

NEGOTIATION

Principles and theoretical underpinnings

Neil Gredecki

Everyday living involves negotiation. Some individuals negotiate flexible working patterns with their managers at work. Others negotiate an early finish from work so they can make their medical appointment at a time that they negotiated with their doctor's receptionist. Beyond the workplace, it is normal for parents to negotiate with their teenage children over the time of their curfew, or their child's desire to go on holiday with friends. We are all negotiators to some degree or another. Consider the following example of a teenager negotiating their curfew with their parent who is keen for them to be in early.

Teenager:	I want to go to Tom's party this evening. Everyone is going. I'm planning to stay until midnight with everyone else.
Parent:	I want you home well before midnight.
Teenager:	I've not got school tomorrow so there's no need for me to come home any earlier.
Parent:	I want you back in the house for 10.00 p.m. so I know where you are.
Teenager:	That's pointless. The party's only starting at 9.00 p.m. so it will not be worth me going.
Parent:	I want you home early and not out all evening. I want you to be home for 10.30 p.m. at the very latest.
Teenager:	I can't come home that early; I'll come home for 11.30 p.m.

And so, the negotiation continues. However, this 'negotiation' may continue for some time, either until a compromise is reached or the negotiation fails altogether. As noted previously, we are all negotiators in some way or another, potentially on a daily basis. Furthermore, many people are in fact very effective negotiators, despite often being unaware of the steps involved in the negotiation process.

Negotiating with individuals in a crisis or conflict situation relies on similar skills, albeit in different situational circumstances: this will be considered later in this chapter.

So, what is negotiation and how is it defined? The current chapter is concerned with reviewing models of negotiation, with a particular emphasis on the psychological literature and theory underpinning these processes. However, it is important in the first instance to establish a definition of negotiation. According to Fisher *et al.* (2001), 'negotiation is a basic means of getting what you want from others. It is back-and-forth communication designed to reach an agreement when you and the other side have some interests that are shared and others that are opposed' (p. xvii).

In short, negotiation involves the ability of two or more parties, with shared or opposing interests and goals, to engage in a form of communication that seeks to establish an agreement. Where individuals share similar goals, then agreement may be achieved more easily. For example, where a mother and a father have similar goals about their child's nursery placement, negotiation may be easier than in the situation where one parent favours stay-at-home parenting over a nursery education and vice versa. The negotiation process is about change. That is, bringing about change in individuals' thinking in order to reach a shared agreement with regard to the way forward. For the parents in the nursery scenario, it is about reaching an agreement regarding their child's care, focusing on their shared goals and using their shared goals and interests to reach some degree of compromise or agreement.

In terms of promoting effective negotiation, it is proposed that three enablers must be present. The first is that *all parties are willing and able to communicate* (Fisher *et al.*, 2001; Vecchi *et al.*, 2005; Wilmot and Hocker, 1998). That is, the individual negotiating has both a willingness and ability to communicate. The second enabler is the ability of *all parties to listen attentively to one another* (Fisher *et al.*, 2001; Vecchi *et al.*, 2005) in that each party listens to what is being said as opposed to simply considering their next response. Finally, effective negotiation requires that *all parties are attuned to clarifying any misunderstandings and/or misinterpretations* in order to ensure that discussions are not misperceived (Fisher *et al.*, 2001; Rogan *et al.*, 1997).

When considering the negotiation process, it is important to understand that negotiation is often needed when individuals have different goals, for example in the scenario above where the two parents have different goals with regard to how their child is cared for. As such, it is important to understand how individuals set goals and how these may impact on the negotiation processes.

According to Ward and Stewart (2003), humans are goal-directed, and the setting of goals can be a useful way for individuals to work towards a particular position and/or way of being. In forensic settings, for example, professionals often seek to set goals with their clients which can be a collaborative way of working towards change. When there is consistency of opinion among the two parties then this is a helpful process. However, where differences exist, this can cause difficulties in moving towards change and collaboratively achieving a goal. For example, consider the scenario where the teenager is negotiating their curfew. If the parent and teenager shared the same view then the situation would be resolved. In the current scenario though, the difference in the perception of the goals leads to some degree of challenge and difficulty in terms of reaching a resolution. As such, the process of negotiation requires an overall awareness of each individual's goals and the potential impact of these on change, particularly in terms of the other person's potential ambivalence towards change (Miller and Rollnick, 2002). According to Locke (1996), the notion of goals is important in understanding human motivation. That is, motivation to change a behaviour (e.g. barricading) or to continue engaging in the named behaviour are both goal choices, based on an individual's characteristics and circumstances. The focus here is therefore on the notion that goals are 'conscious' and involve some level of thought processing on the part of the individual.

In relation to negotiation, humans continue to be goal-driven, and it is important to acknowledge that they will not just have found themselves in the presenting situation. That is, their decision to engage in a particular behaviour will be influenced by their goals which are underpinned by their own views and interests. The decisions made by individuals may relate to the achievement of a particular goal or be a response to the blocking of a particular goal. Within the conflict and crisis communication literature, there is clear reference to the notion of goals and needs in terms of the development of the situation and the potential strategies that are adopted by the negotiator. These will be explored further within this chapter.

The change process

Prior to addressing individual methods of negotiation, it is perhaps important to consider human motivation and change more generally. Negotiation is in essence about the change process and seeking to change an individual's behaviour, cognitions or future goals. As such, understanding the change process is helpful to further understand how and why certain methods of negotiation may, or may not, be effective. Therefore it is important to understand the change process and how individuals bring about effective change.

In relation to the negotiation process, it is important for the individuals involved to commit to change and to have shared goals. Otherwise, there is always the chance for individuals to retreat, resulting in the negotiation process starting again. This is an important consideration, specifically when accounting for crisis and conflict situations. For example, consider the situation where a mentally disordered patient has taken their psychiatrist hostage in their consultation room. At the point where the negotiation process has reached the goal-setting stage and the patient is willing to release the hostage and to exit the room, it is important that the patient is committed to this change in circumstances. That is, should commitment not have been achieved, it is possible for the client to retreat into the consultation room for an extended period of time, thus having further ramifications for all those involved.

Motivation to change and commitment to change are therefore important in the negotiation process. Motivation requires, in the first instance, that the individual be in a position where change is favoured. This too fits with the notion of goal-setting addressed previously, in that the individual is at a point at which they have made a decision (goal choice) to engage in change behaviour. Further to this commitment to change, however, the individual involved needs to have the ability and resources through which to change (see Miller and Rollnick, 2002).

With regard to the change process, Burrowes and Needs (2009) propose the Readiness to Change Framework (RCF), which addresses some of the critiques of the earlier change literature, emphasising the notion of change as a continuum. Specifically, the model addresses previous concerns (see Littell and Girvin, 2002; Orleans, 2000) regarding the need for a fluid model of behavioural change that accommodates unforeseen events and takes into account the context of change (Howells and Day, 2003; Orleans, 2000; Ward, 2002). For example, in a crisis or conflict situation with a prisoner, it would be imperative to be constantly mindful of the potential for impulsivity. Likewise, it would be important to remain mindful of the social support offered by other prisoners to continue with the presenting behaviour which links to the notion of the context of change. For example, on a prison wing/unit, it is potentially unlikely that a prisoner with a grandiose self-view will engage with the requests of prison officers or guards when surrounded by their peers. In this situation, negotiation may be negatively affected by the prisoner's desire to save face in the presence of peers. As such, it is important to consider the context in which change is being sought and to try to manage associated factors in the environment.

Using the metaphor of a river, Burrowes and Needs (2009) conclude that, 'Like a river, change is a rich, dynamic, and not entirely predictable phenomenon over which we have a limited amount of control. Change is viewed as something that we may be able to influence and channel but it is not something over which we have total control.' (p. 43) According to the Readiness to Change Framework (RCF), change is an unpredictable phenomenon over which we have only a degree of control. While it is acknowledged that negotiators do not have ultimate control over the change process and the behaviour and decisions of others, it is acknowledged that they can have some influence over the change process (Van Hasselt *et al.*, 2008). In terms of supporting change, Burrowes and Needs (2009) highlight how change can be blocked by a series of barriers (Barriers to Change Model (BCM)). As such, for change to occur, each of the individual barriers needs to be addressed, as an individual barrier will itself prevent the change process from happening. The barriers identified by Burrowes and Needs (2009) are presented in Figure 2.1.

Let us reflect on how the barriers may be applied to a negotiation. Consider a mother that takes her daughter hostage in their family home. When negotiating with police negotiators, she becomes aware that the resolution of the situation

Barrier 1:	Perceived importance of change in comparison to conflicting goals
Barrier 2:	Perceived need to change
Barrier 3:	Perceived level of personal responsibility to change
Barrier 4:	Perceived cost-benefit analysis of change
Barrier 5:	Perceived sense of urgency to change now
Barrier 6:	Perceived personal ability to change
Barrier 7:	Perceived personal ability to maintain change
Barrier 8:	Perceived costs associated with the means to change
Barrier 9:	Perceived suitability and efficacy of the means to change
Barrier 10:	The realities of change

FIGURE 2.1 Barriers to Change (Burrows and Needs, 2009).

has the likelihood of her being arrested and charged with an offence of false imprisonment. At such a point, the 'perceived cost-benefit analysis of change' (Barrier 4) may indicate that there are more costs associated with ending the situation than there are benefits. As such, negotiation needs to account for the presenting barriers and to address these appropriately before it can be expected that the mother involved will end the situation peacefully.

In terms of understanding the principles underlying change, Self-Determination Theory (SDT – Ryan and Deci, 2000; Deci and Ryan, 2000) goes some way to explaining human motivation and the process of change, and more importantly a commitment to change. Self-Determination Theory is a broad theory of human motivation. The theory assumes that individuals have an innate drive towards their own development and psychological growth; they are driven to manage any ongoing challenges, and to use such challenges to develop their sense of self. The theory postulates that the drive to do this is not an automatic one, but requires continual support from the social environment in order to function as effectively as they can. Ultimately, it argues that the social environment can either maximise or hinder an individual's ability to master their ongoing challenges.

According to Self-Determination Theory, maintenance of behaviours over time requires individuals to 'internalize values and skills for change, and experience self-determination' (Ryan *et al.*, 2008: 2). In addition, the theory postulates that by maximising the individual's experience of *autonomy*, *competence* and *relatedness*, the management and regulation of related behaviours is more likely to be internalised and subsequently behaviour change will be better managed (Williams *et al.*, 1998; Ryan *et al.*, 2008). Autonomy relates to the individual's desire to self-organise their experiences and behaviours. A sense of competence is gained through autonomy whereby once people are engaged and they have a high degree of willingness to both act and engage, they are then considered most able to learn and apply new strategies and competencies (Markland *et al.*, 2005). Finally, relatedness is concerned with the importance of the relationship between individuals as a vehicle of change. La Guardia *et al.* (2000) argue that an individual will gravitate toward those relationships that present the greatest opportunities to meet these basic needs.

Health researchers (e.g. Rothman, 2000) describe the process of change as involving the two tasks of initiating and maintaining change. Self-determination theory is focused on the process through which the individual acquires the motivation for opting for change and the subsequent maintenance of this change. Many individuals attempt behavioural change due to external regulation whereby they seek an external reward or avoid punishment. Negotiators can encourage *external regulation* simply by acting from a position of authority (Ryan *et al.*, 2008). In addition, Ryan and colleagues describe the process of *introjection* whereby an individual may engage in a target behaviour to encourage reward and/or avoid disapproval. Such approaches to behavioural change are reported to be unrelated to long-term adherence (Ryan *et al.*, 2008).

In contrast to the above, self-determination theory argues that maintained change can be a function of *autonomous motivation* and *identified regulation*, whereby an individual identifies the importance or value of a particular behaviour. In terms of the therapeutic process, Ryan *et al.* (2008) suggest that identification is facilitated when 'practitioners provide relevant information and meaningful rationales for change, and do not apply external controls and pressures that distract from a sense of agency or choice'. (p. 3). This is equally important within the context of negotiation where rationales for change can be offered in order to support the change process. However, a challenge for negotiators can be in following command structures which may, for example, change the negotiation strategy, thus applying external controls. In such instances, it is important for the negotiator to provide rationales for any decisions that have been made.

In addition to autonomy is a sense of competence. According to Self-Determination Theory, a sense of competence is gained through autonomy whereby once people are engaged, and they have a high degree of willingness to both act and engage, they are then considered to be most apt to learn and apply new strategies and competencies (Markland *et al.*, 2005). Finally, many models of behavioural change refer to the importance of the relationship between the individuals involved as a vehicle of change. Within negotiation, this could be the relationship between the parties involved. In healthcare settings, it is suggested that vulnerable individuals often look to professionals for their input and guidance. According to Ryan *et al.* (2008: 3), 'in this process a sense of being respected, understood, and cared for is essential to forming experiences of connection and trust that allow for internalization to occur'. As such, it is important for negotiators to have a sense of credibility to support the negotiation process.

In conclusion, Self-Determination Theory promotes the belief that people work at their best and are happiest when they feel they have some level of control over their daily lives (Ryan and Deci, 2000). It is important to consider this when engaging with individuals who are attempting to change their behaviour through the negotiation process.

Models of negotiation

Thus far, this chapter has highlighted how negotiation forms part of day-to-day life, with individuals routinely engaging in negotiation with a plethora of people and situations. As noted previously, individuals try to achieve personal goals, presenting with their own needs in their daily experience of life. These needs can be varied, and may include financial, emotional or, for the teenager in the initial example, staying out later. When these goals are prevented or challenged, negotiation can be the strategy through which to overcome the potential barriers that exist and which prevent the goal from being achieved.

Within the context of negotiation, it is postulated that individuals engage in the negotiation process in order to satisfy particular needs (Harvey-Craig *et al.*, 1997) whether the presenting needs are substantive (e.g. transport in which to escape after a bank robbery) or expressive (e.g. the opportunity to express their feelings and emotions to another person) in content (Vecchi, 2002, 2003). The notion of a *need* is similar to the notion of the *goal* presented above, in that the 'needs' reflect, in part, the goals and purpose of the negotiation process. They are in essence the motivating factors underpinning the presenting situation. According to Wilmot and Hocker (1998), individuals entering the negotiation process do so with four potential categories of needs: content, relational, identity and process.

Content needs reflect substantive needs such as food or transportation and tend to be tangible and substantive. In contrast, *relational* needs are less tangible and refer, for example, to the interpersonal needs of individuals and how they want to be treated. That is, consider a teenager who is mocked by their peers – they may feel disrespected which in turn undermines their basic relational need. For the teenager who feels isolated from their parents and rejected by their peers, they may have *identity* needs associated with feelings of abandonment. Finally, *process* needs refer to the environment in which the needs are communicated. For example, when a couple separate, they may hold discussions through a mediator or, conversely, in a court setting. Based on the identification of needs, it is important that these needs are considered in relation to the individual with whom the negotiation is taking place. That is, without understanding the needs of the other person, it is difficult to effectively pursue the negotiation process. As such, the ability to distinguish between the different needs is important.

General psychological literature regarding motivation and change highlights a number of factors that can potentially enhance communication and favour change. The work of Miller and Rollnick (2002) has focused on the application of motivational literature to practice through motivational interviewing techniques. In short, motivational interviewing suggests that, 'Rather than persuade the client directly, the therapist systematically elicits from the client, and reinforces, reasons for concern and for change, whilst maintaining a warm and supportive atmosphere for exploration of ambivalent feelings' (Miller and Rollnick, 2002).

Although motivational interviewing is not the focus here, the general principles may also be applied in negotiation to assist resolution. Key strategies to support behavioural change and negotiation are presented in Figure 2.2.

While a range of factors and strategies may support change and assist in the negotiation process, the model of negotiation that is adopted is an important consideration. That is, there is a number of different ways of going about negotiating with others. According to Fisher *et al.* (2001: 4), any method of negotiation may be judged by three criteria:

- It should produce a wise agreement if agreement is possible.
- It should be efficient.
- It should improve, or at least not damage, the relationship between the two parties.

- *Express empathy.* Attempting to understand the other person's point of view is fundamental as it can function to facilitate change and negotiation, where attempts are made to see the situation through the other person's eyes. This is also a strategy that is employed in crisis negotiation (see Van Hasselt *et al.*, 2008).
- *Developing discrepancy.* In terms of facilitating negotiation, it is important for individuals to see the difficulties in their own position/argument. To develop intrinsic motivation for change, it should be the client who identifies arguments in favour of change rather than these being presented by the other individuals involved.
- *Rolling with resistance.* Negotiation should guide the other party towards change in order to encourage commitment. Where the other party presents arguments against change, negotiation requires the ability to 'roll' with any resistance. That is, negotiators should not directly challenge any resistance, but rather they should provide opportunities for the individuals involved to begin to challenge their own arguments against change, thus developing discrepancy.

(Based on Miller and Rollnick's (2002) motivational interviewing principles.)

FIGURE 2.2 Strategies for supporting change and negotiation.

Let us again consider the first example in this chapter, the parent and teenager 'negotiating' over the time at which the teenager should return from the party. In this example, it would appear that each participant is taking and potentially giving up a position. While it is postulated that in conflict situations such as these (i.e. situations where an individual's goals are being blocked) rational, problem-solving communication works best in most cases, not all communication styles are effective (Fisher *et al.*, 2001; Slatkin, 2005; Ury, 1991). In terms of negotiation, what is happening here is that each individual is taking a particular position and as such using *positional bargaining* techniques.

Positional bargaining is a common approach to negotiation in which individuals take a position over a particular issue. According to Fisher *et al.* (2001), this can be effective, in that it makes each party's position clear. Furthermore, it provides an anchor (starting point) from which the negotiation can begin, and it can ultimately produce an acceptable agreement. However, it also argued that this approach can further result in difficulties. That is, by adopting a particular position, the individual locks themself into that position for fear of 'losing face', that is, a potential fear of looking foolish by seeming to 'lose' the negotiation. For example, in the scenario of the parent and teenager, the parent adopts the position whereby they want their child home by 10.30 p.m. 'at the very latest' and the teenager does not want to leave the party before 11.30 p.m. at the earliest. As such, each participant has adopted a position that they appear to be sticking to. Where individuals adopt such an approach, an ability to negotiate is restricted and relies on one participant ultimately 'backing down'.

The difficulty here is that both parties have taken a particular stance and are arguing for their own position. The process of positional bargaining can prove very difficult for successful negotiations; often the individuals involved have their own extreme positions that they are negotiating for. While it has been noted above that this form of negotiation provides a starting point, this mode of negotiation fails to meet the criteria of producing wise agreements both efficiently and amicably (see Fisher *et al.*, 2001: 4). This tends to be due to the fact that those involved begin to 'negotiate' over specific positions, becoming fixated on their own position and 'winning'.

In terms of the motivation and change literature reviewed above, positional bargaining also causes some difficulties in terms of addressing the principles of change. First, consider the notion of goal-setting. What happens here is that two (or more) individuals have specific goals which are opposing. From the perspectives of the parent and the teenager they have opposing goals which appear to be conflictual by the very nature of the positions they have communicated. As such, in order to effectively negotiate and move forward, it is important to consider and apply the principles of change and human motivation as discussed previously. In the first instance, it will be important to further clarify the position of each of the individuals involved; often individuals may not make their goal or position very clear. For example, in the current scenario, the parent may be concerned with getting their child home safely, with the timeframe not being important. However, this is very different from the position they have set out. As such, in terms of effective negotiation, what is required is a model of communication which allows an exploration of such issues, that is a process that provides an opportunity for the individuals' goals and needs to be considered while also considering the barriers to achieving a particular goal/outcome. This type of approach to negotiation also supports the principles of self-determination theory in that the individuals involved have a sense of choice and autonomy over the matter and the decision being made, in addition to developing a relationship that may act as a vehicle of change (see Ryan *et al.*, 2003: 3).

The alternative model of communication involved in negotiation is that of *principled negotiation*. Principled negotiation seeks to focus on achieving a collaborative gain for all parties, encouraging ownership on the part of the individual stakeholders involved. As such, this method of communication seeks to satisfy the three criteria of effective negotiation as outlined by Fisher *et al.* (2001). That is, it seeks to produce *a wise agreement* that seeks to address the needs of the individual stakeholders in a collaborative method and without either party having to 'lose face' or lose their goal. Thus the win–win method seeks to *improve or at least not damage the relationship* between the two parties, acting in an *efficient* manner.

It has already been established that, in the earlier example of the parent and teenager, the adoption of a method of communication based on positional bargaining will not be successful. However, adopting principled negotiation techniques may go some way to negotiating a successful outcome that encourages all stakeholders to play a part in the negotiation process. In short, principled negotiation is a problem-solving based approach that addresses four principles (see Fisher *et al.*, 2001):

- Separate the people from the problem
- Focus on interests, not positions
- Create options for mutual gain
- Insist on using objective criteria.

A further exploration of how each of these principles is applied in the negotiation process and the key features of the process is set out below.

Separate the people from the problem

Within the negotiation process, it is fundamental to remember that we are dealing with people, and that we are aware of their potential responses to the negotiation process (Fisher *et al.*, 2001). While stakeholders want to reach an agreement that satisfies their substantive needs, they also need to maintain a relationship with the other party. The relationship is the important factor in some negotiations. A further issue in negotiation is that people often become entangled in the problem (Fisher *et al.*, 2001). For example, a comment such as 'this is a bad situation' in a hostage situation can be interpreted as a personal comment that deems the individual themself to be 'bad'. As such, the first stage of principled negotiation is to separate the person from the problem whereby the focus is on the problem. For example, in a hostage situation, this principle would involve focusing on the behaviour of the perpetrator and not the person as a whole. According to Vecchi (2009), this guards against the perpetrator being seen as a 'bad person' with the focus being on their 'bad behaviour', thus providing an opportunity for the discussion of the behaviour without losing face. According to Fisher *et al.* (2001), there are three categories to consider in order to achieve this principle: perception, emotion and communication. These will be discussed in turn.

Perception

Within negotiation, it is important to understand the other person's thinking as this is what separates the different stakeholders. That is, conflict often exists not in objective reality, but in the thoughts of the individuals involved (see Fisher *et al.*, 2001). Thus it is the reality as each stakeholder sees it that constitutes the problem in negotiation. As a consequence, it is important to consider each stakeholder's view. That is, it is proposed that if you want to influence others then you need to empathically understand their points of view and the emotions underpinning them (Fisher *et al.*, 2001). Being able to understand others' perspectives allows for an exploration of the merits of their position while also considering your own, thus seeking to reduce the amount of conflict. However, when trying to understand their position, it is important not to assume the other stakeholders' intentions based on your own fears, putting the worst interpretation on what the other side says or does. Equally, it is important not to fall into the trap of blaming the other party for your problem as it is likely that they will become defensive.

When talking about the problem, it is important to separate the symptoms from the person, i.e. it is the person's behaviour that is problematic and not the person. It is also important to discuss each person's perceptions and to participate in negotiations where each party is engaged as they will then be more likely to approve or comply with the outcome. This again fits with the principles underpinning Self-Determination Theory.

Emotion

It is noted that emotions have the potential to grow during the negotiation process resulting in negotiations being brought to an end. As such, it is important to label the emotions of oneself and the other people involved. According to Fisher *et al.* (2001), explicitly exploring emotions with the other stakeholders not only highlights the seriousness of the problem, but also makes negotiations less reactive and more proactive. Allowing the other party the opportunity to release their emotions and not responding to emotional outbursts can also be effective in the negotiation process.

Communication

Without communication there is no negotiation (Fisher *et al.*, 2001). However, even among individuals with shared backgrounds and values, communication can still be challenging. Problems with communication during negotiation can be a result of people not talking to each other so that they can be understood, people not listening to what is being said and misinterpretation of what is being said. In order to attend to some of these challenges, it can be important to speak about oneself and not the other party as it is far more difficult for them to challenge a statement about you. It is also important to ensure that information is communicated concisely so that the message is heard and not misinterpreted (Fisher *et al.*, 2001).

According to Fisher *et al.* (2001), it is not enough to separate the person from the problem and then move on; it is something that needs to be worked at. They conclude that 'the basic approach is to deal with the people as human beings and with the problem on its merits' (p. 39). Strategies for achieving this will be explored further below.

Focus on interests, not positions

Within the negotiation process, interests and positions are not the same. That is, the position is something that the individual has decided upon, whereas the interests are what led them to that decision (Fisher *et al.*, 2001). Consider the example of the teenager and their parent earlier. Based on the positions presented, it would appear that the teenager wants to stay out late and their parent wants them home early. As such, they appear to have conflicting positions. However, when another person explores their positions further, the teenager wants to stay out later to 'fit in' and be seen positively by their friends, and the parent wants them to come home earlier as they do not want them to walk home late at night. As such, it is suggested that the parent collect the teenager at 11.30 p.m. so they do not have to walk home alone. By exploring the motivations for the opposed positions or goals, it is often possible to find an outcome that meets the interests of both sides (Fisher *et al.*, 2001).

According to Vecchi (2002, 2003), negotiating interests means negotiating things that people really want rather than what they say they want or need. That is, people often take extreme positions that are designed to counter others' positions. However, when they are asked about why they are taking such positions, it often turns out that the underlying reasons are actually compatible with and not mutually exclusive of the others' interests as previously thought (see Vecchi, 2009; Fisher *et al.*, 2001; Ury 1991). Within the negotiation process, it is therefore fundamental that the negotiators understand not only their own interests but those of the other stakeholders. In order to explore the interests of the other party, it is important to examine each position, exploring why they have adopted the position. It is also necessary to understand what interests of the other person stand in the way of a successful resolution; by understanding this, the negotiator may be in a better position to influence them. However, it should be noted that potentially several interests exist in a particular situation and, as such, it is important not to fall into the trap of thinking that there will be one underlying interest in each situation. In addition to considering interests, it will also be important to consider each individual's basic needs (Fisher *et al.*, 2001).

In order to progress with negotiations, Fisher *et al.* (2001) suggest that it is important to talk about the interests. That is, if the purpose of negotiation is to serve one's interests, this needs to be discussed in order to increase the chances of them being met. However, it is important not to imply that the other person's interests are any less important than your own. The task of impressing your interests on the other party is to present them legitimately, trying to convince them that they might feel the same if they were in your position (Fisher *et al.*, 2001), developing discrepancy in their argument and rolling with any resistance (see Miller and Rollnick, 2002). It is important to present the reasoning and interests first and conclusions later, being mindful of where you are heading, while also being open to new ideas. However, it is advisable that, within negotiations, individuals commit themselves to their own interests, while also remembering to separate the person from the problem and not being closed to the other person's point of view. If you do not listen to the other side's point of view, then it is unlikely that they will listen to your interests. By focusing on interests, disputing parties can more easily focus on the third principle of creating options for mutual gain (Vecchi, 2009).

Creating options for mutual gain

Within negotiations, it is suggested that people rarely see a need to have many options, particularly if they have fixed on a particular position. It is postulated (see Fisher *et al.*, 2001) that there are often four obstacles to generating options:

- *premature judgment* (i.e. becoming more critical and less creative, also fearing that generating options will disclose important information);
- *searching for a single answer* (i.e. becoming fixed on narrowing down the negotiation too soon);
- *the assumption of a 'fixed pie'* (i.e. adopting an 'either/or' approach to the situation);
- thinking that 'solving their problem is their problem' and focusing only on one's own interests.

Given the reported tendency to narrow down thinking, the focus here is on ensuring that new solutions to the problem are sought in order to allow both sides to 'win', rather than fight over their original positions where the assumption is that one side will win while the other loses (Fisher *et al.*, 2001). However, in order to do this, it is important that creative thinking is used. For example, it is not enough to simply 'brainstorm' a range of ideas but to use a range of creative techniques to assist in the generation of options.

Insist on using objective criteria

The final principle of principled negotiation is to use objective criteria. That is, in some cases, using external and objective criteria to help in the decision-making process can be very helpful. Although it may not always be available, where it does exist, objective criteria outside of the negotiation can simplify the process, giving both sides more guidance as to what is fair, thus making it more difficult to oppose the options presented (Fisher *et al.*, 2001). For example, consider a situation where a hostage-taker has killed the hostage and is negotiating with a police officer. Rather than the police officer telling the perpetrator that they will go to prison, they may state 'you've killed someone and as an officer of the law

I can't let you go because that would be breaking the law'. Here, the objective criterion of 'the law' is used to decide on the options available.

When using objective criteria it is important that fair standards and procedures are applied to the negotiation process. That is, it is imperative to apply standards and principles relevant to both parties and to use a procedure of decision-making that is also sensitive to both parties. Once the objective criteria have been established, it is then important to frame each issue as a joint search for objective criteria which involves reasoning and being open to reason (Fisher *et al.*, 2001).

Application of theory to conflict and crisis situations

Depending upon the individuals involved in the negotiation and the dynamics of the situation, the processes followed in a crisis and conflict situation may be somewhat different to those applied in day-to-day negotiations. That is, in a hostage-taking, barricade, domestic or roof-top incident, the process may very well be different to that adopted when negotiating which colour of paint to purchase for the dining-room with a partner. The stakes can be very different and often much higher. The remainder of this chapter will focus on the application of methods of negotiation to what may be termed conflict or crisis situations (see Chapter 1). Such situations can refer to a range of circumstances where an individual may find themselves in conflict or crisis (e.g. hostage and barricade situations or roof-top protests). Despite the seriousness of each of these forms of behaviour, the main focus for the remainder of this chapter will be on the most extreme of these situations: negotiating with hostage-takers.

As detailed previously, there have been many developments in the literature concerning conflict and crisis communication. Chapter 1 explored in detail how the motivations for hostage-taking or engaging in crisis behaviours (e.g. barricading, roof-top protests or suicide attempts) can vary. That is, people engage in the associated behaviours for a number of reasons, with motivations noted to lie on the continuum of expressive to instrumental (see Vecchi *et al.*, 2005). Given the nature of a continuum, individuals have the potential to move between the two extremes throughout the incident and the associated negotiation process.

Typically, an individual presenting with 'instrumental' motivations would be a hostage-taker who is demanding a car in which to escape from the scene of a crime. Such individuals may present with *content*-driven needs in that their needs are substantive in nature (see Wilmot and Hocker, 1998). However, in contrast, engaging in crisis behaviours for 'expressive' reasons may reflect an individual who is unable to manage their emotions effectively to the point where they become overwhelmed and feel out of control, thus having more *relational* and *identity* needs (i.e. they have needs in relation to how they want to be treated by others and in relation to protecting their self-image: see Wilmot and Hocker, 1998). According to Ireland (2008), it is likely that an individual engaging in an expressive manner will be likely to have less clear demands as the needs tend to be expressive in nature. As such, the focus of any negotiation and/or intervention is primarily centred on bringing back more rational thinking.

Consider the following situation: Simon has been serving a seven-year sentence for drugs-related offences. He has engaged in a number of therapies in prison and has recently applied for early release via the parole system. He feels that parole will be important so that he can help care for his sick mother. His psychologist and probation officer have both supported his application for early release under the terms of the parole system. Simon has had his parole hearing and has found that the parole board have refused his early release stating that he needs to engage in more work aimed at reducing his risk of future offending. Simon was very disappointed with the situation and was noted to be verbally aggressive to staff following the decision. On the same evening, a prison officer who knows Simon well comes to his cell and begins to talk to him about the situation and the result of the parole application. Simon becomes upset about the fact that he has not been released from prison, he begins crying stating that 'there's no point in me going on, it's not worth it any more'. As the officer goes to leave the cell, Simon hits her from behind before closing his cell door and demanding that prison staff release him or he will hurt the prison officer whom he has already punched several times.

In a separate situation, the perpetrator (Tom) has monitored staff movements within a forensic psychiatric unit for several weeks. He has noted that in the early evening, staff numbers are lower, especially when medication is being administered. Tom has also noted that, given the time of year, many members of staff are taking annual leave from work, and as such temporary staff with less experience are working on the wards. At 7.30 p.m. when the evening medication is being administered by the qualified staff, Tom grabs a nursing assistant who is on a temporary contract. He holds a pen to their throat and threatens them. Tom then takes the member of staff to the main entrance of the unit, demanding that staff release him or he will stab the member of staff in the neck with the pen. Tom is clear that he wants to be released from the hospital.

According to Vecchi (2009), 'conflict' and 'crisis' have specific meanings within the context of critical incident response, management and resolution. Conflict is defined as the perceived blocking of important goals, needs or interests of one person or group (Wilmot and Hocker, 1998). As such, the negotiation process here is one whereby the individual in conflict requires the negotiator to assist them in attending to and achieving their needs. As such, the focus is on the application of principled negotiation to assist in the management of the situation.

The way in which an individual chooses to respond to a conflict situation can be either constructive or destructive (Vecchi, 2009). For example, consider Simon's situation above. He has a number of options in this situation; however, we will consider the extreme options here. Firstly, he could choose to set himself a number of goals that will assist him in addressing the concerns of the parole panel. Alternatively, he can engage in a more emotional response, barricading himself in his cell and holding a member of staff hostage. The latter would be an example of a conflict gone wrong, that is a crisis. Simon's situation is indicative of a crisis situation whereby he perceives insurmountable obstacles to the achievement of his desired goals or outcomes (Caplan, 1961; Carkhuff and Berensen, 1977). Within a crisis situation, it is further argued that there is a sense that the goals cannot be managed through the usual problem-solving methods (James and Gilliland, 2001). As such, there are demands on the person in crisis to resolve the situation through what may be adaptive or maladaptive methods. However, the extent to which a situation is viewed as a crisis depends upon the individual's perception, previous experiences, level of resiliency and coping skills (Vecchi, 2009).

In the second scenario, it would appear that, based on Tom's presentation, he has clear goals that he wants addressing, i.e. a release from the secure environment. This is an example of a conflict situation. That is, Tom currently wants to be released but the nature of the forensic environment prevents this, thus blocking his goal. Thus in this situation Tom requires the negotiator to assist him in the acquirement of his goal. As such, principled negotiation techniques can be applied to assist in the management of the situation and the problem-solving process. However, the approach used for Simon in the previous scenario will be somewhat different as he presents as an individual who is in crisis and who sees insurmountable obstacles to the achievement of his goals. He further presents as an individual who is not rational in his thinking. As such, in terms of the negotiation process, in the first instance it is important to bring about rational thinking. This is in order to further the ability of the negotiator to later effectively respond to the situation and to problem-solve the individual out of the situation in which they find themselves (principled negotiation). This will involve, for example, the application of the Behavioural Change Stairway Model (Van Hasselt *et al.*, 2008) that is routinely used in negotiation. This model focuses on the negotiator demonstrating active listening and empathy to gain rapport in an effort to influence the individual's behaviour. This is to ultimately bring about behavioural change through the ultimate gain of rational thinking.

It is proposed by Vecchi (2009) that, in both examples, it is imperative that the negotiator applies the correct approach. That is, if they adopt the wrong strategy and tactics then it is likely that the situation may get worse or culminate in violence. As such, Vecchi (2009) argues that 'This is precisely why conflict and crisis communication is both an art and a science that requires both study and practice to be effective' (p. 36).

Let us consider Tom's situation in order to apply the negotiation principles outlined earlier in the chapter. As noted previously Tom is in a conflict situation where he needs the negotiator to assist him in achieving his goal, thus calling for the need for principled negotiation techniques. In terms of the first principle of *separating the people from the problem*, it is important not to allow Tom to become entangled in the problem so that the behaviour becomes the topic of discussion rather than Tom himself. Beyond this, it is important to understand Tom's perception of the situation and to engage in further discussion, to empathically understand his view and the emotions underpinning this. It would be of further importance for the negotiator to be mindful of Tom applying negative interpretations to what is being said and also for the negotiator to be drawn into Tom's views about the hospital and his continued detention. That is, it is important that he does not begin to see the negotiator as the reason why he is being detained. In addition, it is also important that the negotiator monitor Tom's emotions throughout the discussions in order to maintain rational thinking and to support the application of the principled negotiation techniques. Likewise, the ability to self-monitor is also important on the part of the negotiator. The above will be applied consistently throughout the negotiation process.

Having started the process of separating Tom from the problem, the next principle will be to *focus on his interests and not his position*. His current position is that he wants to be released from the forensic hospital. However, as noted previously, his interests may be somewhat different and more compatible with the aims of the negotiator. Thus it is important to understand his motivations for engaging in the hostage-taking behaviour and his underlying goals. As such, and through open communication, it is important to explore why Tom may have made the choice to take a hostage, and for Tom to explore why the negotiator may want him to release the hostage and return to the ward. Once these motivations/interests have been established then it is more likely that options associated with a resolution can be explored. Within a hostage situation such as this, however, it is imperative that the negotiator does not focus solely on their own interests (i.e. resolving the situation) but also focuses on the interests of the perpetrator and how these can be met. For the negotiator, it will be important to legitimately present their interests to Tom, developing some degree of discrepancy in his position and rolling with any resistance that he may present with.

Once the negotiator has been able to facilitate an exploration of their interests and those of Tom, they are in a better position to begin *suggesting options for mutual gain*. Let us suppose that during the discussion about interests Tom identified that his interests were concerned with supporting his child in their education and personal development. Once this has been established then it is possible to generate a range of options that will benefit Tom in supporting his child's education, in addition to securing the release of the hostage and ending the situation. However, research suggests that individuals involved in forensic services, or those involved in offending, often bring with them their own set of challenges in terms of social problem-solving and their ability to solve problems with others. Research suggests that, generally, those individuals involved in forensic services, including those exhibiting aggressive behaviour (e.g. hostage-taking), are known to show deficits in cognitive skills (Donnellan *et al.*, 2000; Howard, 2006) including the ability to solve problems and generate alternatives to assist in the problem-solving process in a social context. As such, the negotiator may need to support Tom in the generation of a range of options. However, it is imperative that Tom feels a sense of autonomy in this process in order to increase his sense of commitment to the outcome, thus maintaining the principles of Self-Determination Theory. Once an outcome has been established, one further barrier may be considering what will happen to Tom after the situation has ended (e.g. will he be able to have access to his child, will he be prosecuted, etc.). Here, it will be important to *use objective criteria* such as considering what the law may say in relation to taking somebody hostage.

The above example aims to demonstrate the application of principled negotiation techniques to a conflict situation. The same process and framework can be adopted in a range of situations such as in Simon's scenario. However, for Simon, it would be important to establish more rational thinking in the first instance through the application of techniques such as the Behavioural Change Stairway Model (Van Hasselt, *et al.*, 2008). As with general negotiation situations, conflict and crisis situations both favour principled negotiation techniques over positional bargaining. Such an approach to problem-solving also upholds the principles of change as outlined earlier in the chapter.

Conclusions

While negotiation is a daily occurrence for many people, the manner in which negotiation takes place is fundamental to resolving the dispute or discussion successfully. As was seen at the start of chapter, many individuals adopt a positional bargaining approach to negotiation. While this is helpful in providing an anchor and starting position, it often culminates with at least one party having to make concessions, with the ultimate outcome being that while one party wins, the other loses. As such, principled negotiation is favoured as an approach that results in a win–win outcome for all parties.

As noted in this chapter, in addition to applying these models of negotiation to everyday situations, they further lend themselves to negotiation in both crisis and conflict communication. While the former requires a degree of emotional regulation before the process can begin, principled negotiation is still a successful option and a strategy noted to be fundamental to the safe resolution of such situations. In short, principled negotiation is a model of communication which has the potential to resolve difficult situations safely and successfully, including hostage-taking, barricades and roof-top protests. Furthermore, it is an appropriate structure for effective problem-solving and seeking a peaceful resolution to what can be very challenging situations.

References

Burrowes, N. and Needs, A. (2009) 'Time to contemplate change? A framework for assessing readiness to change with offenders', *Aggression and Violent Behavior*, 14 (1): 39–49.

Caplan, G. (1961) 'An approach to community mental health', cited in G. M. Vecchi, (2009) 'Conflict and crisis communication. A method for influencing and persuading behavioural change', *Behavioural Sciences*, 34: 34–42.

Carkhuff, R. R. and Berensen, B. G. (1977) 'Beyond counselling and therapy', cited in G. M. Vecchi, (2009) 'Conflict and crisis communication. A method for influencing and persuading behavioural change', *Behavioural Sciences*, 34: 34–42.

Deci, E. L. and Ryan, R. M. (2000) 'The "what" and "why" of goal pursuits: Human needs and self-determination of behaviour, *Psychological Inquiry*, 11: 227–68.

Donnellan, M., Ge, X. and Wenk, E. (2000) 'Cognitive abilities in adolescent-limited and life-course-persistent criminal offenders', *Journal of Abnormal Psychology*, 109: 396–402.

Fisher, R., Ury, W. and Patton, B. (2001) *Getting to Yes: Negotiating Agreement Without Giving In* (2nd edn). New York: Penguin.

Harvey-Craig, A, Fisher, M. J. and Simpson, P. (1997) 'An Explanation of the profiling of hostage incidents in HM Prison Service', *Issues in Criminological and Legal Psychology*, 29, 41–6.

Howard, P. (2006) *The Offender Assessment System: An Evaluation of the Second Pilot*, Home Office Research, Development and Statistics Directorate Research Findings No. 278. London: Home Office.

Howells, K. and Day, A. (2003) 'Readiness for anger management: clinical and theoretical issues', cited in Needs, A. and Burrowes, N. (2009) 'Time to contemplate change? A framework for assessing readiness to change with offenders', *Aggression and Violent Behavior*, 14 (1): 39–49.

Ireland, C. (2008) *Crisis Communication Manual*. Liverpool: Mersey Care NHS Trust.

James, R. K. and Gilliland, B. E. (2001) *Crisis Intervention Strategies* (4th edn). Stamford, CT: Brooks/Cole.

La Guardia, J., Ryan, R. M., Couchman, C. and Deci, K. L. (2000) 'Within-person variation in security of attachment: a self-determination theory perspective on attachment, need fulfillment, and well-being', cited in E. L. Deci and R. M. Ryan (eds), 'The "what" and "why" of goal pursuits: human needs and self-determination of behaviour', *Psychological Inquiry*, 11: 227–68.

Littell, J. H. and Girvin, H. (2002) 'Stages of change. A critique. Behavior modification', cited in N. Burrowes and A. Needs (2009) 'Time to contemplate change? A framework for assessing readiness to change with offenders', *Aggression and Violent Behavior*, 14 (1): 39–49.

Locke, E. A. (1996) 'Motivation through conscious goal setting', *Applied and Preventive Psychology*, 5 (2): 117–24.

McGuire, J. and Hatcher, R. (2001) 'Offense-focused problem solving: preliminary evaluation of a cognitive skills program', *Criminal Justice and Behavior*, 28: 564–87.

Markland, D., Ryan, R. M., Tobin, V. J. and Rollnick, S. (2005) 'Motivational interviewing and self-determination theory', *Journal of Social and Clinical Psychology*, 24: 811–31.

Miller, W. R. and Rollnick, S. (2002) *Motivational Interviewing: Preparing People for Change*. New York: Guilford Press.

Orleans, C. T. (2000) 'Promoting the maintenance of health behaviour change: recommendations for the next generation of research and practice', *Health Psychology*, 19 (Suppl. 1): 76–83.

Rogan, R. G., Hammer, M. R. and Van Zandt, C. R. (eds) (1997) *Dynamic Processes of Crisis Negotiation: Theory, Research and Practice*. Westport, CT: Praeger.

Rothman, A. J. (2000) 'Toward a theory-based analysis of behavioral maintenance', cited in R. M. Ryan, H. Patrick, E. L. Deci and G. C. Williams (2008) 'Facilitating health behaviour change and its maintenance: interventions based on self-determination theory', *European Health Psychologist*, 10: 2–5.

Ryan, R. M. and Deci, E. L. (2000) 'Self-determination theory and the facilitation of intrinsic motivation, social development and well-being', *American Psychologist*, 55 (1): 68–78.

Ryan, R. M., Patrick, H., Deci, E. L. and Williams, G. C. (2008) 'Facilitating health behaviour change and its maintenance: interventions based on Self-Determination Theory', *European Health Psychologist*, 10: 2–5.

Ryan, T. A. (1970) *Intentional Behavior*. New York: Ronald Press.

Slatkin, A. A. (2005) 'Communication in crisis and hostage negotiation: practical communication techniques, stratagems, and strategies for law enforcement, corrections and emergency service personnel in managing critical incidents', cited in G. M. Vecchi

(2009) 'Conflict and crisis communication: a method for influencing and persuading behavioural change', *Behavioural Sciences*, 34: 34–42.

Ury, W. (1991) *Getting Past No: Negotiating with Difficult People*, cited in G. M. Vecchi (2009) 'Conflict and crisis communication: a method for influencing and persuading behavioural change', *Behavioural Sciences*, 34: 34–42.

Van Hasselt, V. B., Romano, S. J. and Vecchi, G. M. (2008) 'Role playing: applications in hostage and crisis negotiation skills training', *Behavior Modification*, 32 (2): 248–63.

Vecchi, G. M. (2002) 'Hostage/barricade management: a hidden conflict within law-enforcement', cited in G. M. Vecchi (2009) 'Conflict and crisis communication: a method for influencing and persuading behavioural change', *Behavioural Sciences*, 34: 34–42.

Vecchi, G. M. (2003) 'Active listening: the key to effective crisis negotiation', cited in G. M. Vecchi (2009) 'Conflict and crisis communication: a method for influencing and persuading behavioural change', *Behavioural Sciences*, 34: 34–42.

Vecchi, G. M. (2009) 'Conflict and crisis communication: a method for influencing and persuading behavioural change', *Behavioural Sciences*, 34: 34–42.

Vecchi, G. M., Van Hasselt, V. B. and Romano, S. J. (2005) 'Crisis (hostage) negotiation: current strategies and issues in high-risk conflict resolution', *Aggression and Violent Behavior: A Review Journal*, 10: 533–51.

Ward, T. (2002) 'Good lives and the rehabilitation of offenders: promises and problems', *Aggression and Violent Behavior*, 1: 513–28.

Ward, T. and Stewart, C. (2003) 'Criminogenic needs and human needs: a theoretical model', *Psychology, Crime and Law*, 9 (2): 125–43.

Williams, G. C., Deci, E. L. and Ryan, R. M. (1998) 'Building healthcare partnerships by supporting autonomy: promoting maintained behaviour change and positive health outcomes', cited in R. M. Ryan, H. Patrick, E. L. Deci and G. C. Williams (2008) 'Facilitating health behaviour change and its maintenance: interventions based on Self-Determination Theory', *European Health Psychologist*, 10: 2–5.

Wilmot, W. W. and Hocker, J. L. (1998) *Interpersonal Conflict* (5th edn). Boston, MA McGraw-Hill.

3

CRISIS SITUATIONS
Communications, goals and techniques

Samuel L. Browning, Andrea M. Brockman, Vincent B. Van Hasselt and Gregory M. Vecchi

Crisis and hostage negotiations are a series of communications between the law enforcement negotiator and the person in crisis (subject). These communications are a means to achieve goals on both sides. The goals of the captive-taker, or subject, can span a wide range (e.g. monetary gain, escape, expression of rage, revenge). This is because barricaded hostage and crisis incidents can reflect either instrumental or expressive motivations on the part of the subject (e.g. Call, 1999; Vecchi *et al.*, 2005). 'True' hostage situations reflect instrumental goals of the subject. In these incidents, the subject has substantive demands, and s/he needs law enforcement, for example, to bargain for hostages in order to have those demands met. The communication and behaviour of subjects in these situations is calculated and methodical. Hostages serve as leverage in a negotiated transaction with law enforcement. In contrast, crisis situations reflect expressive goals of the subject. Illustrative are domestic disputes, workplace/school violence events or crisis situations involving the mentally ill in which the subject has barricaded himself/herself and others from law enforcement. Subjects in crisis situations do not necessarily have any substantive demands, nor do they need law enforcement to accomplish their goals. Further, subjects' communications and behaviours are more erratic and emotion-based in non-hostage crisis situations (Noesner and Webster, 1997).

Results of research by the FBI's Crisis Negotiation Unit (CNU) found that 90 per cent of incidents in the US were the result of expressive motivations in which the captives were, in fact, homicide victims-to-be or 'victims' (Vecchi *et al.*, 2005). In these situations, the subject was highly emotional and the captives were targets of the subject's emotional state (e.g. anger, frustration, humiliation). Therefore the CNU modified the communication goals and techniques involved in crisis negotiations to better fit these situations. Specifically, the unit began focusing on ways of reducing the emotionality of the subject and increasing rationality. This chapter will focus on negotiation strategies that are directed toward amelioration of highly negative emotions in crisis situations.

The negotiator is ultimately seeking one outcome: a peaceful resolution of the situation (i.e. the subject surrenders voluntarily, without violence or injury to on-scene professionals, hostages/victims or the subject). To accomplish this, communication techniques utilised by law enforcement negotiators focus on a specific goal: establishing a relationship between the negotiator and the subject as a means to reduce emotionality and diffuse the crisis. By accomplishing this, it is expected that the subject will be more rational and easily influenced by the negotiator.

Behavioral Change Stairway Model

The FBI's CNU developed a model that describes a process for effective negotiations, taking into account the high proportion of incidents that involve subjects' expressive goals (Noesner and Webster, 1997). These communications involve the establishment of a relationship between the negotiator and the subject, such that the former is able to influence the behaviour of the latter to achieve a peaceful resolution of the incident. This process has been conceptualised as the Behavioral Change Stairway Model (BCSM) (Vecchi *et al.*, 2005) and consists of five stages: (1) active listening skills; (2) empathy; (3) rapport; (4) influence; and (5) behavioural change. The model is viewed as a stairway because each stage is achieved sequentially and cumulatively as the negotiation progresses. Specifically, the negotiator cannot influence the subject (Stage 4) unless rapport has been established (Stage 3) using empathy (Stage 2) and active listening skills (Stage 1). The stairway metaphor is also useful with regard to setbacks in negotiations. For example, if the negotiator says something that damages rapport (Stage 3), the process reverts to an earlier stage of the stairway. The negotiator must then focus on active listening skills (Stage 1) and empathy (Stage 2) to re-establish rapport. A visual representation of this model is provided in Figure 3.1.

Behavioral Influence Stairway Model

The Behavioral Influence Stairway Model (BISM) is a recent modification of the BCSM and includes three stages: (1) empathy; (2) rapport; and (3) influence (Vecchi, 2009). These stages are also attained sequentially and cumulatively, and each is supported by the use of active listening skills *throughout* the negotiation process. As time passes, a relationship forms between the negotiator and the subject (see Figure 3.2). This relationship is critical to the successful resolution of a situation, regardless of whether the subject's motives are instrumental or expressive (Vecchi, 2009). In this model, active listening is not a stage by itself, but rather a continuous process in relationship-building underlying each of the other steps. As with the BCSM, the negotiator may move up or down the stairway, depending on the nature of the communications. An overview of active listening skills is provided in the sections below followed by a delineation of BISM components.

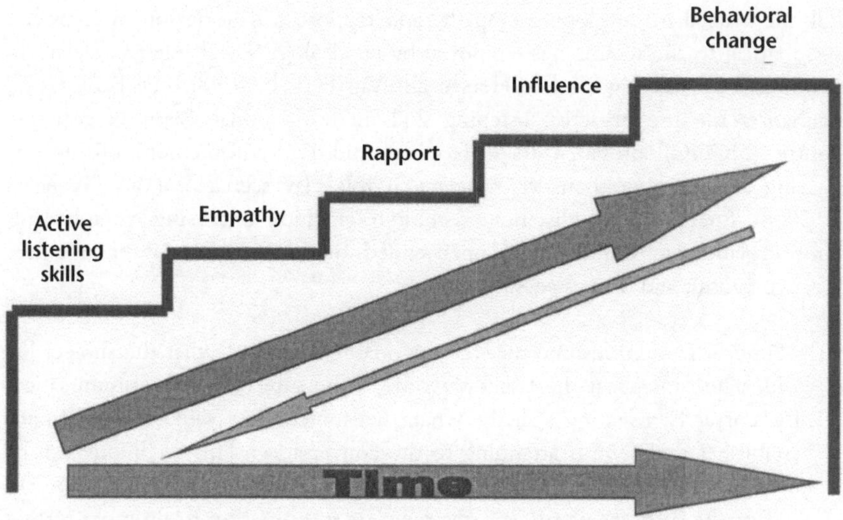

Source: Vecchi *et al.* (2005).

FIGURE 3.1 Behavioral Change Stairway Model.

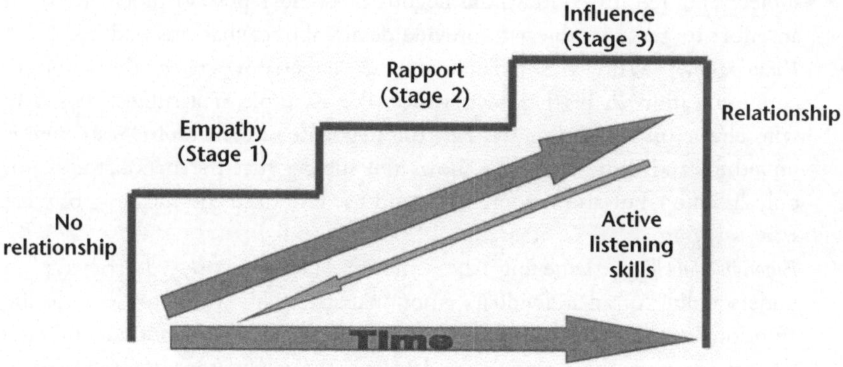

Source: Vecchi *et al.* (2005).

FIGURE 3.2 Behavioral Influence Stairway Model.

Active listening skills: laying the foundation

Although active listening skills are not a formal stage in the BISM, they create the foundation for the relationship between the negotiator and the subject. When dealing with highly-emotional persons in crisis, the most effective negotiation strategy is to listen (Noesner and Webster, 1997). Listening allows the subject to 'vent' the extreme emotions that are often the source of building pressure in the crisis. Use of active listening demonstrates to the subject that the negotiator perceives and is interested in his/her message (Noesner and Webster, 1997). These skills are crucial in developing empathy and rapport with a person in crisis and are identical to the techniques employed by psychologists and other clinicians to accomplish the same goals (see Hersen and Van Hasselt, 1998). The FBI's CNU emphasises the use of active listening skills in its National Crisis Negotiation Course (NCNC), provided to FBI agents and law enforcement officers, by assessing and training them via a series of role-play scenarios (Van Hasselt *et al.* 2008). Specific active listening techniques include mirroring, paraphrasing, emotion labelling, summarising, open-ended questions, minimal encouragers, effective pauses, and 'I' messages.

- *Mirroring.* To demonstrate that the negotiator has heard what the subject has said, s/he can repeat the last few words of the subject's last communication. By correctly restating exactly what the subject just said, the negotiator establishes that s/he is attending to the conversation. This technique can be used in disparate ways. First, the negotiator can use different inflections to mirror the subject's words as a statement or as a question to promote further elaboration on the part of the subject. For example, if a subject stated, 'My father put me through so much stress,' the crisis negotiator might respond, 'So much stress,' to indicate empathetic recognition of the mistreatment the subject endured. In contrast, the negotiator could reply, 'So much stress?' in an effort to get the subject to provide details about what was endured.
- *Paraphrasing.* With this technique, the negotiator states the subject's communication in his/her own words. For example, if a subject says, 'My wife cheats on me and always lies,' the negotiator might reply, 'Your wife is unfaithful and dishonest.' This shows the subject that the negotiator is not only listening, but also comprehends and has processed the meaning of what s/he is saying.
- *Emotion labelling.* Labelling the emotion being expressed conveys an understanding of an individual's emotional state. This works to decrease the emotionality of the subject. Even if the negotiator does not identify the correct emotion, the technique underscores the negotiator's commitment to trying to understand the situation. Examples of emotion labelling are, 'You seem angry,' or 'It sounds like you are overwhelmed.'
- *Summarising.* When a subject has relayed a substantive amount of information to the negotiator, it is helpful to periodically summarise what s/he has said up to that point. This tells the subject that the crisis negotiator has comprehended his/her main points. To effectively summarise the situation, the negotiator paraphrases what s/he has said, and labels any emotions the subject expressed. For example, the negotiator might say, 'Let me see if I have this right: your wife abandoned you for no reason, which makes you feel overwhelmed and angry.' A statement like this lets the subject know that the negotiator 'has the facts' of the situation and the subject's associated feelings.

- *Open-ended questions.* These are questions that require a narrative or expository response. Such questions cannot be answered with a single-word response such as 'yes' or 'no'. By asking questions that require elaboration, the negotiator encourages the subject to provide more information and express more emotion, in an effort to lower his/her emotionality and increase rational thought processes. These questions frequently begin with 'what' or 'when'. Questions that begin with 'why' are avoided due to their tendency to seem interrogatory and place the subject on the defensive (Vecchi *et al.*, 2005).
- *Minimal encouragers.* When the subject is speaking, the negotiator should occasionally express that s/he is listening and attending to what is being said, through the use of minimal encouragers or verbal cues such as 'uh-huh', 'okay', or 'right'. Interjecting such cues provides continuous reinforcement to the subject and encourages him/her to continue.
- *Effective pauses.* All conversations are marked by breaks in which neither person speaks. These pauses can be used to emphasise a point and focus thoughts before resuming dialogue. When employed in this manner in a crisis negotiation, these can be very effective.
- *'I' messages.* Some of the subject's behaviours are likely to be particularly disruptive to the negotiation. To counter this, negotiators employ 'I' messages. These statements take the focus off the subject and place it on the negotiator's feelings or reactions. For example, if the subject continues to hang up on the negotiator, the latter might say, 'When you hang up before I can talk to you, I feel frustrated because I am not able to help you.' This statement confronts the subject on the problem behaviour, but also helps to build rapport and demonstrate concern on the part of the negotiator. Further, it models an acceptable behavioural response to frustration for the subject. Gibbs *et al.* (1998) noted that this technique is effective in constructively framing the consequences of a situation or behaviour and, therefore, useful in training aggressive individuals to use appropriate assertiveness. 'I' statements can additionally be used to relate to the subject through self-disclosure. For example, the negotiator might say, 'I am a husband, too; I can't imagine what it must be like to lose your wife.' This statement establishes common ground between the subject and the negotiator.

Active listening skills have many uses in the context of crisis negotiations. One such benefit is to increase the length of the interaction, which serves to diffuse emotional intensity and lability (McMains and Mullins, 2006a). In crisis negotiations, time is clearly the negotiator's ally. This shift from emotionality to rationality results in more productive negotiations (Hatcher *et al.*, 1998). Moreover, if the negotiator distracts the subject from his/her original intention of harming captives by conversation, the strategy is valuable. This concept is referred to as 'verbal containment' in law enforcement, because the negotiator is limiting the subject's actions to talking rather than committing an act of violence.

Case illustration

Patrol officers requested a police crisis negotiator to respond to a suburban home in the late afternoon after they were unable to make contact with the couple inside. Neighbours had called the police because of sounds of yelling, and crashes from inside the house. The subject was a 29-year-old male who had a history of violent crime and weapons charges. Reports from neighbours indicated that the man had entered the home with a handgun. When the negotiator arrived on the scene, the subject was barricaded in the residence with his wife of five years and their two small children. Officers on the scene informed the negotiator that the subject lost his job approximately five months prior to the incident and that his wife served him with divorce documents earlier that day.

The following conversation occurred during the course of the negotiation with the subject:

> *Subject*: My stupid wife doesn't realise how lucky she is to have me! She's never appreciated me or what I do for our family!
> *Negotiator*: You sound really angry.
> *Subject*: I *am* angry!
> *Negotiator*: It seems like you also feel under-appreciated in your marriage.
> *Subject*: Yeah. I worked hard for four and a half years to put food on the table, and just a couple of months after I get let go from my job, she's ready to leave me.
> *Negotiator*: Ready to leave you?
> *Subject*: Yeah! She served me with divorce papers today. She doesn't want anything to do with me, now that I can't put money in her pocket!
> *Negotiator*: So, let me see if I'm hearing you correctly. You got let go from your job a few months ago, and your wife served you with divorce papers today, and her readiness to divorce you so soon makes you feel angry and unappreciated. Is that right?
> *Subject*: Yeah! That's exactly right.

This example shows how active listening skills can be used by negotiators to encourage subjects to continue talking and ventilate emotions. The negotiator's first two comments in this interaction involved labelling the subject's emotions. This made the subject feel like the negotiator was trying to understand the crisis from the subject's perspective. The negotiator then employed mirroring to encourage the subject to continue relating his story. Finally, the negotiator summarised the events and corresponding emotions to convey a sense of understanding to the subject. In response to these techniques, the subject shows enthusiasm regarding the negotiator's continued interest and continues interacting with him.

Proper use of these active listening skills will allow a negotiator to progress his/her relationship with the subject to the subsequent stages of the BISM. Further, any setbacks in the negotiation require a renewed emphasis on the use of these skills.

Behavioral Influence Stairway Model: Stages

Stage 1: Empathy

As previously mentioned, active listening is fundamental in the negotiator's attempt to demonstrate empathy for the subject in crisis. Empathy involves viewing circumstances from the perspective of another person, in the context of that person's life (see Johnston *et al.*, 1998). Projecting an empathetic attitude builds trust and rapport between the negotiator and the subject (Martinovski *et al.*, 2007; Regini, 2004). In addition to active listening, a negotiator's tone and inflection are important in conveying empathy. The negotiator must maintain a tone of calm sincerity in order to effectively convey empathy. The axiom that 'It is not *what* is said, it is *how* it is said,' is very applicable here.

Individuals in crisis have a desire to be heard and to have someone attempt to understand them (Noesner and Webster, 1997). When a negotiator projects an empathetic attitude, the subject feels that someone is on their side. However, Martinovski *et al.* (2007) point out that rejection of empathy in negotiations not only occurs, but is a normal phase in the process. This may occur because the negotiator has misunderstood the emotional state or needs of the subject. In this case, the negotiator must emphasise active listening to accurately identify these needs. Once empathy has been demonstrated by the negotiator and accepted by the subject, it forges a relationship between them that is requisite to a peaceful crisis resolution (Martinovski *et al.*, 2007; Regini, 2004; Vecchi *et al.*, 2005).

Stage 2: Rapport

When the crisis negotiator has demonstrated active listening and empathy with the subject, rapport develops (Vecchi, 2009). Development of rapport means that the subject places more trust in the negotiator. Consequently, the subject becomes more likely to accept ideas and suggestions. At this stage, the negotiator shifts from nearly exclusive use of active listening skills to inclusion of other verbal techniques. However, it is still too early in the negotiation to incorporate problem-solving strategies. Premature initiation of problem-solving may make the subject feel that: (a) the negotiator is not taking his/her problem seriously or (b) the problem is being minimised. On the other hand, the negotiator can minimise the consequences of the current situation for the subject by reframing the context. This may be accomplished by highlighting the fact that even though the circumstances are not good, they could be worse (e.g. no one has been injured or killed), and the consequences are not likely to be very severe. The negotiator does not want to say that the subject will go free, because such an obviously untrue and insincere message will undermine rapport. Most subjects realise that they will not go free at the conclusion of the situation. In addition, when utilising minimisation, the negotiator should keep in mind what actions the subject has taken up to that point. For example, minimising the consequences will be difficult, if not impossible, if the subject has already injured or killed one or more captives.

It is also important that the negotiator finds ways for the subject to save face and justify his/her behaviour. To do this, the negotiator must agree (when possible) with the subject, minimise differences and find common ground (Vecchi, 2009). It is easier for the subject to come to terms with what has happened, and subsequently surrender, if there is an explanation or justification for his/her behaviour. Helping subjects save face: (1) helps them to displace responsibility for their actions, and (2) serves to give the impression that they are victims themselves, rather than 'bad guys'. To do this, the negotiator and the subject may collude to place blame for the current situation on others (e.g. victims, family members, courts).

Stage 3: Influence

At this stage, the negotiator has established a relationship of trust with the subject. The subject is, therefore, prepared to accept suggestions and input from the negotiator (Vecchi *et al.*, 2005). Problem-solving strategies can now be effectively employed to bring about a peaceful resolution to the crisis. The negotiator and the subject will collaborate to reach a mutually agreed-upon solution for the subject's surrender. Goldfried and Davison (1994) outlined an effective psychological counselling technique that has heuristic value here. Their problem-solving strategy includes: (a) defining the problem; (b) generating all possible solutions ('brainstorming'); (c) eliminating less desirable options; (d) choosing a solution that both the subject and negotiator find acceptable; (e) making a plan for carrying out the chosen solution; and (f) implementing the planned solution. Because the subject is an active participant in the problem-solving, s/he can take ownership of finding the solution.

Getting past no

Ury's (1993) 'getting past no' approach is very popular when it comes to influencing a subject in crisis. According to Ury (1993), the negotiator must work to get past 'no' during the negotiation. This method focuses on getting past the subject's refusal to cooperate in order to employ joint problem-solving. However, there are five barriers which must be addressed before the negotiator can employ problem-solving strategies: (1) the negotiator's reaction, (2) subject's emotion, (3) dissatisfaction, (4) position, and (5) power. First, all involved in the negotiation will have some emotional reaction. Negotiators must be aware of their own reaction, especially when the subject is uncooperative, belligerent or refusing to speak. For example, if the negotiator reacts in a negative manner (e.g. uses derogatory language, dehumanises or displays frustration or anger towards the subject), negotiations are likely to deteriorate. However, if the negotiator remains calm and utilises active listening skills, the subject's emotional response will likely reflect the same demeanour (Ury, 1993).

To effectively work toward compromise, negotiators must acknowledge the emotions, power and position of subjects, as well as their dissatisfaction and distress. Over time, and given the opportunity to vent their feelings, subjects' emotional state will stabilise, allowing increased communication. However, to improve chances for success, negotiators must take their subjects' needs/wants into consideration. To achieve a positive outcome, Ury (1993) suggested five stages in the negotiation process.

Stage 1: Go to the balcony

Negotiators must first overcome their own emotional reaction. Specifically, the negotiator needs to distance him/herself from emotional reactions to the greatest extent possible. In accomplishing this, the negotiator must be able to remain professional, objective and empathetic. This strategy is particularly important when the subject is verbally abusive or combative. By experiencing the interaction as an outside observer, negotiators remove their own emotional biases from crisis situations and are able to move to the next stage of the negotiation process.

Stage 2: Step to their side

At this stage, the negotiator must diffuse the emotions of the subject (e.g. defensiveness, fear, anger). Rather than acting like an adversary, the negotiator gives the impression of taking the subject's side by actively listening, acknowledging feelings, agreeing (when possible) and showing respect. In this way, the negotiator becomes an ally (from the subject's perspective). The negotiator attempts to foster this sense of camaraderie with the subject, even to the extent that the subject feels that the negotiator is a partner, working with him/her against the police agency or other professionals.

Stage 3: Reframe

The subject is still likely to be hesitant to trust the negotiator completely: because most subjects assume that the police, or other professionals involved in the negotiations, will not approve their demands, negotiators can use reframing techniques to 'catch the subjects off guard'. For example, a subject may not expect the demand of a million dollars and a private jet; however, the negotiator does not refuse this demand outright. Instead, the negotiator acknowledges that the subject needs money and transportation, and s/he will see what can be done. In addition to demands, the negotiator may use open-ended questions to encourage the subject to think about his/her plan more closely. The hope is that subjects will realise that the position is unrealistic.

Stage 4: Build them a golden bridge

The goal of this stage is to make it possible for the subject to say 'yes'. Up to this point, both parties may not be satisfied with any of the proposed solutions. Therefore, negotiators must allow subjects to present possible alternatives and subsequently point out the problems with them. If subjects' solutions are not viable, it makes it easier to accept those from the negotiator. Simultaneously, negotiators will be getting subjects to agree to small requests (e.g. continuing to talk, engaging the safety on their weapons). Establishing this pattern of acquiescence to small requests makes subsequent agreements to larger requests easier. Another strategy to ease cooperation is for the negotiator to help the subject 'save face' by providing a justification for their actions and making the solution appear to be a victory for the perpetrator.

Stage 5: Use power to educate

The purpose of this stage is to identify with subjects while showing them that they cannot 'win' without the assistance of the negotiator. Further, the subject must come to the conclusion that surrendering is the most beneficial outcome of the situation. Negotiators must be subtle in utilising their power over the situation. For example, it is likely that if the subject does not surrender, command staff will send in a tactical team. However, when presenting this information to the subject, the negotiator might say something like, 'My bosses are getting frustrated and want to send in SWAT; let's see if we can come up with a better solution, so they don't have a reason to do that.'

The above-mentioned sequence of steps is viewed as requisite to joint problem-solving. Negotiators must first control their own emotions, as well as the emotions, dissatisfaction and position of the subject. The negotiation process will progress when the negotiator is able to put aside emotions and establish rapport with the subject. The negotiator works to develop a relationship so that the solutions they offer are more likely to be accepted. However, as indicated, this problem-solving approach is not based on the needs or wants of the negotiator. Rather, the agreement between the negotiator and subject is paramount (Ury, 1993).

Although the BCSM and BISM, often in conjunction with Ury's (1993) approach to influence, are currently the preferred models of the FBI (Vecchi *et al.*, 2005) and other law enforcement agencies, other models have been offered as well. Most of these share at least some communication strategies (e.g. active listening skills, empathy), but employ them in different ways. These communication models are discussed in the following sections.

Substantive demands, attunement, face and emotion

Originally referred to as the FIRE (Face, Instrumental demands, Relationship and Emotion) model, an acronym that is used to represent frames of communication within the crisis negotiation, the Substantive demands, Attunement, Face, and Emotion (SAFE) model was renamed to ensure that the acronym FIRE was not misinterpreted by the general public as a tactical approach to crisis response (Hammer, 2007). The SAFE model specifies three core interactive processes essential for negotiations. These include: (1) identifying the subject's emotional frame of reference (e.g. anger, jealousy, sadness) through communication; (2) matching the response style of the subject; and (3) attending to the negotiator's need for a peaceful resolution. According to the SAFE model, subjects in crisis will interpret all of the interactions with the negotiator within the context of their emotional frame.

In this model, the negotiator must first determine the predominant frame that reflects the perspective of the subject's communication. Some examples of these are: substantive (bargaining/problem-solving), attunement (trust or distrust toward the negotiator), face (sensitivity to how s/he is perceived), or emotional (the emotional state). The negotiator uses these frames to identify the subject's response pattern and then matches the negotiation style with the appropriate frame (i.e. each frame is synonymous with a 'trigger' for either escalation or de-escalation of crisis situations). The SAFE model proposes a tracking of escalation/de-escalation patterns, thus making it possible to modify the negotiation strategies when necessary (Hammer, 2007).

Once negotiators determine the frame that best demonstrates the subject's communication pattern, they proceed to the second interactive process. At this point, negotiators are encouraged to match their communication to the frame of the subject. Specifically, the negotiator must engage subjects within their SAFE frame by addressing their particular wants/needs. For example, if the subject falls within the 'attunement' frame, the negotiator must portray a sense of trustworthiness. This approach directly addresses the subject's need to be able to place trust in the negotiator.

After the negotiator is able to establish that progress has been made in the de-escalation of the situation, there is a shift to the third process in the model, which focuses on the underlying needs of the negotiator (successful resolution through surrender) (Hammer, 2007). This aspect of the model requires the negotiator to demonstrate influence over the subject. The model proposes that once the subject's wants/needs have been managed, the negotiator will have more ability to assert influence, allowing the negotiation to culminate in a peaceful resolution.

The cylindrical model of crisis communications

The cylindrical model of crisis communications highlights the interaction, motivation and behaviour within the negotiation process (Taylor, 2002). Specifically, this model demonstrates the differences between interpersonal behaviours during crisis negotiations. Taylor (2002) proposed various communication behaviours of negotiators: withdrawn, emotional and rational. The model was developed by analysing nine hostage incidents. Those incidents were representative of both hostage (e.g. during the commission of a crime) and non-hostage (e.g. within the context of domestic violence) situations. Analysis focused on changes in the subject's person or object of focus and in thought units (i.e., a complete idea that an individual expresses). Taylor (2002) proposed three general levels of interaction: (1) avoidance, (2) distributive and (3) integrative; and within each level, three motivational themes were identified: identity, relational and instrumental.

The avoidance level of interaction is indicative of behaviours that depict a tendency to withdraw from interaction, and a tendency to deny responsibility for the hostage situation. At this level, negotiators should make an effort not to assert power over the subject, as this would indicate a refusal in relationship development. Within this level, the identity theme focuses on subjects' attempts to place blame for their behaviour elsewhere. The relational theme deals with behaviours (e.g. withdrawal) that are associated with ineffective communication. The instrumental theme reflects an inability to maintain personal involvement in the crisis. If the negotiator fails to commit to previous agreements, the negotiation will likely regress to earlier stages of negotiation and possibly result in unsuccessful crisis resolution.

The distributive level of interaction is characterised by an uncompromising approach to communication (i.e., the parties involved share unwillingness to compromise). Suggestions made are often unreasonable, with a tendency to reject the other party's offers. The identity theme involves highly emotional criticisms of the other party's actions. If this theme is present, negotiators will likely express commitment to their exaggerated views of self-efficacy. Although the relational theme emphasises relationship development, here the focus is not on the other party but rather on one's personal goals. Through pleas and appeals, negotiators attempt to persuade the subject to agree with their point of view. The instrumental theme is identified by the display of antagonistic behaviours (i.e. both parties reject the other's solutions and place strong emphasis on demands) (Taylor, 2002).

The integrative, or cooperative, level of interaction is described as a negotiator's willingness to fulfil the demands of the subject (Taylor, 2002). During times of disagreement, the negotiator provides a solution by utilising empathy. The identity theme enhances communication through displays of empathy. Patterns of interaction become collaborative, with solutions being met with reduced conflict. The relational theme is reflected by interactions in which the negotiator incorporates active listening into their interaction. When the negotiator begins to focus on compromise and flexibility, the communication level is classified as instrumental.

Thus the cylindrical model demonstrates the differences between interpersonal behaviours during crisis negotiations. Taylor (2002) identified various communication behaviours of negotiators: withdrawn, emotional and rational. At each level, the communication was further shown to revolve around three themes. The basis of the research was to identify the underlying features of communication during negotiation. The value of this approach is the ability to identify the relationship between the context of the negotiation and the outcome (Taylor, 2002).

Structured Tactical Engagement Process

The Structured Tactical Engagement Process (STEPS) is based on the Transtheoretical Stages of Change model developed by Prochaska and DiClemente (1985) for behaviour change in the therapeutic context. STEPS views the negotiation process as proceeding through a series of stages or steps. The negotiator's responsibility is to identify the step that applies to the subject and proceed from that point. According to Keeln and McMurtry (2007), STEPS is based on four assumptions: (1) peaceful surrender is a common behavioural goal in all crisis situations; (2) barricaded subjects may be at different steps of readiness for change; (3) a negotiator's goal is to move the subject through the different steps; and (4) a subject must move through all steps for a peaceful resolution.

Step 0: Pre-contemplation

Subjects in this step are unwilling or unable to acknowledge that they are in a crisis situation. The subject is uncooperative, argumentative and unrealistic. S/he is unwilling to accept a peaceful resolution. The negotiator must work to move the subject toward Step 1 by building rapport. As the subject begins to feel a connection with the negotiator, s/he is less likely to be defensive and becomes more open to suggestions.

Step 1: Contemplation

When the subject begins to acknowledge that s/he is in a situation that will require cooperation with the negotiator, s/he has moved into Step 1. Now, the subject may begin offering an explanation or justification for his/her behaviour. The subject may realise there is a need to make a change, but feels like s/he does not have the necessary options or resources to do so. The negotiator provides hope and optimism by indicating that together they can resolve the situation.

Step 2: Preparation

In Step 2, the subject acknowledges that there is a problem and is ready to consider a resolution. Problem-solving occurs at this stage, as the subject attempts to identify a number of alternative solutions and consequences. As the subject shifts into this stage, the negotiator must become more directive in order to proceed to the final step.

Step 3: Action

The subject is now willing to peacefully surrender by following an agreed-upon resolution. The negotiator must remain highly directive and supportive, because subjects may retreat to a prior step if they become anxious or distrustful.

According to Keeln and McMurtry (2007), this model should be used as a guideline to determine the subject's level of readiness for change. The negotiator must be aware of the potential movement of the subject back and forth through the stages; therefore, the negotiator must be flexible. The STEPS model is broad and originally designed for application across many types of crisis situations. As with other approaches, the basis of negotiation is the use of active listening skills.

Negotiations involving special settings or populations

In addition to different models of negotiation communication in crisis situations, there are certain strategies that are more or less beneficial, depending on the unique setting or type of subject involved. Some examples of circumstances include negotiations that take place in correctional settings or involve the mentally ill or fellow police officers as subjects.

Negotiation in correctional settings

Crisis situations in correctional settings are unique in several ways. First, hostage situations in correctional settings may include staff members as victims and, therefore, invoke a strong emotional response from crisis response team members. Also, many of the demands made by prisoner subjects pertain to relatively minor issues (e.g. living conditions), some of which are negotiable. However, the following items are non-negotiable: (1) a reduction in the subject's sentence; (2) drugs or alcohol; (3) weapons; or (4) hostage exchanges. As with other crisis situations, prisoners can be categorised into three groups: the mentally unstable, the criminal who takes hostages primarily to cause harm and the 'crusader' (hostage-taking is employed as a means of making a statement). Negotiation team members need to be familiar with the different types and trained to deal with each (Strentz, 2006).

Beyond these motives, prisoners are under institutional stress, used to being told what to do and accustomed to routine; therefore, when providing prisoners with options, these should not be open-ended. For example, the negotiator should not ask a prisoner what they want to eat as they may not be used to having choices and may find this frustrating. Rather, the negotiator should provide limited choices, 'Do you want a burger or pizza?' (Strentz, 2006). The elements requisite for a successful negotiation in a prison setting are similar to those needed in other settings, and include: (1) show of force by authorities; (2) containment; (3) substantive demands made by the subject; (4) communication; and (5) expanded time frame for establishing of emotions. Negotiations should be based on the institution's response plan and strategies should focus on prison-specific aspects of negotiation (Souvenir, 2009).

Case illustration

During a routine prisoner count in a housing unit, a prisoner pulled the floor officer into his cell. The second officer present during the count called for assistance and locked the unit down. The subject was a 43-year-old male who had a history of aggression toward staff and fellow prisoners. When the negotiator arrived on scene, the subject had barricaded himself, his roommate, and the officer in his cell. Fellow prisoners indicated that the subject possessed a 'shank' (e.g. homemade knife) which he had planned to use on the captives.

The following conversation occurred during the course of the negotiation with the subject:

> *Subject*: I have been falsely accused; I do not belong behind bars.
> *Negotiator*: You sound very upset.
> *Subject*: Yeah, I'm upset. I have been in here for 10 years and have another 20 years to go. I never get mail, I don't get to go to the store, and the officers are always hounding me about shaving.
> *Negotiator*: It sounds like you feel that you are not getting your needs met.
> *Subject*: I'm not! But I will now. I've got your buddy in here, and I know you're going to do what I want to get him out. I have been in here all day waiting for this very moment.
> *Negotiator*: Well, my goal is to help you get everyone out of there safely, and that includes you. My focus is more on you right now. What is it you hope to accomplish?
> *Subject*: I've wanted to get a new (work) detail for five months, and several staff members have insisted they will help and no one has done so yet.
> *Negotiator*: That can be very frustrating. Would you like to work in lawn maintenance or horticulture?
> *Subject*: Horticulture sounds good!

This example shows how negotiators in correctional settings face special challenges. For example, the subject chose a correctional officer as a hostage because he knew that the other staff members knew him personally. It appears that his hope was that the negotiator would comply with any request he made due to the emotional connection between the negotiator and the hostage. Further, the negotiator had to be aware of institutionalisation effects on the subject. When the subject requested a new work detail, the negotiator gave him limited options to avoid overwhelming him with decisions. Using these context-specific strategies, in conjunction with active listening skills, the negotiator was able to diffuse the subject's emotion and begin to influence the subject.

Negotiating with individuals who have mental illness

The ability to influence another's behaviour is hindered in crisis situations, especially when the subject has a mental illness. Individuals with a mental illness (e.g. mentally disordered subjects) present unusual challenges to the negotiator. However, the basic principles of negotiation can still be applied, as long as negotiators remain aware of the mental disturbance and its potential impact on the subject in crisis. Lanceley (2003) indicates that the following five disorders are of particular relevance: (1) schizophrenia, (2) bipolar disorder, (3) major depressive disorder, (4) antisocial personality disorder, and (5) borderline personality disorder. For a detailed discussion of the application of crisis communication to mental disorder, see chapters 4 and 5 (this volume).

Negotiating with law enforcement officers

Law enforcement officers (LEOs) have highly stressful jobs that involve ongoing exposure to traumatic events (Van Hasselt *et al.*, 2003; Violanti, 2004). Officers must respond to dangerous situations on a regular basis. They must be able to react quickly and effectively to this danger. In addition, they must make important decisions in a short period of time. LEOs are held accountable for these decisions by a bureaucratic agency, the media/public and the court system. Not surprisingly, rates of post-traumatic stress disorder (PTSD), alcoholism, relationship problems and suicide are high in this population (see Chapter 10, this volume, and also reviews by Miller, 2006; Stephens *et al.*, 1999; White and Honig, 1995).

While the limited amount of available research suggests that prevalence of LEOs as barricaded subjects is relatively low, it is still of concern for negotiators (Terhune-Bickler, 2004). There are several special considerations for negotiators dealing with fellow officers, including: personality factors, the prior relationship of responding officers to the officer in crisis, increased risk of trauma to responding LEOs, media exposure and the in-crisis officer's knowledge of a fellow law enforcement professional. Further, LEOs share some common traits that warrant consideration by negotiators (McMains and Mullins, 2006b). For example, they tend to be disciplined, driven and somewhat perfectionist. These traits result in effectiveness on the job, but can cause problems when an officer is in crisis. Specifically, they can lead to an increased fear of shame, failure and loss of control, due to the fact that LEOs place high value on their reputations. Crisis situations constitute a significant threat to their reputations; therefore, such fears may be paramount in negotiations.

LEOs are also a part of a tight-knit, closed group. Officers, crisis negotiators and tactical operators responding to an officer in crisis often have a prior relationship with that individual. This situation can impact on the negotiation process in different ways (Terhune-Bickler, 2004). For example, the voice of a trusted friend and colleague can be reassuring to the officer. Also, when the employing agency responds, there is easy access to intelligence information on the officer, as well as potential third-party intermediaries. However, when the officer expresses enmity toward the agency, s/he may view the negotiator as part of the problem. Command staff should contemplate the benefits of allowing/asking another agency to respond to the incident if the officer displays hostility or feelings of persecution from his/her agency.

The prior relationship with the in-crisis officer poses a concern for responding law enforcement personnel themselves as well. If the situation must be resolved tactically, there is an increased risk of trauma to on-scene negotiators and tactical operators (Terhune-Bickler, 2004). In these circumstances, the responding LEOs may experience feelings of failure, frustration and anger due to the inability to resolve the situation without harm to their colleague. The connection to the officer in crisis increases the stress and effect of the trauma on the responding officers.

Although these incidents are rare, there is significant media attention when they occur (McMains and Mullins, 2006b). Consequently, law enforcement administrators feel increased pressure to resolve the situation rapidly. This can result in questionable decision-making that is not consistent with agency policy and that may constitute a safety risk for everyone involved. Further, the in-crisis officer is likely to feel that his/her career is being threatened given the increased media attention.

Finally, officers in crisis are more aware of law enforcement policies and procedures than civilians (Terhune-Bickler, 2004). This is especially true when the responding officers are from the officer's employing agency. In that case, the officer is aware of the average response time, rules of engagement, negotiating style/tactics and philosophy of the agency. Therefore the officer may not trust promises made by negotiators or administrators. However, McMains and Mullins (2006b) caution that officers may not know negotiation/SWAT tactics as well as might be expected. They caution that assumption of knowledge may lead to the in-crisis officer misunderstanding what is happening during the crisis. According to McMains and Mullins (2006b), when dealing with a fellow officer in crisis, negotiation teams should: (1) decide what agency will respond to the officer in crisis, based on indications of the subject officer's level of enmity or trust with the employing agency; (2) select a negotiator carefully, based on the existence/quality of a prior relationship between the negotiator and the subject; (3) minimise fault and help the officer in crisis save face; (4) be prepared for the officer to have advanced knowledge of policies/tactics, but avoid making assumptions; and (5) carefully assess for signs of suicide.

Communication patterns to avoid in crisis situations

Several strategies and issues in crisis negotiation have been discussed. However, there are some techniques that should be avoided in crisis negotiations due to their propensity to exacerbate the situation. First, while mirroring is a very effective active listening technique, Miller (2005) contends that, with subjects who use much profanity, the negotiator should avoid matching this type of language. Individuals under stress are more likely to use profanity; the role of the negotiator is to model calm, appropriate interactions for the highly emotional and volatile subject. The use of certain words or phrases may have a negative effect on crisis negotiations as well. For example, saying 'I understand' often causes the subject to feel as though the negotiator is minimising the problem or not taking it seriously. Whatever the subject's situation, it is likely that s/he has been dealing with it for quite some time. Therefore to have someone say they fully comprehend the difficulties of that situation creates the impression that the negotiator is simply trying to put a 'plaster' on the issue. Instead, the negotiator should give the impression that s/he is trying to take the perspective of the person in crisis.

'Listen' is a word that law enforcement officers use frequently when trying to solve problems. However, the same word in a crisis negotiation may come across as a demand (i.e., the negotiator is giving an 'order'). Similarly, the negotiator should avoid telling the subject to 'calm down'. The subject took captives so that s/he would be in control; taking that control away by force will escalate the situation. Eliminating options early in the negotiation leaves the subject with few perceived alternatives other than harming captives. Examples of words that eliminate options are 'don't', 'won't', 'can't', and 'no'. Rather than eliminate options, it is better for the negotiator to advise the subject that the request/demand must be cleared through higher-level administrators and that the negotiator will get back to the subject regarding the request.

Summary

Crisis negotiations consist of a series of communications between a negotiator and a subject. The goals of subjects' communications vary as a function of their motivation. Those who display instrumental motivation make substantive demands, are more in control of their emotions and think of their captives as leverage or capital in the negotiation. Alternatively, subjects who display expressive motivations make no substantive demands, are emotionally volatile and their captives are usually the target of their extreme emotions. The negotiators' communications are aimed at diffusing intense emotions and convincing subjects to release their captives without injury.

The most salient model of crisis negotiation communication is the Behavioral Influence Stairway Model (BISM), which was derived from the Behavioral Change Stairway Model (BCSM), developed by the FBI's Crisis Negotiation Unit (CNU). Proponents of BISM conceptualise negotiator communications through the metaphor of a stairway. The negotiator completes all stages of the model sequentially and cumulatively in order to reach the 'top' of the stairway. The model stipulates that the negotiator begin by utilising active listening skills and continue to employ these skills throughout the negotiation. The negotiator then demonstrates empathy (Stage 1), establishes rapport (Stage 2) and exerts influence (Stage 3) with the subject.

A popular approach to exerting influence was outlined by Ury (1993) and is referred to as the 'getting past no' method of negotiation. This technique advocates the use of five stages in attempting to influence the subject. The different stages delineate tactics for gaining the trust of subjects and psychological strategies for influencing behaviour.

Several other models also have been developed to conceptualise the process of communications in crisis situations. SAFE, for example, emphasises the importance of: substantive demands (bargaining/problem-solving), attunement (trust or distrust toward the negotiator), face work (sensitivity to how s/he is perceived) and emotional state (Hammer, 2007). The cylindrical model highlights the interaction, motivation and behaviour of subjects and negotiators within the negotiation process (Taylor, 2002). The Structured Tactical Engagement Process (STEPS) model, derived from Prochaska and DiClemente's (1985) Transtheoretical Stages of Change model, views the negotiation process as proceeding through a series of stages in which the negotiator's responsibility is to: (1) identify the stage that reflects the subject's readiness for behaviour change and (2) proceed from that point (Keeln and McMurtry, 2007).

Beyond the disparate theoretical models for crisis negotiation, there are context-specific strategies designed for use in special settings or populations as well. Some examples of these include giving prisoner subjects limited options so as not to overwhelm them and using a 'buddy' approach with antisocial subjects. In cases where the subject is a police officer, it is important to assess feelings about his/her own agency to determine which department should respond to negotiate the crisis.

Finally, negotiators need to know not only what strategies are effective in crisis negotiation communications, but also what techniques to avoid. For example, negotiators should avoid eliminating options perceived to be available to the subject or using language that sounds like the negotiator is giving orders to the subject. These strategies may escalate the emotional volatility of the situation, and detract from the negotiator's goal of a peaceful resolution.

References

Call, J. A. (1999) 'The hostage triad: takers, victims, and negotiators', in H. V. Hall (ed.), *Lethal Violence: A Sourcebook on Fatal Domestic, Acquaintance, and Stranger Violence.* Boca Raton, FL: CRC Press.

Gibbs, J. C., Potter, G. B., Goldstein, A. P. and Brendtro, L. K. (1998) 'How EQUIP programs help youth change', *Reclaiming Children and Youth*, 7: 117–22.

Goldfried, M. R. and Davison, G. C. (1994) *Clinical Behavior Therapy.* New York: John Wiley & Sons.

Hammer, M. R. (2007) *Saving Lives: The S.A.F.E. Model for Resolving Hostage and Crisis Incidents.* Westport, CT: Praeger Security International.

Hatcher, C., Mohandie, K., Turner, J. and Gelles, M. G. (1998) 'The role of the psychologist in crisis/hostage negotiations', *Behavioral Sciences and the Law*, 16: 455–72.

Hersen, M. and Van Hasselt, V. B. (eds) (1998) *Basic Interviewing: A Practical Guide for Counselors and Clinicians.* Mahwah, NJ: Lawrence Erlbaum Associates.

Johnston, F. E., Van Hasselt, V. B. and Hersen, M. (1998) 'Rapport, empathy, and reflection', in M. Hersen and V. B. Van Hasselt (eds), *Basic Interviewing: A Practical Guide for Counselors and Clinicians.* Mahwah, NJ: Lawrence Erlbaum Associates.

Keeln, B. and McMurtry, C. M. (2007) 'STEPS – structured tactical engagement process: a model for crisis negotiation', *Journal of Police Crisis Negotiations*, 7: 29–51.

Lanceley, F. (1981) 'The antisocial personality as a hostage taker', *Journal of Police Science and Administration*, 9: 28–34.

Lanceley, F. (2003) *On Scene Guide for Crisis Negotiators* (2nd edn). New York: CRC Press.

McMains, M. J. and Mullins, W. C. (2006a) 'Demands and the effects of time', in M. J. McMains and W. C. Mullins (eds), *Crisis Negotiations: Managing Critical Incidents and Hostage Situations in Law Enforcement and Corrections* (3rd edn). Cincinnati, OH: Anderson, pp. 113–51.

McMains, M. J. and Mullins, W. C. (2006b) 'Unique incidents: negotiating with special groups', in M. J. McMains and W. C. Mullins (eds), *Crisis Negotiations: Managing Critical Incidents and Hostage Situations in Law Enforcement and Corrections* (3rd edn). Cincinnati, OH: Anderson, pp. 459–81.

Martinovski, B., Traum, D. and Marsella, S. (2007) 'Rejection of empathy in negotiation', *Group Decision and Negotiation*, 16: 61–76.

Miller, L. (2005) 'Hostage negotiation: psychological principles and practices', *International Journal of Emergency Mental Health*, 7: 277–98.

Miller, L. (2006) *Practical Police Psychology: Stress Management and Crisis Intervention for Law Enforcement*. Springfield, IL: Charles C. Thomas.

Needham, J. (1977) 'Neutralization of a prison hostage situation', *Criminal Justice Monographs*, 8: 1–48.

Noesner, G. W. and Webster, M. (1997) 'Crisis intervention: using active listening skills in negotiation', *FBI Law Enforcement Bulletin*, 66: 13–19.

Prochaska, J. O. and DiClemente, C. C. (1985) 'Transtheoretical therapy: toward a more integrative model of change', *Psychotherapy: Theory, Research and Practice*, 19: 276–88.

Regini, C. (2004) 'Crisis intervention for law enforcement negotiators', *FBI Law Enforcement Bulletin*, 73: 1–6.

Souvenir, A. (2009) *Crisis Negotiations in Correctional Settings*. Presentation given at FBI Crisis Negotiations Selected Topics Course, Fort Lauderdale, Florida, October.

Stephens, C., Long, N. and Fleit, R. (1999) 'Vulnerability to psychological disorder: previous trauma in police recruits', in J. M. Violanti and D. Paton (eds), *Police Trauma: Psychological Aftermath of Civilian Combat*. Springfield, IL: Charles C. Thomas, pp. 65–77.

Strentz, T. (1983) 'Negotiating with the hostage-taker exhibiting paranoid schizophrenic symptoms', *Journal of Police Science and Administration*, 14: 12–16.

Strentz, T. (2006) 'Crisis negotiations in the correctional setting', in T. Strentz, *Psychological Aspects of Crisis Negotiation*. Boca Raton, FL: CRC Press, pp. 149–61.

Taylor, P. (2002) 'A cylindrical model of communication behavior in crisis negotiations', *Human Communication Research*, 28: 7–48.

Terhune-Bickler, S. D. (2004) 'Too close for comfort: negotiating with fellow officers', *FBI Law Enforcement Bulletin*, 73: 1–5.

Ury, W. (1993) *Getting Past No: Negotiating Your Way from Confrontation to Cooperation*. New York: Bantam Books.

Vecchi, G. M. (2009) 'Conflict and crisis communication: the Behavioral Influence Stairway Model and suicide intervention', *Annals of the American Psychotherapy Association*, 12: 32–9.

Vecchi, G. M., Van Hasselt, V. B. and Romano, S. J. (2005) 'Crisis (hostage) negotiation: current strategies and issues in high-risk conflict resolution', *Aggression and Violent Behavior: A Review Journal*, 10: 533–51.

Van Hasselt, V. B., Romano, S. J. and Vecchi, G. M. (2008) 'Role playing: applications in hostage and crisis negotiation skills training', *Behavior Modification*, 32: 248–63.

Van Hasselt, V. B., Sheehan, D. C., Sellers, A. H., Baker, M. T. and Feiner, C. (2003) 'A behavioral–analytic model for assessing stress in police officers: Phase 1. Development of the Law Enforcement Officer Stress Survey (LEOSS)', *International Journal of Emergency Mental Health*, 5: 77–84.

Van Hasselt, V. B., Baker, M. T., Romano, S. J., Schlessinger, K. M., Zucker, M., Perera, A. L. (2006) 'Crisis (hostage) negotiation: a preliminary evaluation of program efficacy', *Criminal Justice and Behavior*, 33: 56–69.

Van Hasselt, V. B., Baker, M. T., Romano, S. J., Sellers, A. H., Noesner, G. W. and Smith, S. (2005) 'Development and validation of a role-play test for assessing crisis (hostage) skills', *Criminal Justice and Behavior*, 32: 345–61.

Violanti, J. M. (2004) 'Predictors of police suicide ideation', *Suicide and Life-Threatening Behavior*, 34: 277–83.

White, E. K. and Honig, A. L. (1995) 'Law enforcement families', in M. I. Kurke and E. M. Schrivner (eds), *Police Psychology into the 21st Century*. Hillsdale, NJ: Lawrence Erlbaum Associates, pp. 190–206.

Note: The views expressed in this chapter do not necessarily represent the views of the FBI.

4

APPLICATION OF MENTAL ILLNESS AND COGNITIVE IMPAIRMENT TO THE CRITICAL INCIDENT

Considerations and implications

Carol A. Ireland

The preceding chapters have discussed the theoretical underpinnings of crisis and conflict communication, alongside the importance of a clear and well understood negotiation strategy. This has focused upon the goals and techniques of the negotiation process, and key considerations for the negotiator and other individuals involved in the management of the situation. Following such clear underpinnings, the importance of flexibility in the negotiation process can be paramount. This is of particular relevance when a negotiator and associated team are faced with other factors that may influence the outcome of the negotiation process. Such factors may impact upon its consequent potential for successful resolution. Such factors may include the mental health of the individual or issues of cognitive impairment (for example, as a result of an acquired brain injury). As such, this chapter will focus upon some of the considerations in regard to negotiations when an individual presents as mentally ill and/or has issues with cognitive impairment.

Mental illness

Mental health problems are not found in just a small proportion of the population. It has been estimated that around one in four of the general population will experience some form and degree of mental illness during their lifespan (Stewart, 2009). While there remains much debate around how its aetiology and the most effective methods of treatment, it is nonetheless found in a substantial proportion of the population. Mental illness can have a potentially negative impact upon an individual's life, affecting their relationships with others and impacting upon their quality of life. This is especially so if it is not successfully managed, such as through the prescribing of medication and/or supportive mechanisms. Importantly, individuals with mental health problems can lead productive lives with the right support, such as medication and/or therapies.

In respect of crisis and critical incidents, Fuselier (1981) and Strentz (1985) argue that people with mental disorder, including mental illness, can make up 50 per cent of all hostage-takers. Despite the potential for such considerable proportions of incidents to present with individuals who have challenges in their mental health, there is a lack of empirical research in this area. While there has been consideration in the field of some management strategies, such as the work of Strentz (2006) and Lanceley (1999), these are based solely on clinical judgments and practical experience in the field. Such judgments would be worthy of empirical research. Yet, they nonetheless further the discussion as to the importance of examining individual factors as part of the negotiation process. The first part of this chapter will explore the impact of mental illness on the negotiation process, before moving on to explore the impact of cognitive impairments. It is equally notable that there is a need for more detailed research in this area.

Depressive disorder

According to the DSM-IV (DSM-IV-TR, 2000), an individual with depressive disorder can experience a range of symptoms. Such symptoms must be consistent and last for at least a two-week period. First, there is an obvious depressed mood. This must be indicated by either their own self-report, such as reporting feeling sad, or observations made by others, such as them becoming withdrawn and/or tearful. It must further be noted that they demonstrate a clearly diminished interest or pleasure in all, or almost all, activities. For example, they may have been noted by relatives to have had a keen interest in jogging and a range of sports, yet they have been observed more recently to have little or no interest in such activities. An individual with a depressive disorder may further show a significant loss in weight while not actually attempting to diet. They may, for example, show little interest in eating and present with a diminished appetite. In contrast, they may demonstrate a gain in weight through an increase in their appetite. Such individuals may demonstrate levels of insomnia or hypersomnia (excessive daytime sleepiness), psychomotor agitation or retardation (DSM-IV-TR, 2000). They may generally present with a loss of energy and high levels of fatigue, with a diminished ability to think or concentrate.

Individuals with a depressive disorder may further present with feelings of worthlessness or excessive or inappropriate guilt. They may further have recurring and overwhelming thoughts of death, recurrent suicidal ideation without a specific plan, or a suicide attempt or a specific plan for committing suicide (DSM-IV-TR, 2000).

In summary, and in the absence of a diagnosis, an individual with possible depressive disorder may present as follows:

- appear low in mood;
- have little interest in anything around them (e.g. even engaging in conversation);

- appear fatigued and tired;
- feel worthless/display extensive feelings of guilt;
- struggle to make a decision (indecisive);
- struggle to concentrate on activities, distractible;
- have thoughts of self-harm/suicide.

Depending upon the circumstances of the negotiation, it may not be known that an individual presents with depressive disorder. Such a disorder may be undiagnosed in an individual, or they may not present with sufficient symptoms to meet the criteria. Or, if they do present with the disorder, then there can be an assumption that all the criteria are met. Indeed, a diagnosis takes place only if *most* symptoms, not all, are present. In the absence of a formal diagnosis the aim then is not to diagnose depressive disorder, but to take note of any presentations in the individual (or individuals) where considerations of negotiation strategies relating to depressive disorder may be of benefit. In any event, it may still be helpful to consider modifications to the negotiation strategy, which may potentially enhance the opportunity for a positive outcome.

Management considerations

There is a range of considerations for the negotiator and their team when engaging with an individual who presents with some or all of the above symptoms. It may be considered more likely for such an individual to present as 'in crisis' as opposed to 'conflict' as a result of an overwhelming feeling of low mood. Such an individual may be difficult to engage in any level of conversation, and they may not wish to engage. They may present with little motivation to engage in any requests, and this may also include any need to make a decision. Their presentation may be noted by negotiators and those around as 'flat' in affect, such as a lack of emotional expression. With reference to the BCSM (Van Hasselt *et al.*, 2008), the use of active listening and empathy would be of benefit. For example, it may be helpful for the negotiator to demonstrate that they are clearly listening to the issues inferred or referred to by the individual in crisis/conflict, and showing an appreciation for the difficulties that the individual may be experiencing.

Feelings of worthlessness and guilt may be real issues for this individual, and as such it can be helpful for the negotiator not to focus on these. To do so may only escalate negative feelings, and may worsen the situation. Importantly, it may be of benefit to encourage them to focus on times when they have felt of low mood in the past, but when things have then become more positive for them. As part of this, it may be helpful to focus on the successes in their lives, both past and current (Ireland, 2007).

In respect of a lack of motivation and difficulties in thinking and concentration, it may be of benefit to allow them additional time to respond to questions asked. They may indeed struggle to engage in a conversation, and, if this is the case, the negotiator needs to persevere. There may be times when the negotiator is fundamentally 'having a conversation with themselves', such as 'talking about nothing'. A further strategy in some negotiations may be to withdraw food and water in an effort to make the situation more uncomfortable for the subject and to encourage them to consider exiting the situation. Yet with these individuals, the withdrawal of food and water may have little impact, as there may already be a loss of appetite (Ireland, 2007).

It is noted that a risk of self-harm and suicide may be a real possibility with such individuals. In this case it can be helpful to determine the nature of any threats of self-harm or suicide made. While a detailed summary of the function of self-harm and suicide is outside the remit of this chapter, the negotiator may seek to explore the following with them:

- How long have they thought like this?
- Is their plan of self-harm/suicide well considered?
- Have they attempted this in the past? (If so, what happened?)
- Have they thought of it in the past, but changed their mind? If so, what caused them to change their mind?
- Have they the means of carrying out their plans?

As part of this, it is crucial that the negotiator and team are wary of any 'sudden improvements' unrelated to the negotiations themselves. For example, they may begin to note that they feel better once they have made a decision. This may reflect a decision to commit suicide. McMains and Shannon (2007) identify a number of clues that may indicate that suicide could be a real possibility. These may include behavioural issues, such as giving away treasured possessions, telling others of their 'final wishes' or saying 'goodbye' to people they see all the time. There may be situational verbal clues, such as the individual stating to the negotiator that 'Nothing will make this better', 'I have nothing to live for' or 'I want out'. McMains and Shannon (2007) make further reference to the issue of time, where the individual may remark that 'It won't matter after today', 'I can't live this way anymore' and 'It is time to finish things off'. They may make further reference to relationships, reporting 'They will be better off without me' or 'They don't need me anymore [my children], they'll be okay'. Importantly, McMains and Shannon (2007) emphasise the importance of the context in which these take place. For example, a depressive individual may remark that 'I can't live this way anymore' more in the context of their frustration at dealing with stress poorly as opposed to a direct statement of wishing to take their own life. Further, McMains and Shannon (2007) identify a number of questions that may be helpful for the negotiator in situations of uncertainty around self-harm and suicide. These include:

- *What* is the context in which statements are being made?
- *Where* is the crisis event taking place? (*Generally*, the more public, the less likely the risk of suicide.)

- *When* – are they threatening to take their life *now* or much later (e.g. within the next week) if a particular event does not work out?
- *Why* – what is the extent and depth of the crisis for the individual? Have they experienced a loss that is very substantial for themselves?
- *How* do they plan to take their life, and do they have the means?

Furthermore, determining the nature of the injury may be of assistance. Some researchers have argued that if the method an individual chooses to harm themselves is not a highly lethal one (e.g. superficial cuts to limbs), then this act can be perceived as 'deliberate self-injury' as opposed to attempted suicide (Ireland, 2000). This research argues that such deliberate self-injury presents in an individual who has little or no intention to kill themselves. Yet, even here, the context needs to be considered. For example, in prison environments, Livingston (1997) argues that 'deliberate self-injury' in other contexts cannot be readily applied to a prison environment, arguing that it can be common for prisoners and young offenders in particular to select a highly lethal method of self-injury, such as hanging, but actually have a low level of suicidal intent.

If there are real concerns that an individual may attempt to take their own life, the negotiator may make efforts to encourage them to postpone any suicidal action as opposed to changing their mood. This is with the view that support and counselling around any suicidal ideation can take place immediately after the crisis. As such, the negotiator avoids getting into a debate with the individual as to whether they may choose to take their own life now.

Another key consideration for the negotiating team here is that the negotiations themselves are not about offering therapy to resolve any depressive symptoms, but more the offering of support as to how they are feeling at the current moment in time in seeking a resolution. As part of this, the negotiator may enquire if the individual is on medication, and if so, the type of medication, when it is due and what may happen if they do not take this.

Manic episode

According to the DSM-IV (DSM-IV-TR, 2000), a manic episode is a distinct period of abnormally and persistently elevated, expansive or irritable mood which lasts at least one week, or certainly long enough where hospitalisation is felt to be necessary (DSM-IV-TR, 2000). During this period of disturbance of mood, three (or more) of the following symptoms need to have persisted (four if the mood is only irritable) and to have been present to a significant degree (DSM-IV-TR, 2000). These include an elevated level of self-esteem or grandiosity, a decreased need for sleep, such as claiming to feel rested after only a few hours of sleep, and reported to be more talkative than usual or under pressure to keep talking. They may further present with a 'flight' of ideas where there can be a rapid shifting from one thought to another, with each thought not necessarily linking clearly to the first. There may be a further report by the individual that their thoughts may be 'racing'. Unsurprisingly they may further present as distractible, where their attention is too easily drawn to unimportant or irrelevant external stimuli. They may show an increase in goal-directed activities, such as through work or school, or psychomotor agitation (DSM-IV-TR, 2000). They may further show an excessive involvement in pleasurable activities, which have an elevated potential for painful consequences (e.g. engaging in unrestrained spending sprees, sexual indiscretions or careless business investments) (DSM-IV-TR, 2000).

In summary, and in the absence of a diagnosis, an individual with possible manic disorder may present as:

- having an inflated view of self, such as feelings of supreme importance;
- appearing to take little time to rest;
- irritable and argumentative;
- excessively talkative, such that it may be difficult to 'keep up' with their conversation;
- distractible (including progressing on to often irrelevant issues);
- potentially having lots of impulsive and 'wild' ideas (e.g. grand opinions as to what they may do).

Depending upon the circumstances of the negotiation, it may not be known that an individual is experiencing a manic episode. As with depressive disorder, such an episode may be undiagnosed in an individual, or they may not present with sufficient symptoms to meet the diagnostic criteria. Or, if they do present with a manic episode, then there can be an assumption that all the criteria are met. Indeed, and as with depressive disorder, a diagnosis takes place only if most symptoms, not all, are present. In the absence of a formal diagnosis the aim then is not to diagnose a manic episode but to take note of any presentations in the individual (or individuals) where considerations of negotiation strategies relating to a manic episode may be of benefit. In any event, it may still be helpful to consider modifications to the negotiation strategy which may potentially enhance the opportunity for a positive outcome.

Management considerations

There is a range of considerations for the negotiating team when engaged with an individual who appears to present with some of/all the characteristics of a manic episode. Importantly, it is helpful for the negotiator to maintain the pace of discussions and not to allow the individual to control this. For example, if they allow the individual to maintain the pace of dialogue, the negotiator is likely to become exhausted trying to 'keep up'. It is helpful to consider that, due to the pressure of speech and flight of ideas, it may be difficult for the negotiator to fully understand the discussions taking place. Distractibility may be a real challenge, and it may be important to redirect the individual back to the conversation if they become distractible and to do this in a sensitive way. The negotiator needs to be mindful that the individual may behave impulsively, and there is a need to be prepared for this. For example, the negotiator will need to consider how to keep the attention of the individual. In further efforts to manage impulsivity, the negotiator may need to adopt a more directive style, as well as being prepared for the likelihood of impulsive and unexpected behaviours. For instance, the individual may quickly decide to end the situation, walking out of a room they had locked themselves into without any discussion with the negotiator.

Making efforts to 'tire out' an individual experiencing a manic episode may be less helpful as a strategy. Generally, their ability to maintain their energy levels may far exceed that of the negotiator. They may, for example, require little time to rest and the negotiator is likely to tire before them. Further, the negotiator may focus on information-gathering around certain aspects. For example, they may sensitively enquire as to any medication the individual may have been prescribed and which may be related to their mental health. This would include the type of medication, when it is due and the problems likely to arise if it is not taken.

Such individuals may present with a somewhat inflated view of themselves, believing they present with a high level of self-importance. It is helpful for the negotiator not to challenge such a perception but to simply accept this. They may, for example, present as irritable and argumentative. It is important for the negotiator not to respond negatively to this. With regard to levels of grandiosity, they may potentially enjoy taking risks, being further stimulated by the presenting situation and not fearful of it. With reference to the BCSM (Van Hasselt, *et al.*, 2008), the use of active listening would be of particular benefit here as well as the use of empathy.

Schizophrenia

In accordance with the DSM-IV (DSM-IV-TR, 2000), schizophrenia is a severe mental disorder that can be characterised by a range of symptoms, including delusions, hallucinations and disorders of thought. According to the DSM-IV (DSM-IV-TR, 2000), for a diagnosis of schizophrenia an individual must present with two or more of the following, with each being present for a considerable period of time during a one-month period (or less if successfully treated).

- *Delusions*. These include 'False ideas' which individuals from the same culture would also regard to be false. Cultural considerations are important here. For a delusion to be regarded as existing, it is required not to be held by society. If it were, then it would not be a delusion. Delusions may be varied, and may be held strongly despite evidence to the contrary. Indeed, an individual firmly believes them to be real. For example, one delusion may be an individual believing that they are constantly under police surveillance, or that someone is plotting to murder them, despite no evidence that this is the case.

- *Hallucinations*. Here the individual may hear, see, feel, smell and/or taste things that are not real. The hearing of voices may be the most common and can be very distressing. Such voices may be in constant conversation, they may ridicule and belittle the individual, they may argue with the individual or give them orders to undertake. The voices may present in a number of ways, such as the voice of an older or younger person, male or female, or a combination. For example, the voice may tell the individual that they need to act violently towards others. An individual may be seen to respond to the hearing of voices, such as seemingly talking to or arguing with themselves, laughing for no apparent reason and out of context, or continually listening to music via headphones in an effort to drown out the voices.
- *Disorganised speech/thought*. Here the individual may experience difficulty in their thinking and/or speech which fails to follow a logical and coherent pattern. The individual may report to experience a 'thought echo', where they hear their own thoughts as if they were being spoken aloud. 'Knight's-move thinking' may be another, where the individual appears to transfer from one train of thinking to another which makes no logical sense. An example of 'knight's-move thinking' would be 'I told the doctor I was not very happy about the care I have received, umm, I suppose you always wonder how you can pick the right puppy, I suppose they always pick you, that's what they say, but then I suppose I need to think about dying my hair tonight…'

  Here an individual may also 'invent' new words, or repeat a single word or phrase out of context, or attribute a different and potentially 'special meaning' to more ordinary words. An example may be regarding use of the term 'shop' in conversation by others as a sign that something terrible is about to take place.
- *Disorders of thought possession*. Here the individual can present with a range of disorders of thought possession. This can include 'thought insertion', when an individual believes that the thoughts in their mind are not their own and that they are being put there by an 'outside agency'. It can also include 'thought withdrawal', where an individual believes that thoughts are being removed from their mind by an 'outside agency'. 'Thought broadcasting' may be another where the individual believes that their thoughts are being broadcast or heard by others. 'Thought blocking' may be another feature where there can be a sudden interruption of thinking before it is completed, leaving a 'blank' for the individual. Here the individual may suddenly stop talking and be unable to recall what they have been saying.
- *Grossly disorganised or catatonic behaviour*. These can be one of the symptoms less seen in individuals who have schizophrenia, primarily felt to be a result of the improvements in medication. Nonetheless, it can include the very extremes of behaviour, such as being unable to speak, move or respond. It may be possible, for example, for an individual with catatonic behaviour to remain motionless or to hold a grimace for many hours on end.

- *Negative symptoms, i.e. affective flattening.* The above symptoms are what may be regarded as 'positive symptoms' of schizophrenia, i.e. what is regarded as more 'abnormal behaviours'. Negative symptoms on the other hand are those considered to be an 'absence' of normal behaviours. One example of the more negative symptoms may be a lack of motivation, where everything seems to be an effort. Tasks may not, for example, be finished, there may be a desire to be alone, concentration is poor and there is a loss of interest in social activities. Such individuals may present with long periods of inactivity, and facial expressions may remain the same with a potentially monotonous tone of voice. They may be described by others as 'flat' in their emotions, or their emotions may appear out of context, such as laughing at what should be a sad event.

In summary, and in the absence of a diagnosis, an individual with possible schizophrenia may present with the following:

- having 'false ideas' not based on fact (e.g. unfounded claims of persecution);
- reporting to see, smell, feel, hear, taste that which is not recognisable by others;
- having speech and thought processes which seem incoherent and difficult to follow;
- having the belief that others are 'messing' with their thoughts;
- having low motivation;
- being emotionally flat;
- displaying 'bizarre' behaviour (e.g. laughing at inappropriate times);
- having poor concentration;
- showing loss of interest in what is going around them.

Management considerations

There is a range of considerations for the negotiating team when engaged with an individual who appears to present with some of/all the characteristics of schizophrenia. Importantly, it is helpful for the negotiator to be mindful that an individual presenting with symptoms of schizophrenia does not mean that negotiation cannot be successful, nor does it mean that a negotiator not trained in mental health is not able to successfully negotiate with such an individual. It is important for the negotiator to be mindful that the crisis situation is stressful, and as such symptoms for the individual may be exacerbated. Negotiation should not be about challenging the delusional beliefs of the individual. The individual strongly regards such beliefs as facts, and to challenge otherwise can only exacerbate the situation and negatively impact on the relationship between the negotiator and person/s in crisis. Negotiation is not about therapy here – it is about resolving the situation safely and peacefully for all. Treatment for symptoms can come later.

The negotiating team may find it difficult to engage the individual in conversation, yet it is important to be persistent here. Talking 'about nothing' may in fact be a key strategy, for example discussing a variety of topics such as the weather, hobbies, interests, simply to keep the conversation going. It can be important for the negotiating team to ensure that the lead negotiator is not getting drawn into the individual's delusional network. For example, the individual in crisis may hold the view that some individuals may be part of a secret service sent to spy on them, and they may begin to form the view that the negotiator is part of this conspiracy. If the negotiator becomes drawn into the delusional network this may still be manageable, although there may be some potential consideration given to rotating the negotiator team. Although gathering information around the type, frequency and severity of the delusions may be helpful, it needs to be done carefully. The same sensitivity is required for any discussions around medication; does the individual take medication, and if so, when did they last take it, what type of medication are they on, as well as any insight they may have about what may happen if they don't take their medication. As part of this, it is important for the negotiator to relay key messages about the mental state of the individual to the rest of the team, and not to assume that the team has also identified such information. For example, if the individual appears to be responding to voices, it is important for the lead negotiator to relay this carefully and sensitively to the team, such as, 'I'm sorry, are you speaking to me? You seem to be saying something about how you "won't do that", but I'm not sure if you are directing that to me …' It is important if the negotiator can get the individual to say what they see to assist the rest of the team, but to do so in a careful and considered way, such as, 'You seem to be smiling a lot and looking toward the corner of the room. I'm wondering what might be going through your mind at the moment…'

If the negotiator is in a position where they are able to see the individual in crisis, there may be some difficulty in reading their facial expression; their expression may be minimal. Even if the negotiations are over the phone, the negotiator may experience some difficulty in forming a judgment as to the emotional state of the individual in crisis as a result of their flatness in emotion, tone and expression. Furthermore, if the individual in crisis appears to present in an unusual way, such as laughing out of context, it is important for the negotiator not to respond negatively toward this as to do so may only exacerbate the situation.

In reference to the BCSM (Van Hasselt *et al.*, 2008), rapport may not be possible with these individuals as it may be difficult to ensure the level of interaction required to develop a relationship. Further, and if there are any hostages involved, it may be important for the negotiator to reassure the hostages, as they may be unnerved by the presentation of the person in crisis conflict.

Cognitive impairment

If an individual presents with a cognitive impairment, such as through an acquired brain injury, then this can impact upon the negotiation strategy and the individual's ability to engage in a successful negotiation. For this chapter, we will focus on cognitive impairment as opposed to an individual who has been diagnosed with a learning disability. Learning disability is one example of learning disorder where an individual has presented with difficulties prior to adulthood, and where they show a significant impairment in their intellectual functioning, as well as a significant impairment in their ability to engage socially and in their general adaptive functioning (British Psychological Society, 2000). Cognitive impairment difficulties on the other hand can also reach the same level of severity that learning disability may potentially reach, but may have been acquired in adulthood, for example through traumatically acquired head injury. Cognitive impairments may also be found in much higher numbers in the general population as opposed to the more severe learning disability. Yet, importantly, an impairment in even one area of an individual's cognitive functioning can present with a substantial difficulty in their ability to engage and interact with others and to generally function in society. Importantly, even the management considerations discussed here would still have applicability with individuals classified as learning disabled.

A brain injury is not necessarily difficult to acquire, and an individual does not have to have experienced a period of unconsciousness in order to do so. To use the UK as an example, Mateer and D'Arcy (2000) argue that there are 290,000 to 325,000 new cases each year in the UK alone of acquired brain injury, with 131 per 100,000 requiring hospitalisation as a result. They argue that 85 per cent of all traumatic brain injuries can be classified as mild, with continued advancement in medical research meaning that more individuals are surviving acquired brain injury (Brooks *et al.*, 1997) than ever before. Importantly, those with injuries can recover, yet 25 to 35 per cent continue to report symptoms three to six months later, with 10 to 15 per cent reporting continued symptoms for longer than six months. Such injuries can arise from a knock to the head, long-term substance misuse and neurological difficulties such as strokes and brain tumours.

An individual with cognitive impairments can experience a range of difficulties. This can include challenges in receiving information (selection, acquisition and classification of information), difficulties with memory and learning (information storage and retrieval), challenges in thinking (mental organisation and reorganisation of information) and expressive functioning (how information is communicated or acted upon) (Pitman and Ireland, 2003). Individuals can experience a range of difficulties as a result, such as problems in their ability to express themselves and challenges in holding and manipulating information, processing information, responding to novel situations and flexible thinking. Importantly, such challenges may not be immediately apparent in an individual, as some individuals may mask their difficulties or appear very functional in other areas. As a result of such challenges, they may present as easily distracted, finding it difficult to concentrate and experiencing difficulty in their emotions such as becoming easily irritated; they may be impulsive, easily overwhelmed and rigid in their thinking, finding it difficult to work through the management of a problem and generate different ways of dealing with a situation.

In summary, and in the absence of a formal assessment of cognitive difficulties, an individual with possible cognitive impairments may present as:

- distractible, appearing to lose concentration quickly;
- irritable and experiencing difficulty in managing their emotions;
- impulsive;
- finding it difficult to move from one topic to the other, always coming back to an earlier topic and discussing it over and over;
- having an impaired ability to appreciate the distress or discomfort of others;
- having poor planning ability;
- having poor problem-solving skills, including the identification of a problem, the generation of solutions and/or its successful management;
- having an impaired ability to manage novel situations;
- having an impaired ability to generate alternative ways of managing a situation;
- being easily overwhelmed;
- lacking inhibition and engaging in socially inappropriate behaviour.

Management considerations

There is a wide range of considerations when engaging with an individual who is suspected of having cognitive impairments. For example, the situation itself may be an impulsive and poorly considered one. As such, they may have considered little about any demands they wish to make, if at all. Indeed, it may be more likely an expressive act as opposed to instrumental, where the goals are more determined. Ultimately they may have little idea as to what they wish to achieve from the situation.

When a negotiator is engaged with such an individual it is important to consider that they tire quickly, particularly if they are required to engage in a conversation that involves a lot of careful thought and consideration. As they become more fatigued, their judgment may deteriorate and their stress levels may begin to increase. There can thus be a risk of escalation in the situation if it is not carefully managed. As the negotiator is engaged with them it can be crucial to observe that their ability to retain information may be difficult, along with a risk of poor attention, concentration and greater distractibility. They may find it more difficult to manage their emotions successfully and become more irritable.

A helpful management strategy can be for the negotiatior to consider their questioning style. It is helpful to ask one clear and unambiguous question at a time. To account for possible difficulties in processing information, allowing time for them to respond is crucial. In fact, they may still be processing the question when the negotiator is expecting an answer. The negotiator needs to allow for this. As part of the negotiator's discussion with the individual in crisis, it is important not to engage in hypothetical 'imagine if' scenarios, or ask them to consider a novel situation of which they have no experience; there is a risk they may become overwhelmed and respond to the question asked in literal terms. As part of efforts to develop a relationship with the individual, the use of humour and joking may be best avoided; there is a risk that any jokes made may be taken literally. Also, the use of humour and joking can lead to an increase in arousal, which is best avoided in individuals with cognitive impairments. There can be a risk that such heightened arousal may become difficult for them to control, and they may show an increase in emotion that may be difficult for the negotiation team to manage.

It can be helpful for a negotiator to remain empathic toward the impairments the individual experiences and to appreciate the challenges of this. It can be helpful if the negotiator is in view of the individual for there to be no sudden movements. There is a risk that such movements may be interpreted as a threat. Further, and if the negotiator is in view of the individual in crisis, it can be helpful to ensure there is the least distraction possible. Too much activity around them may potentially overwhelm and distract them. In order to account for any challenges in processing information, it is important for all conversations to be at a slow pace, and as such the negotiator needs to be aware of their use of language and speed of conversation. As part of any discussions, it is important that only one thing is done at a time. The negotiator must not attempt to discuss lots of different things all at once; they need to consider their pace of delivery, with new topics introduced slowly, and with a preference to continually recap and clarify discussions made. For example, it would not be unusual for such an individual to appear to understand an issue, only to lose this understanding some time later. Because of this, regular recaps of important issues are crucial.

Putting it in to practice: illustration through case examples

Importantly, whether or not an individual meets a formal diagnosis for mental illness, or if there is a lack of information to indicate a possible cognitive impairment, this should not impact upon the negotiation approach. Rather, consideration should be made of those characteristics and behaviours that may impact negatively upon the negotiation. Further, it is not unusual for individuals in crisis or conflict to potentially demonstrate a range of characteristics which may match across a range of different possible disorders. The fictitious case examples below illustrate how a negotiator may modify their approach based on the behaviours they observe as part of the situation, further illustrating the planning that may be considered part of this approach. These examples focus solely on mental illness and/or cognitive impairment, rather than on any other issues that would need to be considered as part of a crisis or conflict situation. Also, to help understanding, only one individual in crisis has been considered as opposed to multiple individuals.

Case A: Preparing for the negotiation

Jane is a law enforcement officer and a trained negotiator. She is on call as a negotiator and is called to a disturbance at a bar. It is 2 p.m. on a Thursday. She works as a negotiator with a colleague, Steve. This afternoon, Jane is rostered to undertake the lead negotiator role, whereas Steve is to act as support negotiator. Steve's support role is to compile relevant notes and gather further information. When they arrive at the scene, they are provided with the following brief:

> Law enforcement officers were informed by the owner of the bar that there was a disturbance at 12.30 p.m. A man entered the bar following it opening, and appeared agitated. At this time present were the owner, three regular customers and the cleaner. The owner noted that the man appeared to be smiling to himself, and at times appeared to make a number of angry statements seemingly directed at no one, such as 'it's not right, you can't do that'. The owner further noted that the man was not a regular customer, and he did not recognise him. The man was dressed in an unkempt fashion, was approximately 45 years of age, and it appeared from his level of hygiene that there might be every chance that he might be of no fixed abode. The owner noted that the man then became more and more agitated, and threw some glasses on to the floor, smashing them. He then picked up a large shard of glass and ran towards one of the customers. The customer ran out of the way, and the owner, customers and cleaner promptly ran into the back of the bar, barricading themselves into the upstairs living quarters of the owner and where he cannot get access. The owner is not sure if there were any more customers in the bar, and thinks there may have been a young man who had gone to the bathroom just a few minutes before the glasses were smashed.
>
> The man still remains in the premises, and appears to have hold of the shard of glass. This has been noted as he had opened the door of the premises slightly to shout at officers outside to 'go away and leave me alone'. It is not clear if there is anyone else in the bar near the vicinity of the person in crisis.

Jane makes the decision to begin the initial negotiations via a phone, and rings through to the phone near the bar area where the individual is thought to be. Jane asks Steve to gather as much information from officers who have spoken to the individual already and from the owner, customers and cleaner currently barricaded in the living quarters of the owner where a phone is available. Jane asks Steve to ensure that all information gathered from the owner and others is done so safely, and does not then place them at risk. Jane says that, as well as information about what has happened, it is important to gather information on the individual's apparent mental state. The decision is taken to do this quickly, gathering as much information as possible within a short time frame. From this Jane notes the following:

- The individual has named himself as 'Paul' to officers.
- He is presenting with possible hallucinations. These seem to include possibly smelling things that are not real. The owner and one of the customers noted that he commented that he could smell excrement all around him, but they were unable to smell this themselves. They further noted that this appeared to distress him very much, and he commented, 'Can't you smell it? It's awful, it won't stop,' becoming more agitated when they told him they could smell nothing. It was also felt that he might be hearing voices, as he seemed to be smiling and talking to himself. When questioned further, the cleaner stated that he had said, 'I won't do it, I just won't' just prior to throwing the glasses on to the floor.
- He does not appear to have entered the bar with any apparent focus – he did not wish for a drink or anything else in particular. The owner and one of the customers felt that he had almost 'stumbled' in.

From this, Jane and Steve began to develop some initial ideas that Paul might be showing some symptoms of schizophrenia, such as possible hallucinations. They noted that it would be helpful to try to gather some more information around these symptoms for him, and to do this sensitively. They also noted that it appeared Paul was distressed by these possible hallucinations. They both noted that, while not making any attempt to diagnose Paul as having schizophrenia, they were simply identifying a strategy for best engaging with him that was most likely to lead to a peaceful resolution.

With the help of her support negotiator, the following list of 'dos and don'ts' in regard to Jane's interactions with Paul were drawn up based on his suggested symptoms of schizophrenia. These were not considered to be concrete, and were modified and changed as time progressed. In particular, Jane noted what appeared to work effectively, and which strategies were less helpful. From this, they drew up the following list to help Jane in her initial negotiations with Paul:

Do

- Do be aware that a crisis situation is stressful – any symptoms may become exacerbated.
- Do be persistent in trying to get into a conversation – talking about 'nothing' can be key.
- Do relay back to the team what you can hear in regard to the person's mental state – don't assume the team have picked up on the same issues.
- Do try to sensitively find out if he is on any medication, the type, when he last took it, what happens if he misses the medication.
- Do be aware that he may present as distractible and may lose his concentration.
- Do remember that you can still negotiate, even if the person is unwell – perseverance is key!

Don't

- Don't challenge his beliefs, no matter how 'odd' or 'bizarre' they may seem – this is not therapy!
- Don't respond negatively to any unusual behaviours – stay calm and reasoned.
- Don't expect rapport – this may be more difficult.

Case B: Managing the negotiation

Adrian works in a secure forensic hospital in the UK for individuals detained with a mental disorder. He works as a psychiatric nurse and is trained as a negotiator. He has been called to one of the wards to negotiate with a patient, Jason Jones, who has barricaded himself into the day room using a cupboard and a snooker table. He also has a snooker cue in his hand and appears to be threatening staff who attempt to get close to the day room. The negotiations have been going on for one and a half hours, and there appears to have been little progress. At the hospital, the negotiators work in teams of three. There is the lead negotiator (Adrian) who talks to the patient. He has a support negotiator, Jackie, who is writing down relevant information and supporting him. There is also a third negotiator whose job is to pass important messages to and from the negotiations to the commander of the incident. Jason Jones is new to the hospital, and had been transferred from HM Prison Service custody four months previously. The brief that the negotiation team were given is as follows:

> Jason Jones
> 33 years of age
> Index offence: Rape
>
> Mr Jones reported to staff on the morning, just prior to the barricade, that he was not happy to be here. He was aware that he had come here to be assessed for his mental health, but felt there was nothing wrong with him. He told staff that he wanted to return to prison, where he could 'serve my time and get out to see my family', reporting that, 'If I stay in here, I'll just rot.'
>
> Mr Jones was still being assessed for his mental health. If was felt that he might have bipolar disorder, previously referred to as manic depression, and where there can be symptoms of depressive disorder as well as manic disorder. The diagnosis has not yet been confirmed, yet staff had noted him to have been displaying some potentially depressive-like symptoms over the last few months, which had also been apparent some months prior to him coming to the hospital. These included the following:
>
> - low in mood, with little interest in what was going on around him;
> - fatigued and tired, which was not felt to be a result of medication;
> - difficulty in concentrating on a task;

- previous thoughts of self-harming, having self-harmed on at least six known previous occasions. His self-harm usually involved opening a vein on his forearm with one of his finger nails or using a knife if one was available.

Mr Jones has also recently undertaken a cognitive assessment at the hospital which revealed a number of cognitive impairments. These included:

- a poor ability to process information given to him;
- a poor ability to express himself and to get his views across;
- a poor ability to hold and manipulate information in his mind;
- a poor ability to respond to novel situations that he has not previously had experience of;
- a poor ability to think flexibly and creatively.

After two hours of negotiation, the team began to feel that they were developing a reasonable impression of Mr Jones. The team managing the incident also gathered information on Mr Jones' cognitive impairments by speaking to staff on the ward. From this the following impressions began to take shape around his impairments:

- He can become easily overwhelmed when new information is discussed or if hospital rules change. He appears to find it difficult to remember these changes or new information, often mixing the information and rules up. This appears to frustrate him. When he becomes frustrated, he appears to lose his temper, and will shout and threaten staff. It has been noted that he has never previously carried out any of his threats. He finds it difficult to unlearn an over-learned routine.
- He can often present with an understanding over an issue, only to lose this understanding some hours later.
- He responds well if staff tell him what he is doing well and are specific about this for him.

From this, the support negotiator, Jackie, drew up a list of 'dos and don'ts' in regard to Jason Jones, and some suggested strategies to maximise a successful engagement with him. In order to do this, Jackie drew knowledge from Mr Jones' potential depressive traits as well as from his particular cognitive impairments. This list was not considered concrete, and was modified and changed as time progressed. In particular, Jackie noted what appeared to work effectively, and which strategies were less helpful. From this, they drew up the following list to help Adrian in his negotiations with Mr Jones:

Do

- Do persevere in getting him to have a conversation with you ('talking about nothing' may be helpful here).

- Do be aware that he may find it difficult to make a decision – you may need to support him with this.
- Do use lots of active listening and show lots of empathy;
- Do try to focus on the successes in his life, when possible and when appropriate – aim to turn the situation into a positive one (without supporting the decision for a barricade).
- Do be aware that the withdrawal of food and water may not have the desired effect.
- Do explore any indication of self-harm/suicide (e.g. how long has he thought like this? is it a well considered plan?).
- Do be aware that he may tire quickly.
- Do expect that he may forget some decisions that he has made earlier – regular recaps can help here.
- Do be prepared that he may be distractible.
- Do remain neutral – don't show any frustration.

Don't

- Don't give him too much information at once – go at his pace.
- Don't joke – humour is best avoided.
- Don't have any hypothetical discussions – keep it concrete, and in the here and now.
- Don't speak too fast, and use a vocabulary he understands.
- Don't expect him to have understood even if he says he has – check this out with him carefully and sensitively.
- Don't be afraid to change the topic of conversation if his emotions become elevated.

Conclusion

The aim of this chapter was to draw together the importance of considering characteristics and behaviours during a crisis and/or conflict situation which relate to an individual's mental illness and/or cognitive impairments. The chapter has focused upon suggestions as to how to respond to these effectively to maximise the potential for a successful and peaceful resolution. The importance here is to observe for behaviours that may interfere with a successful negotiation, and not to over-focus on the need to seek a formal diagnosis. Even a formal diagnosis of mental illness, for example, can only offer suggestions as to how an individual is most likely to present. For instance, two individuals may be diagnosed with symptoms of schizophrenia, but their individual presentations may be very different. Confidence and trust in the observations of the negotiator and the support team can be critical here, while maintaining the importance of retaining the structure of the negotiation.

References

British Psychological Society (2000) *Learning Disability: Definitions and Contexts*. Leicester: Professional Advisory Board for the BPS.

Brooks, W. M., Wesley, M. H., Kodituwakku, P., Garry, P. and Rosenberg, G. A. (1997) '1H-MRS differentiates white matter hyperintensities in Subcortical Arteriosclerotic Encephalopathy from those in normal elderly', *Stroke*, 28: 1940–3.

DSM-IV-TR, (2000) *Diagnostic and Statistical Manual of Mental Disorders*. American Psychiatric Association.

Fuselier, G. D. (1981) 'Hostage negotiation consultant: emerging role for the clinical psychologist', *Professional Psychology: Research and Practice*, 19 (2): 175–9.

Ireland, C. A. (2007) 'Crisis negotiation with a mentally disordered offender population: development of a training package in a high secure forensic hospital', *Forensic Update*, 91: 20–6.

Ireland, J. L. (2000) 'A descriptive analysis of self-harm reports among a sample of incarcerated adolescent males', *Journal of Adolescence*, 23: 601–13.

Lanceley, F. J. (1999) *On Scene Guide for Crisis Negotiators* (2nd edn). New York: CRC Press.

Livingston, M. (1997) 'A review of the literature on self-injurious behaviour amongst prisoners', in G. J. Towel (ed.), *Suicide and Self-Injury in Prisons: Issues in Criminological and Legal Psychology*. Leicester: British Psychological Society.

McMains, M. J. and Shannon, K. (2007) 'Suicide assessment: being able to say it out loud', *Journal of Police Negotiations*, 1 (2): 131–6.

Mateer, C. A. and D'Arcy, R. C. N. (2000) 'Current concepts in assessment and management', in S. Raskin and C. Mateer (eds), *Neuropsychological Management of Mild Traumatic Brain Injury*. New York: Oxford University Press.

Pitman, I. and Ireland, C. A. (2003) 'Cognitive ability sex offender therapy', *Forensic Update*, 73: 14–19.

Stewart, G. (2009) *Understanding Mental Illness: Diagnoses and Treatment*. London: Mind. Available at: http://www.mind.org.uk/help/diagnoses_and_conditions/mental_illness.

Strentz, T. (1985) 'A Statistical Analysis of American Hostage Situations'. Unpublished manuscript, FBI Academy, Quantico, VA.

Strentz, T. (2006) *Psychological Aspects of Crisis Negotiation*. Boca Raton, FL: CRC Press.

Van Hasselt, V. B., Romano, S. J. and Vecchi, G. M. (2008) 'Role playing: applications in hostage and crisis negotiation skills training', *Behavior Modification*, 32 (2): 248–63.

5

APPLICATION OF PERSONALITY DISORDER TO THE CRITICAL INCIDENT

Considerations and implications

Carol A. Ireland

As discussed in Chapter 4, a variety of factors may influence the negotiation process, its goals and strategies, including personality-interfering considerations from the perspective of the individual in crisis or conflict which are the focus of this chapter. I will concentrate on the continuum of personality disorder, and examine particular traits, characteristics and consequent behaviours that a negotiator and team may need to take into consideration when undertaking a negotiation.

Personality disorder

In western society in particular, personality disorders are regarded as psychiatric conditions that relate to the psychological distress for an individual, and which result from inflexible and maladaptive personality traits (McMurran, 2002). A personality disorder can be defined as unhelpful traits, characteristics and behaviours that impact upon an individual's day-to-day functioning, including their interactions with others. A formal diagnosis of personality disorder, such as through the DSM-IV-TR (2000), requires an individual to present with stable and enduring experiences and behaviours that are substantially different to those expected within the prevailing culture. Such presentation can be noted in two or more of the following areas (DSM-IV-TR, 2000):

- a difference in the individual's perception and interpretation of themselves, others and events they experience;
- a difference in the extent, fragility and intensity of an individual's emotional response;
- their ability to engage in an appropriate and meaningful way with others;
- their ability to manage and control their impulses.

The understanding of what personality and personality disorder is can be complex (Livesley, 2007) and is outside the focus of this chapter. Yet, in order for an individual to be diagnosed as presenting with a personality disorder, the challenges in their presentation must be consistent and found across a broad range of situations and interpersonal interactions. Such challenges must leave an individual with considerable distress and/or difficulty in their ability to function and interact appropriately with others, and can be found in their day-to-day interactions. Importantly, such difficulties must be observable in the long term, and can be identified at least from early adulthood or adolescence. For example, it is important to look for a five-year period of stability in their personality presentation. Importantly, such a presentation cannot be accounted for by another mental disorder such as mental illness or as a result of substance misuse.

This chapter does not aim to offer an overview of the literature of personality disorder, but rather a more practical examination of some approaches that may be considered when presented with such traits, characteristics and behaviours. This will also include those that may not amount to personality disorder but nonetheless present with challenges in the negotiation process. This chapter does not encourage the diagnosis of a possible personality disorder by a negotiator, but simply considers traits, characteristics and behaviours that may possibly interfere with a successful negotiation. It further encourages the importance of observation in the negotiator in the consideration of factors that may potentially impact upon the negotiations. Some key personality disorders will be discussed below, although greater emphasis will be placed upon the observation of key traits, characteristics and behaviours as opposed to any effort to diagnosis personality disorder in any individual case. This is an important distinction to make, as even in cases where a diagnosis of personality disorder is present, this does not necessarily lead to the individual demonstrating all of the traits, characteristics and behaviours that fall within a formal diagnosis. As such, and in cases where personality disorder is diagnosed, there can be a risk that a negotiator assumes a particular presentation when this may in fact be absent. This would have an impact upon their method of negotiation, such as assuming an individual may be manipulative or aggressive, when this is not the case.

The approach taken in this chapter reflects more the view of personality disorder as developing along a continuum as opposed to a categorical 'yes or no' in regard to diagnosis. That is, the characteristics of personality disorder are considered simply extreme or exaggerated forms of normal behaviour (Costa and Widiger, 1994). Arguably, when following the dimensional approach to personality, it is likely there may be people with elements of personality disorder who have avoided the attraction of a categorical label as they have not come to the notice of psychiatric or forensic services (Board and Fritzon, 2005). Indeed, community surveys estimate that up to 11 per cent of the adult population may present with a personality disorder (Zimmerman and Coryell, 1990; Ekselius *et al.*, 2001). As such, there can be a risk that others may not observe some of the more unhelpful traits and characteristics in an individual's personality unless they have a formal diagnosis of personality disorder.

While reference will be made in this chapter to personality disorder and its definition, it will also move more towards the identification of traits, characteristics and behaviours that may impact upon the negotiations, rather than seek to understand the condition through a formal diagnosis of personality disorder. Also, not all types of personality disorder will be discussed in this chapter. For brevity, only some key disorders will be focused on, in the context of crisis and conflict situations.

Anti-social personality: traits, characteristics and behaviours

An individual with a diagnosis of anti-social personality disorder can present with a failure to conform to social norms (Loranger, 1999; Adshead and Jacob, 2009). For example, they may have engaged in a range of criminal activities. They do not necessarily engage in what we may consider in society as moral behaviour; they can often be deceitful, with a reckless disregard for the safety of themselves and others (McMurran and Howard, 2009), such as knowingly driving while under the influence of drink or drugs or speeding excessively. They may further demonstrate little evidence of long-term planning, tending to live for the 'here and now'. For example, they may show little evidence of engaging in long-term employment, and when working they may be absent on a number of days, or they may leave one job without another being lined up. They may present as impulsive in their behaviour, such as travelling from place to place with no clear direction or plan. Their behaviours may be regularly regarded as irresponsible, with a lack of remorse for any unhelpful activities they engage in, believing their behaviour to be justified. In order for an individual to meet a diagnosis of anti-social personality disorder, they must further demonstrate elements of aggression, physical cruelty, criminal activity and the 'conning' of others before the age of 15. In addition, before the age of 15, they must present with a range of difficulties, such as poor school attendance and truanting, along with possible episodes of running away from carers (Loranger, 1999).

In the majority of cases where an individual is in crisis or conflict, a formal diagnosis of anti-social personality disorder may not be available, possible or appropriate. For example, they may not demonstrate sufficient traits to meet a formal diagnosis, or such a diagnosis may not be necessary. Further, the dimensional approach to personality, regarding the characteristics of personality disorder as simply extreme or exaggerated forms of normal behaviour (Costa and Widiger, 1994), may be the more appropriate approach. Yet, nonetheless, an individual in crisis or conflict may demonstrate certain traits, characteristics or behaviours that reflect aspects of the anti-social personality, which would be worth taking into consideration in the negotiation approach. In summary, such traits would include (Loranger, 1999; McMurran and Howard, 2009):

- deceitfulness and persistent lying;
- impulsivity;
- poor planning (for the future);
- irritability;
- aggressiveness;
- reckless disregard for themselves and others;
- lack of remorse for, indifference to or inappropriate justification of their actions.

Management considerations

There are a range of considerations for the negotiator and the team when engaging with an individual presenting some or all of the above traits. Such an individual may be focused on 'what's in it for me' as part of the negotiations. A negotiator can potentially use this to their advantage, emphasising the value to the individual of continuing to engage with them. It is important to ensure that the focus is maintained on the individual in crisis or conflict. This is concerned with the importance of managing their impulsivity, keeping them occupied and ensuring that attention is maintained on them by the negotiator. Such individuals may have a heightened risk of aggression. In such a case, coupled with a lack of remorse, it can be helpful not to over-focus on the hostage/s, as to do so may draw unnecessary attention toward them and increase their risk of harm. This is not to say that any hostages should be ignored, but rather that careful consideration should be given to how the hostages can be informed that they have not been forgotten without raising their profile significantly. Furthermore, the risk of potential aggression, and even irritability, may be heightened if the person's demands are not met. Within negotiations, it may be clear what is negotiable and what it not. The negotiator may therefore have to consider carefully how an individual's unreasonable demands are discussed, while preparing for the possibility that such discussions may increase the risk of aggression. Importantly it can be helpful here for the negotiator to ensure at such times that the focus is on themselves and distracted away from any hostages.

One of the possible challenges with individuals who present some or all of the anti-social traits and characteristics is that they can give the impression that a positive relationship may be developing between the negotiator and themselves when this is in fact not the case. This has the potential to have been orchestrated by the individual, where the negotiator may wrongfully have believed that rapport has been developed. The importance of maintaining professional boundaries can be crucial here, as well as the negotiator not assuming that a positive relationship has developed and being mindful that information the individual provides them with may not always be accurate.

Such challenges in the development of a positive relationship between the negotiator and individual in crisis and conflict may further extend to the hostages, if present. For example, a negotiator may make efforts to humanise the hostage/s and develop a positive relationship between them and the individual in crisis or conflict in an effort to reduce the risk of harm to them. Yet, with this type of individual, such an action may have a reduced potential for positive effect. For example, they may have little concern for the safety of the hostage/s, and may even seek some pleasure from the distress and even harm caused to the hostage/s.

An individual who presents with some or all of these traits may further present with a negative view of authority. If the individual perceives the negotiator to have some level of power, control and influence, they may respond negatively toward them, wishing not to engage with them or making unnecessary demands. For example, they may request the negotiator meet certain demands for them, feeling they have the power to do so and reacting negatively when this does not take place.

Narcissistic personality: traits, characteristics and behaviours

An individual who presents with a diagnosis of narcissistic personality disorder can present with a grandiose sense of self-importance (McMurran and Howard, 2009). This may include an exaggeration of achievements and talents, with an overarching desire to be seen as superior. For example, in a conflict situation, the individual may state that they wish to speak only to a senior member of the team, as discussing issues with individuals they consider more junior and 'ordinary' is not helpful to them and does not reinforce their need to be regarded as 'unique' and 'special'. They may further exaggerate their talents, claiming to possess a range of university qualifications or specific expertise, none of which are accurate. Such individuals may present with a preoccupation with fantasies of unlimited success, power, brilliance, beauty or ideal love. For example, they may discuss experiencing daydreams where they are very beautiful or handsome. They may further talk with conviction as to their belief they will be able to develop substantially successful businesses, having given little detailed consideration as to the specifics of these businesses and how they could achieve this.

Such individuals can have a further sense of entitlement, focusing very much on their own wants and needs with unreasonable expectations that individuals will simply comply with their demands. They may, for example, expect to be treated in a different or special way as a result of who they are or what they believe they have accomplished (Loranger, 1999). They can further be exploitative, taking advantage of others for their own needs and requirements. Not surprisingly, they can lack empathy, showing an unwillingness to recognise or identify the feelings and needs of others. Indeed, they can present with a desire to be excessively admired, they can be envious of others or believe others are envious of them. Fundamentally, they may be regarded by others as arrogant and present an air of superiority over others (McMurran and Howard, 2009).

In summary, an individual in crisis or conflict may potentially demonstrate certain traits, characteristics or behaviours that are in accordance with aspects of the narcissistic personality such as (Loranger, 1999):

- inflated self-importance – a belief that they are 'special';
- a need to be seen as powerful and brilliant;
- a need for a lot of admiration;
- expression of entitlement – '*I* want what *I* want, and *I* want it *now*';
- a lack of the ability to empathise;
- arrogance/'haughtiness'.

Management considerations

There is a range of considerations for the negotiator and the team when engaging with an individual presenting with some or all of the above traits. It can be important not to challenge their perceived sense of 'self-importance'. Indeed, such a perception could potentially be used to an advantage. For example, the negotiator could involve them in the negotiations, working with their traits of feeling important, such as stating to the individual 'You strike me as the kind of person who knows what you want, and you aren't afraid to speak your mind …' By doing so, the need for the individual to be admired can be further reinforced. Using active listening from the BCSM (Van Hasselt *et al.*, 2008) can be helpful, as it can link to their need to be listened to and valued. One of the challenges with their sense of self-importance can be their decision not to negotiate with an individual they feel to be inferior to themselves. A key tactic of the negotiator is to be seen as someone who does not make executive decisions; by doing so, the negotiator can reduce the risk of conflict and play for time when managing the situation (Hatcher *et al.*, 1998; Vecchi *et al.*, 2005). However, this may cause some problems as the individual in crisis or conflict may decline to converse with the negotiator. It is important for the negotiator to persevere here, not enter into conflict and make effective use of active listening.

As part of the individual in crisis or conflict's need to be recognised as important, it can be crucial for the negotiator to consider how requests are declined. For example, it can be important that potentially inflammatory terms such as 'no' are not used, with a preference for reframing the decision not to meet a demand. For example, if the individual is demanding to have a meal sent to them and the person in charge of the situation has declined this, but agreed they can have a meal later, the negotiator may state to the individual: 'It is not that you won't get a meal, but there will be a hot meal waiting for you when you get out. That is the message from my boss …' If it is clear that their requests will not be met, it is important that this is dealt with sensitively and carefully.

As with an individual who has some of the anti-social traits outlined above, it can be important for the negotiator to convince them that the safe return of any hostage/s is in *their* best interest and to *their* own personal advantage. As previously indicated, such individuals may come across as arrogant and 'haughty'. In this case, the negotiator needs to remain calm, further emphasising the need to monitor their own feelings and expression and to have the support of their team in this. The expressions of arrogance and inflated self-importance of the individual in crisis or conflict may have a negative impact upon the negotiator if not carefully monitored by the negotiator and other team members.

One of the challenges with narcissistic traits may be the potential need of the individual to seek attention from others. The crisis situation itself may indeed offer the attention they crave. As such, it is important that the negotiator and the team ensure that onlookers to the crisis or conflict situation are kept to a minimum.

In a crisis or conflict situation, any hostage/s may be a 'means to an end'. For example, the individual may be prepared to use hostages to meet their own needs and furthermore may find it difficult to appreciate or recognise the hostages' distress. As with those with anti-social traits, a negotiator may make efforts to humanise the hostage/s and develop a positive relationship between them and the individual in crisis or conflict in an effort to reduce the risk of harm to the hostage/s. However, with this type of individual, it may have a reduced potential for a positive effect.

Histrionic personality: traits, characteristics and behaviours

An individual who presents with a diagnosis of histrionic personality disorder may appear to be uncomfortable in situations where they are not the 'centre of attention' (Loranger, 1999). They may in fact seek situations which can fulfil their need to be seen as the centre of attention, this need being regarded as an insatiable one (Loranger, 1999). Furthermore, they may use their physical appearance to draw attention to themselves, such as by wearing provocative clothing. They may be suggestible, and easily influenced by others or the circumstances they find themselves in. Their interactions with others may at times be regarded as sexually inappropriate, seductive or even provocative. As part of this, they may have a tendency to consider their relationships with others as more than they really are. For example, they may consider themselves to have a substantially intimate relationship with an individual they met only a few hours previously and regard them as a close friend.

Such individuals may present with rapid shifts between emotions, with a further shallow expression of emotion. Moreover, if emotion *is* demonstrated, it may be exaggerated, dramatic and almost theatrical in its expression. Furthermore their conversation may lack detail and depth (Loranger, 1999).

As previously indicated, in the majority of cases where an individual is in crisis or conflict, a formal diagnosis of histrionic personality disorder may not be possible. It may further not be appropriate; they may not demonstrate sufficient traits to meet a formal diagnosis or such a diagnosis may not be necessary. Nonetheless, an individual in crisis or conflict may demonstrate certain traits, characteristics or behaviours that are in accordance with aspects of the histrionic personality and which would be worth considering in the negotiation approach. In summary, such traits would include (Loranger, 1999):

- a keenness to be the centre of attention;
- flirtatious/seductive behaviour;
- a tendency to dramatic displays of emotions;
- a tendency to be easily suggestible;
- a belief that relationships with others (including negotiators) are more intense than they actually are.

Management considerations

There is a range of considerations for the negotiator and the team when engaging with an individual presenting some or all of the above traits. Such an individual is keen to ensure that attention remains on them, and it is important that the negotiator looks to achieve this by ensuring that they appear actively engaged and interested in the conversation. A failure on the part of the negotiator to ensure the individual feels attention is on them can lead to the individual potentially feeling they may have to 'act out' or 'entertain' in some way, in order to ensure the attention is placed on them. This may include behaving impulsively.

As referred to earlier, individuals with histrionic traits and characteristics have the potential tendency to misinterpret their relationship with the negotiator, for example feeling the depth of their relationship is more than it is in reality. One of the key strategies of a negotiator is to actively listen to what the individual in crisis or conflict is stating in order to demonstrate empathic concern and develop rapport and trust, all of which leads to the development of a relationship where the negotiator can influence the individual's behaviour. One of the challenges is that this basis for relationship development can also be found in the development of close relationships with others such as friends. Coupled with the potential tendency for the individual in crisis or conflict with such traits and characteristics to over-interpret the nature of the relationship, there is a real risk that they may feel their relationship with the negotiator is a close one. This may further extend to a belief that there could be a sexual nature to their relationship. It is important for the negotiator to continually assess for this, and to be further mindful of any precursors to efforts to engage in an inappropriate sexual interaction. For example, behaving in a sexually inappropriate way may be an effort to 'act out' or 'entertain' as they feel the necessary level of attention they crave has been removed from them. In any event, the negotiator must carefully consider their management of the situation once the individual becomes aware that the depth of the relationship is not as substantial as they previously thought, and discussing this in a sensitive manner, keeping calm and remaining focused, can be paramount. Such an individual may demonstrate dramatic changes in emotion, and the realisation that their perceived relationship between the negotiator and themselves is not as substantial as they initially thought may provide an example where such dramatic changes in emotion are displayed. Active listening on the part of the negotiator here would be critical.

As a result of the potential risk of suggestibility, there can also be an added challenge that the negotiator may wrongfully believe that the influence stage in the relationship, where the negotiator feels they can influence the behaviour of the individual in crisis or conflict, has been reached. Also, the development of rapport and consequent trust may be more challenging for the negotiator, as the individual in crisis or conflict may experience difficulties in demonstrating a depth of emotion that may be central to the development of trust. As such, and when exploring the BCSM (Van Hasselt *et al.*, 2008), the achievement of rapport may not be realistic.

Paranoia: traits, characteristics and behaviours

An individual who presents with paranoid traits as part of their personality can have a tendency to suspect, without sufficient basis, that others are exploiting, harming or deceiving them (McMurran and Howard, 2009). They may be preoccupied with doubts about the loyalty or trustworthiness of friends or associates. They can be reluctant to confide in others, fearing such information will be maliciously used. For example, they may tend to keep personal problems and issues to themselves at all costs, fearful that such information may be used against them maliciously if they confide it to another (Loranger, 1999). For instance, if they are experiencing problems with their anger, a friend may ask them what causes the anger in an effort to support and help them. They may refuse to answer this, claiming that their friend is only asking them this in order to identify the triggers for their anger which can then be used against them. In addition, they may read hidden, negative or threatening messages into relatively harmless situations or comments. For instance, they may walk past a stranger in the street who appears to turn their head away from them. They may interpret a hidden meaning to this, such as feeling that the individual dislikes them. They can further bear persistent grudges against others which can last for many years, as well as perceive attacks on their character or reputation which are not apparent to others and react angrily. They can, moreover, be suspicious, without grounds, as to the fidelity of their partner (Loranger, 1999).

In summary, such paranoid personality traits would include (Loranger, 1999):

- feeling that others are exploiting or deceiving them;
- struggling to trust others;
- fearing that any information they give about themselves may be used against them;
- reading threats into messages or situations where most people would not;
- bearing a number of strong grudges for a long time (e.g. over 12 months);
- perceiving attacks to their character or reputation without foundation;
- being suspicious of others.

Management considerations

There is a range of considerations for the negotiator and the team when engaging with an individual presenting some or all of the above traits. They may regard the negotiator with suspicion and question their motives. Sincerity and active listening can be important here. It can be very important for the negotiator not to lie. The negotiator needs to present as trustworthy. In order to ensure that this can be maximised, the less the negotiator is informed by those managing the situation, such as the person in charge (i.e. 'the boss'), the better. The individual in crisis or conflict may present as suspicious of any agreements or decisions made. For example, if the negotiator states that they will 'pass the message on' for them, they may be suspicious as to how this may be taking place. It is of paramount importance that the negotiator prepares for such queries. One of the tactics used by negotiators is to 'play for time', in the understanding that to do so may assist in increasing rational thinking among all involved (Hatcher *et al.*, 1998). This may involve the negotiator in generating conversation and generally 'talking about nothing'. However, such a strategy may raise suspicion in the paranoid individual. Ultimately, developing the trust of and gaining rapport with this type of individual may be challenging, and as such a simple acknowledement by the negotiator that this can be difficult for them can be of benefit.

The very role of the negotiator in developing a relationship with the individual in order to influence their behaviour can be challenging here. For example, efforts by the negotiator to gather information may meet with limited success, as the individual may be fearful of confiding. If they feel that the negotiator is attempting to get 'too close' to them in terms of a relationship, then they may react angrily. It can be important for the negotiator simply to be mindful of such possibilities and to remain calm as part of the negotiation. Importantly, the negotiator must be mindful that the individual may perceive hidden meanings in what is discussed. For example, the negotiator may simply state, 'So tell me why you are feeling so upset', and the individual may respond, 'I'm not telling you that. If I do, you will only use it to wind me up further, that's the only reason you are asking that, you just want to do me harm.' While the risk of such a response cannot be avoided altogether, it may help to reduce the risk by carefully considering the nature and format of the discussions. For example, it can be helpful to ensure there is little ambiguity in the discussions undertaken.

Borderline personality disorder: traits, characteristics and behaviours

An individual who presents with borderline traits as part of their personality can suffer from a real sense of abandonment. As such, they can make quite 'frantic' efforts to avoid real or imagined abandonment by others (McMurran and Howard, 2009). Moreover, such individuals can have difficulty in their interpersonal relationships which may be characterised as unstable and/or intense, alternating between extremes of idealisation and devaluation (Loranger, 1999). For instance, they may idolise their intimate partner on one occasion and demonstrate intense dislike towards them on another.

Their self-image may be unstable and they may feel that they lack a clear definition of themselves. They may also engage in impulsive behaviours which can be potentially damaging to themselves, such as substantial spending sprees, substance misuse, reckless driving and binge eating (Loranger, 1999). In addition, these individuals may display recurring suicidal behaviour, gestures, threats or self-mutilating behaviour, and their moods may be extreme along with chronic feelings of emptiness (Loranger, 1999). Such extreme emotions may present as intense anger or as having difficulty in controlling and managing their anger. Extreme levels of stress may further lead to paranoid ideation or even severe dissociative symptoms.

In summary, such borderline traits would include (Loranger, 1999):

- fear of being 'abandoned' and 'left' by others, where they may go to great lengths to prevent this from happening;
- extreme reactions within relationships (all types);
- impulsiveness;
- a real risk of suicide/self-harm which they may talk of;
- demonstration of extreme emotions quite quickly;
- possible demonstration of intense anger which they find difficult to deal with;
- heightened paranoia when stressed.

Management considerations

There is a range of considerations for the negotiator and the team when engaging with an individual presenting some or all of the above traits. For instance, developing rapport may be particularly challenging here. The individual may have a fear of rejection, and may even look to encourage the negotiator to reject them in some way in order to prove that this fear of rejection is a reality. For example, the negotiator may further feel that a relationship has been reached, where there can then be quick rejection. When negotiating with this type of individual, any change of negotiators can be a critical time, and there can be a real risk that the individual will feel that the negotiator is abandoning them in some way. In such circumstances, the negotiator needs to think through carefully how they exit the situation so that the individual does not feel they are being rejected.

The use of active listening and demonstration of empathy can be very helpful and effective in assisting the individual to accurately label and manage their emotions and self-validate. They may experience and display some powerful and/ or extreme emotions. As well as active listening and empathy, there is a need for the negotiator to remain calm, even at times where the individual's fear of abandonment makes little logical sense. Importantly, the negotiator should ensure that any 'venting' of emotions should be carefully controlled. For such individuals, significant 'venting' of their emotions can potentially lead to a situation where they feel less in control of themselves. Redirecting them to another, safer topic, or distraction, can be helpful here (Borum and Strentz, 1992).

It can also be helpful for the negotiator to consider that while a crisis or conflict situation can be stressful for all those involved, the high levels of stress experienced by this type of individual can potentially lead to evidence of paranoid thinking. For the negotiator, it can be important that the individual feels they are 'with them', supporting them through this difficult time. Reassurance can be key, such as emphasising that everyone wants to end the situation unharmed, and that there will be a safe way out of this.

The very nature of negotiation means that the individual is in receipt of attention. Individuals with these traits and characteristics may crave attention as a need to feel valued, and they may go to great lengths if they feel they are losing this. For example, they may threaten self-harm if they feel that attention on them is slipping.

It can be critical here for the team to monitor the emotions of the negotiator, so team work is essential. The emotions of the individual in crisis may more likely be the result of a crisis, and may further be a need to express the distress they are experiencing, as opposed to a material demand (Borum and Strentz, 1992). Thus they may often make unachievable demands from the situation when in fact the demands are not actually the focus. Indeed, if the material demands were met, it might potentially exacerbate the situation as their expressive needs are not being realised. For example, an individual in crisis with these traits who is residing in a secure forensic unit may indicate that they are holding someone against their will as they want access to cigarettes, something not allowed in the unit. The provision of cigarettes may actually exacerbate the situation, as the individual does not really want them. Indeed, it is only after careful dialogue that the negotiator may realise that they are actually distressed about the loss of a loved one and are feeling unable to cope. They felt unable to say this safely and so requested the cigarettes simply as a distraction. Thus, the provision of the cigarettes can potentially send the message that they have not really been listened to. Moreover, it can be important not to evoke any feelings of 'failure'. Thus it is essential that the negotiator avoids terms such as 'surrender' as these can evoke feelings of failure and exacerbate the situation (Strentz, 2006). More helpful terms should be used such as 'coming out'. Finally, with such individuals, it can be helpful to monitor the risks of suicide and self-harm, assessing the level of risk and the ability to undertake any threats made.

Putting it in to practice: illustration through case examples

Importantly, whether or not an individual warrants a formal diagnosis for a personality disorder should not impact upon the negotiation approach. Rather, consideration should be made as to those personality traits, characteristics and behaviours that may impact negatively upon the negotiation. In addition, it is not unusual for individuals in crisis or conflict to potentially demonstrate a range of traits and characteristics which may fit across a range of different disorders or extreme and exaggerated personalities. The fictitious case examples below illustrate how a negotiator may modify their approach based on the traits, characteristics and behaviours they observe as part of the situation, further illustrating the planning that may be considered part of the approach. These examples focus solely on personality issues, and not on any other issues that would also need to be considered as part of a crisis or conflict situation.

Case A: Preparing for the negotiation

Peter is a law enforcement officer and a trained negotiator. He is on call as a negotiator and is called to a disturbance at a house. It is 8 p.m. on a Friday. He works as a negotiator with a colleague, Jennifer. This evening, Peter is down to undertake the lead negotiator role while Jennifer is to support him in this. As his support negotiator Jennifer is to compile relevant notes and gather further information. When he arrives at the scene, he is provided with the following brief:

> Law enforcement officers were informed there was a disturbance in the home at 7 p.m. Jason Smith, 43 years old, is at the residence with his 10-year-old daughter. Officers have already attempted to talk to him over the phone and it is noted that he is very angry. He has reported to officers that his wife left him this morning, saying that she no longer loved him. He has reported to officers he is very angry 'that she can dare to do this to me', and that 'she can't have her daughter back, I'll keep her here'. It is reported that he has been heard to smash things within the property, but it is not clear what. It is further noted that his daughter has been heard to be crying in the background when officers have been speaking to him. It is further confirmed that there is no one else in the residence. Officers are currently attempting to contact his wife but have been unsuccessful.

Peter makes the decision to begin the initial negotiations via the telephone, but before he does, he asks Jennifer to gather as much information from officers and others who have already spoken to Jason Smith, or know him regarding his presentation, in terms of their impressions of both his personality and behaviour. Jennifer does this, and talks to two of Jason Smith's neighbours, and officers who have spoken to him. This is done quickly to gather as much information as possible in a short time frame. From this Jennifer notes the following:

- Officers and neighbours reported Jason Smith to be a bit 'full of himself' – he appeared to 'like the sound of his own voice' and would tend to talk over the officers who were speaking to him. Neighbours also reported that he was a difficult person to talk to as he would always talk about himself and his 'next great big business plan'. Neighbours further reported that they were under the impression that Mr Smith was currently unemployed.

- Both officers and neighbours reported him to be quite an arrogant and opinionated individual. He was keen to get his views heard. The officers reported that this was really difficult to deal with, as they found his arrogance frustrating themselves.
- The officers reported that he appeared to find it difficult to trust them, questioning all time what the officers were planning on doing and stating that 'you can only trust yourself'. One of neighbours also reported that he appeared to sometimes get angry with his wife over the smallest thing. They identified an argument that they could overhear through their kitchen wall, as their house adjoined Smith's. They reported that he was shouting at her, saying that she was lying and deceiving him, stating that she would come home from work ten or fifteen minutes later than he expected her, and from this he deduced she must have been having an affair.
- His neighbours reported feeling he could be a little cold. They mentioned an occasion when his daughter had fallen off her bicycle and grazed her knee. She went to him crying but he said he was too busy and that she needed to go to her mother instead.

From this, Peter and Jennifer began to develop some initial ideas that Mr Smith might be showing some possible traits of narcissism, specifically, inflated self-importance and arrogance, with possible evidence of needing to be seen as special. They also noted that Mr Smith might possibly not have good empathy skills and so might not appreciate the distress of his daughter. They both noted that, while not making any attempt to diagnose Mr Smith as having narcissistic personality disorder, they were simply identifying a strategy for best engaging with him. Jennifer also noted that there could potentially be some paranoid traits, possibly a belief that others were attempting to exploit or deceive him in some way, suspiciousness and finding it difficult to trust people.

With the help of his support negotiator, the following list of 'dos and don'ts' in regard to Peter's interactions with Jason were drawn up, based on his suggested personality presentation. These were not considered concrete and were modified and changed as time progressed. In particular, Jennifer noted which strategies appeared to work effectively and which were less helpful. From this, they drew up the following list to help Peter in his initial negotiations with Jason Smith:

Do

- Do use lots of active listening – really listen to him!
- Do work with him and make it seem a 'team effort' – lots of 'we's.
- Do stay calm!!
- Do think about how unrealistic requests are to be declined – do this sensitively.

- Do try to be clear in what you say – no ambiguity!
- Do expect that he may see 'hidden meaning' in what you say – prepare for this!
- Do expect that he may find it hard to confide in you.

Don't

- Don't challenge him – 'It's all about me' – he is important.
- Don't let him annoy you (check your emotions).
- Don't get into an argument.
- Don't say 'no!' (unless the request is unrealistic, *but* use this carefully).
- Don't forget his daughter (so she knows you are there, *but* not so much that he thinks the attention has moved away from him).
- Don't expect him to appreciate that his daughter is upset.
- Don't lie.
- Don't expect him to trust you (may not get rapport).
- Don't rush the negotiation.

Case B: Managing the negotiation

Neil works as a prison officer and is trained as a negotiator. He has been called to negotiate in a prison nearby where two prisoners have barricaded themselves in the games room. One of them has a piece of broken glass in his hand and the other is brandishing a table leg. They are threatening to assault anyone who comes into the room. The negotiations have been going on for two hours and there appears to have been little progress. At the prison, the negotiators work in teams of three. There is the lead negotiator (Neil) who talks to the prisoners. He has a support negotiator, Michael, who is writing down relevant information and supporting him. There is also a third negotiator whose job is to pass important messages to and from the negotiations to the commander of the incident. Both the prisoners are new to the establishment so there is not a lot of information on them. The brief that the negotiation team are given is as follows:

> *Prisoner A*
> Paul Jackson
> 44 years of age
> Index offence: Assault and grievous bodily harm
> Mr Jackson reported to staff the previous day that he was unhappy that his legal appeal against his sentencing had failed, and that he would be 'making his views known to everyone'. He was then seen to argue with staff about being told to leave the exercise yard, as the time on the yard had finished.
>
> *Prisoner B*
> John Littleton
> 24 years of age

> Index offence: Theft and aggravated burglary
> Mr Littleton reported to staff that he had received a letter from his girlfriend to say that she was ending their relationship, and that she could not wait for his release in three years. Mr Littleton reported to staff that he blamed the courts for this and felt his sentence has been too long. He became very emotional with staff, and reported that 'I just can't carry on'.

After two hours of negotiation, the team began to feel that they were developing a reasonable impression of Mr Jackson and Mr Littleton. The team managing the incident also gathered information on their personalities by speaking to staff on the prison wing. From this the following ideas began to take shape around their personalities.

Paul Jackson

It was noted that Mr Jackson appeared keen to do a lot of the talking, and did not react positively when the negotiator did not engage with him or appeared to have looked away from him. From this, it was also noted that he appeared to be quite impulsive, making what appeared to be quick decisions about issues and becoming angry very quickly. He also appeared very aggressive and would threaten the negotiator with violence, reporting to the negotiator, 'if you come in here I will rip your head off'. It was also noted by wing staff that staff would regularly speak to him about his behaviour, reporting that he had threatened a number of other prisoners on at least six different occasions over the last month. Staff further noted that he presented with little appreciation as to the impact of his threats on these prisoners and those around him.

It was further noted by the negotiation team that he would appear to present with quite dramatic displays of emotions, moving from intense anger one moment to laughter the next. He also made a few comments toward the negotiator in 'feeling' they were starting to have a good understanding.

From this, Michael, with the support of the third negotiator, wondered if there might be some anti-social traits in Mr Jackson, specifically some possible impulsivity, irritability, aggression and lack of remorse. They further wondered if there were some histrionic traits, in this instance a possible keenness to be the centre of attention, some dramatic displays of emotion and a potential to regard relationships with others as deeper than they were. They noted that, while not making any attempt to diagnose Mr Jackson as having anti-social and histrionic personality disorder, they were simply identifying a strategy for best engaging with Mr Jackson to test some of their hypotheses in order to make the negotiations as effective as possible.

The support negotiator, Michael, drew up a list of 'dos and don'ts' in regard to Neil's interactions with Mr Jackson and based on his suggested personality presentation. These were not considered concrete, and were modified and changed as time progressed. In particular, Michael noted which strategies appeared to work effectively, and which were less helpful. From this, they drew up the following list to help Neil in his negotiations with Mr Jackson:

Do

- Do keep the attention on him as much as possible.
- Do be aware that he may not like people in authority.
- Do be aware that he can get irritable – think of your strategies to manage here!
- Do focus the discussion on 'what's in it for me'.
- Do keep him occupied.
- Do look interested!
- Do be aware he may show dramatic changes in emotion.
- Do lots of active listening!
- Do keep focused!

Don't

- Don't trust what he says (shouldn't anyway!).
- Don't get frustrated – stay calm.
- Don't get 'pulled in' (e.g. watch 'the relationship' that is developing).
- Don't challenge (i.e. confrontational).
- Don't expect to get rapport – if you think you have, you may be wrong!

John Littleton

It was noted that Mr Littleton did spend some of his time talking about his girlfriend who had ended their relationship. The negotiation team noted that he would offer differing views of the relationship. Initially he reported how 'she was amazing, the best, no one could come close', but then expressed extreme anger at her for ending the relationship. At these times, he appeared to show strong levels of anger and appeared almost unable to cope with this – he would pace around the room and smash some of the furniture. He further made comments such as, 'It's no use me being here anymore', and, 'What's the point?' Staff on the wing also reported that he would show an extreme reaction if one of the staff forgot a planned appointment, reporting to staff 'they are all the same, no one gives a damn'.

From this, Michael, with the support of the third negotiator, wondered if there might be some possible borderline traits in Mr Littleton, specifically some possible impulsivity, extreme reactions to relationships, the demonstration of extreme emotions and difficulty in managing his anger. They noted that, while not making any attempt to diagnose Mr Littleton as having borderline personality disorder, they were simply identifying a strategy for best engaging with him to test some of their hypotheses in order to make the negotiations as effective as possible.

The support negotiator, Michael, drew up a list of 'dos and don'ts' in regard to Neil's interactions with Mr Littleton and based on his suggested personality presentation. These were not considered concrete, and were modified and changed as time progressed. In particular, Michael noted what appeared to work effectively, and which strategies were less helpful. From this, they drew up the following list to help Neil in his negotiations with Mr Littleton:

Do

- Do actively listen!
- Do be aware he may feel abandoned – think of your exit strategy if needed.
- Do show empathy.
- Do expect him to 'reject' you if it is felt a good relationship is developing.
- Do watch for risk of self-harm/attempts to take his own life – gather information here!
- Do expect the display of extreme emotions.
- Do stay calm.

Don't

- Don't let him vent too much.
- Don't focus on his failures.
- Don't over-focus on demands (the demands may not be the point).
- Don't forget to re-assure him.

Conclusion

The purpose of that this chapter has been to demonstrate the importance of considering the traits, characteristics and behaviours during a crisis and/or conflict situation, and which relate to an individual's personality. The chapter has focused on suggestions as to how to respond to these effectively in order to maximise the potential for a successful resolution. The importance here is to recognise traits and characteristics that may interfere with a successful resolution and not to over-focus on the need to seek a formal diagnosis. Even a formal diagnosis of personality disorder can only offer suggestions as to how an individual may present; it does not offer a guaranteed presentation. Observations from the negotiator and the team are critical. While it is crucial to identify possible personality presentations, it is equally important to be flexible in modifying and altering these if required.

References

Adshead, G. and Jacob, C. (2009) *Personality Disorder: The Definitive Reader*. London: Jessica Kingsley.

Borum, R. and Strentz, T. (1982) 'The Borderline Personality: Negotiation Strategies', *FBI Enforcement Bulletin*, August, pp. 6–10.

Board, B. J. and Fritzon, K. (2005) 'Disordered personalities at work', *Psychology, Crime and Law*, 11 (1): 17–32.

Costa, P. T. and Widiger, T. A. (1994) *Personality Disorders and the Five Factor Model of Personality*. Washington, DC: American Psychological Association.

DSM-IV-TR (2000) *Diagnostic and Statistical Manual of Mental Disorders*. Washington, DC: American Psychiatric Association.

Ekselius, L., Tillfors, M., Furmark, T. and Fredrikson, M. (2001) 'Personality disorders in the general population: DSM-IV and ICD-10 defined prevalence as related to sociodemographic profile', *Personality and Individual Differences*, 30: 311–20.

Hatcher, C., Mohandie, K., Turner, J. and Gelles, M. G. (1998) 'The role of the psychologist in crisis/hostage negotiations', *Behavioural Sciences and the Law*, 16: 455–72.

Livesley, J. W. (2007) 'The relevance of an integrated approach to the treatment of personality disordered offenders', *Psychology, Crime and Law*, 13 (1): 27–36.

Loranger, A. W. (1999) *International Personality Disorder Examination (IPDE) Manual*. Odessa, FL: Psychological Assessment Resources.

McMurran, M. (2002) *Personality Disorders*, Expert Paper, NHS National Programme on Forensic Mental Health Research and Development, University of Liverpool, UK.

McMurran, M. and Howard, R. (eds) (2009) *Personality, Personality Disorder and Violence*. Chichester: John Wiley & Sons.

Strentz, T. (2006) *Psychological Aspects of Crisis Negotiation*. Boca Raton, FL: CRC Press.

Van Hasselt, V. B., Romano, S. J. and Vecchi, G. M. (2008) 'Role playing: applications in hostage and crisis negotiation skills training', *Behavior Modification*, 32 (2): 248–63.

Vecchi, G. M., Van Hasselt, V. B. and Romano, S. S. (2005) 'Crisis (hostage) negotiation: current strategies and issues in high-risk conflict resolution', *Aggression and Violent Behaviour*, 10: 533–51.

Zimmerman, M. and Coryell, W. (1990) 'Diagnosing personality disorders in the community: a comparison of self-report and interview measures', *Archives of General Psychiatry*, 47: 527–31.

6

ETHICAL CONSIDERATIONS IN A CONFLICT AND CRISIS SITUATION

Martin J. Fisher

The issue of ethics in professional practice is one which is coming increasingly to the fore in considerations of both public and private sector roles for those individuals engaged in the provision of specialist professional services. When considering the UK, for example, the implementation of the Human Rights Act 1998 into UK legislature, the more recent enactment of the Health Professions Order 2000, and in particular section 60 of the order (as of 1 July 2009) which regulates applied psychologists through the Health Professions Council in the UK, are important considerations. These all make a review of the relevance and impact of ethical considerations in conflict and crisis situations timely. The UK has thus joined other jurisdictions such as the US with the implementation of a formal, legislated regulatory process for professional conduct at least increasing the cross-Atlantic if not cross-continental pertinence of ethical considerations in critical decision-making situations.

This chapter therefore seeks to review, consider and offer examples of how the practitioner or other such professional might account for and manage ethical issues which will inevitably arise in the context of conflict and crisis management. The work of applied psychologists will often be referred to as a reference point as this is a field in which much consideration has been given to issues concerning ethical practice, but the principles generalise to any person acting as a practitioner or professional in a crisis or conflict situation. In addition it seeks to provide the reader with the opportunity to reflect on their own thought processes and decision-making practices when encountering dilemmas over the need to take decisions in a conflict or crisis situation.

Ethical principles

In considering the issues around ethics in conflict and crisis situations there is a need to reflect on what it is that is meant by 'ethics' in this context. Where the boundaries of the definition lie and how such matters might be determined by situational as opposed to individual factors are central. Often, the practitioner will be engaged with the conflict or crisis in the context of an expert consultant. Cooper and Fisher (2010) discuss the impact of ethical codes and their operation on the broader role of psychologists consulting in forensic practice. They observe that, critically, ethical codes such as those produced by the Health Professions Council (HPC, 2009) and the British Psychological Society (BPS, 2006, 2009) rely on the practitioner using the codes to inform their decision-making processes. This is as opposed to using them as an absolute set of 'rules', which indeed is not inherent in their primary design. Muir-Gray (2001) expresses the additional view, in the context of appropriateness of psychological intervention, that the processes of decision-making are different to those of decision-taking. In the former, scientifically gathered information and observation are reviewed and analysed in order that the approach taken to resolution of the issue at hand is well informed, evidence-based and replicable. In the latter, other features come into play such as resource availability, political context and time-related considerations. This is particularly pertinent to conflict and crises as the latter situational demands of the set of circumstances may weigh more heavily than the former, and thus potentially impact upon the choice made (Koocher and Keith-Spiegel, 1998). Indeed, in the UK, in the HPC Standards of Conduct, Performance and Ethics (HPC, 2009) specific reference is made to the demands of 'emergencies' in terms of service-user informed consent (Figure 6.1 below). This also applies to the American Psychological Association (APA) Code of Conduct (APA, 2002).

Thus, in discussing the impact of ethical considerations in conflict and crisis, there is a need to take into account the interaction between person and situation, individual factors (heuristics) (Tversky and Kahneman, 1974), the role of 'codes' (BPS, 2009) and, statutory requirements (HPC, 2009), the impact of morals on judgments and how the practitioner or 'professional' might seek to navigate effectively through these decision-making and decision-taking obstacles without adversely affecting their professional integrity.

In the context of this chapter then the term 'ethics' refers within its scope to both the decision-making and decision-taking processes of conflict and crisis management, and the set of principles through which the practitioner might operate to ensure that each process is handled effectively and with integrity. Understanding and being as comfortable as possible within a framework of principles is critical to the effective delivery of services: conflict and crises can often present the practitioner with tensions and dilemmas that are unlikely to appear in broader situations and the ability to approach these issues in a user-focused, ethical and defensible manner is a priority.

Francis (2009) outlines a set of principles which may be utilised in assisting ethical decision-making, and while some principles are more pertinent than others to conflict and crisis situations, all apply to some degree. Taking each in turn:

- *Dignity*. In providing professional psychological services, as an example, to the client, the needs of the client should be considered as paramount and above other presenting issues. Francis (2009) argues that this in effect means dealing with the client with due courtesy and respect for their individual rights without offering or being influenced by judgments about outcomes other than the needs of the client. This principle reflects the need for due concern to heuristics or factors which may intervene to influence judgments. For example personal knowledge of someone involved in an incident might impact on objectivity, or beliefs about a given social group might influence judgment about likely responses to circumstances: stereotyping female colleagues as less resilient to stress, for example, may not be helpful and indeed untrue (Tversky and Kahneman, 1974). These are briefly discussed below.
- *Equitability*. This principle reflects the issue that in a professional relationship with a client there needs to be a fair balance of rights and duties. Boundaries reflecting the potential power imbalance need to be considered. As such, whatever decision is taken or advice offered by the practitioner or professional in the presenting situation needs to be self-assured that negative consequences (if any) are minimised for the practitioner, the client and the profession. For example, if a practitioner engaged in advising on a crisis situation were to advocate the use of an intervention where the outcome would be likely to be injurious to the health of a perpetrator with whom the practitioner has had a previous negative interaction, then this might be considered unethical as the practitioner has not fully considered the level of power that they are exerting in influencing the outcome for one of the parties involved in the situation, about whom they have a possible negative opinion, and have not considered the future reputation of the profession in such circumstances.
- *Prudence*. In making decisions the practitioner should always seek to improve the situation through their actions and or advice and not worsen it. Within this principle is the concept of 'do-no-harm' (Francis, 2009: 70). If, in a conflict or crisis situation, irrespective of the level of demand being placed upon the practitioner by the person in charge of the incident, no advice can be offered that would improve the situation, then no advice should be offered which would worsen the situation – this links to the power dynamic of the *equitability* principle in terms of adverse influence on judgment from a perceived authority. In the conflict and crisis situation it is highly unlikely that the perpetrator(s) would be in a position to give informed consent to a 'noxious reinforcement' (Francis, 2009: 70), even if it were to be of longer-term benefit. For example, a perpetrator who demands a particular solution is unlikely to see that it is in their longer-term best interests not to have their demands met. Such advice from a practitioner not to concede to demands may be deemed in the short term to increase the distress of the perpetrator.
- *Honesty and openness*. While recognising the overriding right of the client to privacy (within any ethical standards this is the case), it is important to

avoid any unnecessary or overtly confusing or distracting behaviour that may render the advice or intervention to be that which it does not purport to be. The practitioner needs to be clear that the service offered is all that it says it is, no more, no less. The concept of integrity in professional conduct falls within this principle such that behaviour is consistent, perceived as honest and providing advice and interventions that are in the best interests of the client. The issue of who should be considered the 'client' in conflict and crisis situations is discussed below.

- *Goodwill.* This principle refers to the need for practitioners to be other-orientated rather than self-orientated: focusing on the needs of service users and recipients is paramount. The observation of adherence to legal or statutory minimum standards is unlikely to be beneficial to the client and fall short of professional best practice. Given the often critical and swiftly varying nature of conflict and crisis situations, it is unlikely that any decisions, advice or actions which fall short of deliverable best practice will adversely impact on the outcome. Action in the best interests of the client should always supersede the needs of the practitioner or professional within the boundaries of competence and reasonableness – if a commitment to assist is made then this should be realised.
- *Suffering prevention.* To an extent this is the obverse of *prudence*: the practitioner should not act to increase the suffering of a client. This is particularly pertinent in the case of conflict and crisis situations as on occasion some short-term suffering may be warranted to enhance the greater good: where a victim is involved in the situation, for example, and their unwilling detention is lengthened by the negotiation process. (See Chapter 2 of this volume for a review of this process, and its primary aims and considerations.) In such circumstances consultation with peer(s) may assist in resolving the issue through a 'committee' approach.

As observed, not all of these principles will be generically evenly weighted in all conflict and crisis situations, but clearly each may be considered to have its part to play in informing the decisions made, advice given and actions taken. For example, consider:

> When faced with a client who threatens suicidal behaviour, who has an underlying acute medical condition that means their life expectancy is very short and who specifically requests in consultation that their suicidal ideation is not shared with others, what advice should be given? What information could/should be shared and with whom?

The purpose of this chapter is not to provide 'solutions' to such dilemmas, but the principles drawn from Francis (2009) for example outlined above, along with the principles in the discussion of the area below, are aimed at assisting the reader to consider how they might approach such a situation. In the case above, for example, the principles of *equitability, prudence* and *suffering prevention* seem more weighted but, as discussed below, any set of principles must be considered in the context of ethical codes which in themselves are derived from more generic principles and philosophies (BPS, 2009) and intended to offer clear boundaries for ethical decision-making.

Codes of ethics

As stated above, psychologists operating as practitioners are bound by and expected to adhere to a number of codes. In the UK for instance, the regulatory body since July 2009 has been the Health Professions Council (HPC). In its Standards of Performance, Conduct and Ethics, the Council sets out 14 standards to which registrants must statutorily adhere or be formally investigated for malpractice. Figure 6.1 shows these. In addition psychologists who are also members of their professional body (in the US the APA, in the UK the BPS and across Europe the EFPA,[1] for example) are required by their member states to adhere to these bodies' respective Member Rules (e.g. BPS, 2009) – see Figure 6.2 for the Principles of Ethical Conduct and Ethical Guidance Codes (e.g. APA, 2002; EFPA, 2005; BPS, 2009;[2] OPSI, 2008; New Zealand Police, 2009; New South Wales Police, 2009a).

Clearly the ability of the practitioner to apply all these guidances and principles and remain within regulated boundaries of practice requires careful and reflective consideration of the context and demand characteristics of the situation in which they are working.

These codes generally provide guidance for practitioners and are underpinned by explanatory notes and principles which the practitioner is expected to access and incorporate into their decision-making processes. As will be seen below, and in conflict and crisis situations in particular, this is a challenging task not to be undertaken lightly.

1. You must act in the best interests of service users.
2. You must respect the confidentiality of service users.
3. You must keep high standards of personal conduct.
4. You must provide (to us and any other relevant regulators) any important information about your conduct and competence.
5. You must keep your professional knowledge and skills up to date.
6. You must act within the limits of your knowledge, skills and experience and, if necessary, refer the matter to another practitioner.
7. You must communicate properly and effectively with service users and other practitioners.
8. You must effectively supervise tasks that you have asked other people to carry out.
9. You must get informed consent to give treatment (except in an emergency).
10. You must keep accurate records.
11. You must deal fairly and safely with the risks of infection.
12. You must limit your work or stop practising if your performance or judgment is affected by your health.
13. You must behave with honesty and integrity and make sure that your behaviour does not damage the public's confidence in you or your profession.
14. You must make sure that any advertising you do is accurate.

FIGURE 6.1 HPC Standards of Performance, Conduct and Ethics (HPC, 2009: 8).

BPS:	**NSW Police:**
1. Respect	1. Excellence
2. Competence	2. Trust
3. Responsibility	3. Honour
4. Integrity	4. Impartiality
APA:	5. Commitment
1. Beneficence and non-maleficence	6. Accountability
2. Fidelity and responsibility	7. Leadership
3. Integrity	
4. Justice	
5. Respect for people's rights and dignity	

FIGURE 6.2 British Psychological Society Code of Ethics and Conduct Principles (BPS, 2009), American Psychological Association Principles (APA, 2003) and the New South Wales Police Statement of Values (New South Wales Police, 2009b).

Decision-making and decision-taking

Muir-Gray (2001) makes consideration that the processes of decision-making and decision-taking can be thought of as distinct yet integral aspects of how (scientifically at least) conclusions (and therefore by inference actions) are arrived at.

The process of decision-making can be seen, in the context of ethics, as the process through which the practitioner considers all the different aspects of the presenting issue. Decision-taking is the point at which the practitioner arrives at a balanced point of view about which is the optimal (most ethical) direction to take in their advice, intervention or behaviour. To minimise the importance of the former is folly in the field of conflict and crisis, as the latter is unlikely to be optimal (and potentially lethal) for any party unless due process has been followed.

Francis (2009) refers to the role of a 'gradualist' approach to the development of ethical conduct and thinking processes. This approach suggests that the improvements in ethics arise through a gradual approximation of moral consideration, personal reflection and learning. They do not arrive in a fully-integrated and complete form; rather ethics mature over time and are dynamic. This approach links to models of moral development (e.g. Kohlberg's six-stage model: Kohlberg and Likona, 1976) in addition to the way in which individuals experience the context of ethical practice and the biases, attributions and thinking styles they bring to the learning and developmental environment (Tversky and Kahneman, 1974). Clearly there are limitations to this approach in that certain actions can never be appropriate (e.g. theft from the client or physical assault). However, the gradualist approach to understanding ethical decision-making in the context of conflict and crisis is a helpful one. It recognises the complexity of the issues that are likely to be presenting to the practitioner in the conflict/crisis situation and how this will impact on both the individual's self-reference framework and their ability to respond in terms of taking an effective course of action. As an illustrative example, a practitioner may have applied a set of ethical principles to their decision-making process over a period of time successfully in that the outcome has not been queried. However, a fresh situation may arise in which a feature of the situation is novel (e.g. the victim is an ex-intimate partner). This facet of the presenting situation should cause the person concerned to reflect on how their knowledge of the victim might affect their judgment and consideration. As such the person's ethics will evolve with experience to incorporate developing practice.

Ethical decision-making within a framework of options should, where possible, have a clear set of foundations (principles) that facilitate a point of reference for the basis of considerations. Such an approach allied with the gradualist approach described can assist the practitioner in the process of integrating new information, clarifying their approach and recognising the influences on their decision-making processes. Mason (2000) provides a useful consideration of various philosophical positions on ethical decision-making in a mental health context where protest behaviour by patients needs to be managed, and more generally Francis (2009) considers a similar range of philosophical bases in a broader context over and above conflict and crisis situations. There is a need therefore to use principles of ethical decision-making to guide reflection (APA, 2002), rather than seeking a specific approach and working to that in the absence of other considerations. Adopting a single stance for the basis of ethical decision-making is not necessarily a helpful approach, and in a persistently varying set of situations a flexible starting point in terms of a thinking base can be of benefit. The following two stances, for example, highlight the issues and difficulties arising from the choice to operate within a single ethical paradigm, that is sticking rigidly to a given set of 'rules'.

The utilitarian approach

This is an ethical doctrine that seeks to determine right from wrong and thus seeks to arrive at a clear solution which delivers the most good for the most people. Although this is at face value a useful approach, in conflict and crisis scenarios it can be problematic if applied exclusively (Francis, 2009; Mason, 2000). Consider the following example:

> Fifteen members of the public are held hostage in a public service bus by two armed perpetrators. The incident is a mobile one with the bus driver having a weapon held to his head. The police commander has a set protocol available that states in such situations the vehicle should be disabled as a primary measure. Consequently, a trained marksman is deployed and shoots out a tyre of the bus, causing it to crash into a wall. The driver and the perpetrators are seriously injured, but the 15 passengers are unharmed physically.

Although the action benefitted the majority, the minority suffered. The key ethical weakness of the approach is therefore the minimisation of the rights of the minority, irrespective of their status in the scenario (Francis, 2009).

The beneficence approach

As a doctrine this approach advocates a set of principles which refer to not inflicting harm on others: in short, proactively seeking to do good for others. As with utilitarianism above, this approach seems initially to be promising as an ethical approach to crisis situations at least. However, consider the following example:

> A person in crisis of self-harm has barricaded themselves in a doctor's surgery/consulting room after having been denied medication. A practitioner is consulted by the police commander to advise on a negotiated solution, given concerns for the health of the individual and the likelihood of them self-harming lethally during an intervention. Based on the advice given the situation is resolved and the individual is subsequently detained against their will in a mental health facility as the authorities now deem them to be a 'mentally disordered offender' – in effect, an involuntary 'medical hostage'. (Mason, 2000)

To what extent has the person been helped 'ethically'? In a crisis situation there will inevitably be consequences for the perpetrator(s) and any notion of pure beneficence as a guiding principle will be adversely impacted by this. Smith *et al.* (1991) observe that there is a difference between what a professional will say they should do and what they will do, indicating that an absolute pursuit of a principle is not realistic in the 'real' world – in this example it is not possible to deliver an effective and ethical service on the one hand without consequences for the client on the other (Beauchamp and Childress, 1979).

To moderate the doctrine of ethical principles as the situation demands is a more realistic approach and in that pursuit Koocher and Keith-Spiegel (1998) suggest a stepwise approach that may be used to deliver an effective ethical decision-making process. The initial steps in this process referring to the considerations to be made are listed in Figure 6.3. Considering the foregoing discussion, it is important in the conflict and/or crisis situation that the specialist practitioner is able to act and advise in a defensible manner so that the final decision taken and the advice provided or the action(s) taken are based on reasoning that is not only meaningful and effective, but also justifiable in the context of ethical reference.

Often, the reality of the presenting situation can be far removed from the practice of working through ethical dilemmas in the classroom setting, and their application in conflict and crisis situations means that familiarity with key principles and a set of broad approaches or tools can be of great use to the operative in the field as it were (Schafer, 2002). The steps noted in Figure 6.3 are transposed into the description of a situation below (page 122) in support of this observation.

1. Determine that the matter is an ethical one.
2. Consult the guidelines already available that might apply to a specific identification and possible mechanism for resolution.
3. Consider, as best as possible, all sources that might influence the kind of decision you will make.
4. Locate a trusted colleague with whom you can consult.
5. Evaluate the rights, responsibilities and vulnerability of all affected parties.
6. Generate alternative decisions.
7. Enumerate the consequences of making each decision.

FIGURE 6.3 Suggested approach to ethical decision-making – initial steps (Koocher and Keith-Spiegel, 1998: 12–14).

As such, when incidents go awry (which, while regrettable, will occur), the practitioner will be assured that, irrespective of the outcomes, the advice offered or the actions taken were based in sound, reasoned thinking within the framework of an ethical approach appropriate to the presenting situation, accounting for the individual circumstances, with which ultimately they should feel comfortable.

Babad and Salomon (1978) discuss how (within an organisational framework) the particular features of a crisis situation may adversely impact upon the usual practitioner expectations ('anchor, availability and representativeness' in heuristic terms: Tversky and Kahneman, 1974) of such decision-making processes. Impairment of the preferred process is likely to arise in terms of insufficient time to undertake the usual considerations of pertinent information in the formulation of strategies and plans for interventions, the opportunity for proper consultation with colleagues, identification of the primary party to whom service allegiance is owed, personal stress management techniques (facilitating maximisation of objectivity) and the maintenance of the ongoing evaluation of the intervention being conducted. These issues are covered below in a more practical context with a consideration of the potential means by which moderation might be achieved.

Having made the above considerations, then, the need to proceed to decision-taking naturally follows. In terms of process, the practioner will have little realistic opportunity to undertake testing of the solution arrived at: while this is seen as preferable in terms of broader problem-solving approaches as discussed by D'Zurilla and Goldfried (1971) and D'Zurilla *et al.* (2004), such time allowances are often not realistic in conflict and crisis situations (Schafer, 2002). Consequently, the importance of the sequential decision-making process described above is emphasised. In taking an ethics-based decision the process of communication to recipients/clients and others affected is a very important component. As far as possible the rationale for the decision should be explained so that the level of understanding on the part of the recipient/client/others is maximised (Koocher and Keith-Spiegel, 1998). In crisis and conflict situations, misinterpreted or poorly understood communications can have catastrophic outcomes (Marsh, this volume) and adversely damage the reputation of, and confidence in, the practitioner in the longer term. This in itself would constitute a potential breach of the HPC Standards (2009 – see Figure 6.1, Standard 13) in the UK, for example, rendering the practioner liable to regulatory enquiry. Thus the decision-making outcome should ideally be communicated in a manner which is comprehensible to the recipient/client/others in a format which pertains or is responsive to the context of the conflict or crisis (i.e. visual, verbal, written, etc.) ensuring, of course, that the ethical issues around confidentiality are not inadvertently breached. This may present as rather a simplistic and apparent approach whose description in the current context is seemingly of little value. Yet, as Smith *et al.* (1991) have observed, practitioners may at times act and respond more readily to their own values and out of expedience than with reference to ethical and professional guidelines (APA guidelines in this case).

Finally, in the chain of events and on reflection, the decision taken should be actioned and implemented. It is only at this juncture that the practitioner can begin to evaluate the outcomes of their ethical approach in terms of its rationale, implementation and outcomes (Francis, 2009). Indeed, until the outcome of the cumulative effects of the ethically based professional advice is known then the effectiveness of the resolution ultimately arrived at in the conflict or crisis and its bearing on the ethical approach of the practitioner cannot be assessed and incorporated into future practice. This then leads to the need to review how the practitioner determines what might and might not be considered as ethical practice in a conflict or crisis situation.

Fisher and Ireland (2010) summarise the role of the psychologist as consultant to crisis situations such that the practitioner will need to reflect on their style of engagement and the pertinent areas of expertise and competence to bring to the situation. Appraisal of the presenting conflict or crisis using the available information will assist. The process of triangulating self-report (from those involved), observation and consulting available documentation ('testimony') is a reliable and effective way of gathering the information which will inform the rationale for the decision-making process.

Approaching the conflict or crisis situation

The key ethical aspect which the practitioner approaching a conflict or crisis situation involving hostage-taking, barricading, protesting, rioting or other perpetrator-led complex scenario will face is the existence of multiple relationships where a potential range of stakeholder affiliations is present. Assuming that the practioner is familiar with the role of the consultant advisor (see Fisher and Ireland, 2010, for a review, but also see below) then the ethical issue of competence to engage with the situation should have been considered based on the information provided from the scene/situation by the person managing the conflict or crisis and the expectations made of the practitioner in terms of resolution.

In terms of determining competence, the issue of boundaries of practice is worthy of brief consideration. Consider the following example:

> Tom, a registered practitioner psychologist with lengthy experience and knowledge, receives a call asking that he attends a crisis situation to assist the local police force in resolving a domestic dispute. He is advised that a local man has chosen to take his children onto the roof of his house to protest at the likelihood of having his children taken away from his care as a result of his recent marital breakdown. Although Tom has lengthy experience, this does not encompass domestic-related disputes and, moreover, Tom has a fear of heights.

What are the competence issues arising in this situation? How might Tom seek to resolve them to meet the needs of the scenario without compromising his professional ethics?

A simple step in information gathering would be to request more information from the caller about the height of the property at the incident scene and determine whether or not he will be expected to work at height – clearly working at height may adversely influence Tom's objectivity as he is likely to be preoccupied with his own safety. Second, Tom should reassure himself that he is adequately familiar with the psychological literature surrounding domestic dispute as this may inform judgments about perpetrator motivation. Third, the level of threat posed to the children should be queried based on the information available to him at the time of the call – this will help him to determine what the time parameters are in terms of urgency of attendance – threat assessment (Borum *et al.*, 1999) is a key component in managing time and thus allowing due time for reflection on competence.

Only when Tom is certain that his attendance to assist in the management of the situation will increase the likelihood of success and not increase the likelihood of worsening the issues should he agree to the consultation.

Having arrived at a conclusion concerning appropriateness of attendance prior to arrival, the practitioner will need to undertake an initial consideration of the stakeholders in the situation and judge the affiliations of each party, the role of each party in terms of client status and the principles of ethical decision-making (and thus engagement) with each party.

In considering a multiple client scenario, Francis (2009) suggests a hierarchical approach to thinking. Identification of the client hierarchy may be considered thus:

- *Perpetrator* - method of communication and the balance between caring for the needs of the person and assisting in the management of the harm that they may seek to cause.
- *Agencies* – managing expectations and remaining within the boundaries of competence, confidentiality and responsibility; clarity of the advisory and strategic role as opposed to an authority role; managing the sustainability of the profession's reputation in such situations; compliance with statutory and legislative requirements.

- *Victim* – primarily assisting in advising on managing the level of threat, assessing likely reaction and needs, but above all else protecting life, seeking to ensure the minimisation of harm within the sphere of their responsibility.

Within each of the aspects of the hierarchy, varying levels of allegiances to associates (friends, family, acquaintances, colleagues) will need to be attended to as will consideration of the impact of professional activity on the reputation of the profession and all those concerned (the *dignity* aspect as it were: Francis, 2009).

In each case, the issue of consent to intervention/advice/action will also need to be considered. Consent (as opposed to informed consent per se) can usefully be defined in conflict and crisis situations where parties are unable to give informed consent as 'agreement to receive the services proposed'. Such an approach fits the HPC standard requirements (Standard 9, Figure 6.1 above), for example, meeting a basic medico-legal requirement (Andrews, 2009) in the UK and in the US the requirements of the APA Code (2002). This issue of resolving consent in such circumstances will at the minimum involve communicating the presence of the consultant practitioner to those at the conflict or crisis scene. Unknown to the consultant, those involved at the point of communication may have adverse views as to the presence of a given individual which may hinder the advisor in their role, for example if the victim/perpetrator is an ex-intimate partner, work colleague or family member. Certainly some popular films and television series use such a plot device to engage audiences, but in the real world of conflict and crisis management such scenarios would not be permitted, at least ethically, to persist. At least three of the main errors in negotiation practice noted by Greenstone (2007) are within this area of practice and in ethical terms (both in terms of principles and codes) are avoidable and serious errors in judgment. Recognising the ability to be objective is critical.

Thus, having reflected on the issues of client hierarchy and aspects of consent in the approach to the conflict or crisis situation, the practitioner is able to consider their level of competence to assist in the management of the presenting situation, in effect the ethical aspects of performance, advising and acting during the progression of the conflict or crisis.

Provision of advice, consultancy and guidance in the management of a conflict or crisis situation

Fisher and Ireland (2010) and Ireland (2010) provide reviews of the processes of specialist advice to conflict and crisis situations specifically and more generally in terms of consultancy practice respectively. Suffice it to note in the current context that the literature has broadly established effective and helpful ways for specialists, specifically practitioners, to assist in the successful resolution of conflict and crisis situations. Any practitioner seeking to engage in an advisory (or indeed other supplementary capacity – see Chapter 9 by Tucker and Capelin, this volume) role in the management of a conflict or crisis situation should do so within the parameters of evidenced, acknowledged practice in the field. This is an issue of competence requiring that the practitioner is personally familiar with the relevant literature and practice in the area relevant to the situation presenting (BPS, 2009; APA, 2002; HPC, 2009). Presenting conflict and crisis situations are by their very nature dynamic and often in a continuous state of flux. As such all situations are demanding emotionally, cognitively and physically on those involved, not least due to the often protracted process of successful resolution. The 'siege' crisis at HMP Manchester ('Strangeways') in the UK lasted for 25 days, for example (Home Office, 1990), and the riot at Attica Prison in New York State in the 1970s lasted for a number of days with considerable consequences, not least the loss of life. In any protracted series of events, however, there is a series of subordinate events which together form the overall event. In effect each crisis or conflict situation consists of a series of smaller, cumulative crises or conflicts, and it can be useful ethically to reflect on the overall situation.

Cooper (2007: 6) observes that 'all crises may be seen to embody a certain decisive moment in time, which is truly a turning point'. Approaching the situation in a strategic way (e.g., Ireland and Vecchi, 2009) allows the practitioner to assess and reflect on each step, and judge the presence of an ethical issue and as necessary proceed with due cognisance of the relevant issues in their actions (cf. Figure 6.3 above: Koocher and Keith-Spiegel, 1998).

The impact of stress on decision-making processes equally cannot be underestimated, and in the context of military conflict, for example, the US Marine Corps has developed a training protocol to assist commanders in taking tactical decisions under stress (TADMUS – Tactical Decision-making Under Stress: Cohen *et al.*, 2009). This programme is not dissimilar in its structure and approach to an ethical code (although there are clear and apparent differences) in that it refers to the need to consider how one might balance the benefits of intuitive (i.e. based on prior experience alone) against analytic (i.e., a structured and reflective approach akin to D'Zurilla and Goldfried (1974) or DeBono (1995) approaches. This is equally a useful ethical distinction in terms of processing available information and arriving at a conclusion.

Continuing the example above:

> Having arrived at the scene of the domestic disturbance, and established that the protest is occurring in a single-storey building, Tom has determined that the perpetrator of the crisis, a local man, has a primary grievance against the local social care officials, his boss who sacked him last week and the mortgage company which is threatening to repossess his house (the scene of the crisis). As such the crisis is not a domestic dispute as Tom had initially considered, but one involving protest against what the perpetrator (Gary) sees as interference by the authorities and mistreatment by his boss. Tom has a lot of experience with such conflicts and although there are minors involved (Gary's children) he feels confident that the advice he can offer to the police commander for arriving at a successful resolution will

be salient and helpful. He has told the police commander this and through the negotiators talking to Gary has made him (and therefore the victims on the roof) aware of his presence. There has been no adversarial response to this information.

Tom has now been involved in the management of the crisis for about four hours and, all factors considered, he feels comfortable with his progress. Gary is talking to the negotiators and a rapport has developed. Although Gary has some history from his medical files of a histrionic personality disorder diagnosis following a brief hospital admission ten years previously, Tom hasn't shared this with the commander, as he learned it by reading the confidential medical file passed to him by Gary's medical practitioner who was concerned for Gary's well-being. This means that Gary is likely to act in extreme ways to draw attention to himself and his feelings will tend to be more important to him than rational thinking. He is likely to follow his 'gut' instinct and feel that people who don't respond positively to him are just 'rotten'.

Tom is focusing on the safety of Gary and his children as the primary clients at the moment as other aspects of the crisis are being handled effectively by the police team.

However, Gary now becomes annoyed and upset with one of the negotiators, grabs one of his children by the waist and threatens to run and jump off the roof if he cannot have one of his demands met (which one is irrelevant).

What advice should Tom offer? His primary focus is on the safety of Gary and his children. His intuition tells him that he should advise the fire service to intervene with the police to bring Gary down from the roof before any of the parties are physically harmed. However, that may increase the likelihood of harm to Gary and his children if the intervention goes wrong, and given his reassurances to the police commander about the effectiveness of negotiation, it may call his judgment into question. Equally, as a practising psychologist, Tom knows well the likely behaviour of individuals showing traits of particular personality disorders (see Ireland, Chapter 5, this volume) so he could offer advice on likely outcomes based on that knowledge. At the same time, having consulted with a colleague, Tom is aware of the likely medium- to long-term traumatic reactions of teenagers to life-threatening situations, although he is also aware of the prevalence of parents killing their children during crises.

In the context of the developing scenario it is clear that in order to act ethically, given all the pressures, Tom needs to approach the situation analytically rather than intuitively. The latter is not only a decision beyond Tom's control, but ignores a range of features highly salient to Tom's presence and expectations of his judgment being both helpful and ethical. Having reflected on the appropriate analysis it is then for Tom to weigh the options presented concentrating on the issues being presented as salient to the decision-making process: ensuring that actions are congruent with an ethical approach is critical (Francis, 2009). Balancing emotional and intellectual competence in demanding circumstances is additionally a core tenet of ethical reflection (Pope and Brown, 1996).

Consideration should be given by practitioners during the course of such deliberations in crisis situations to how, on reflection and after the event, others may come to view their actions. Francis (2009) makes the following suggestions:

- 'Imagine that the knowledge of the circumstances (of the situation) then becomes public in a court case: further, imagine that *you* are in the witness box and have to defend *your* decision. Would *you* be able to supply such a defence?'
- 'Imagine the same circumstances as above, but instead of having to defend yourself in court, *your* family asks *you* to explain. After the explanation would they still be proud of *you*?'

(Francis, 2009: 94, parentheses and italics added)

In short, in considering the prevailing issues within an ethical context, has the decision-making process been a rational one based upon the professional knowledge and practice capabilities of the practitioner, and have the interests of the relevant stakeholders been recognised with due attention to the client hierarchy at the time of the consideration? In many cases factors which can adversely impinge on this process are rooted in heuristics, and a short discussion of their operation is warranted at this point.

Tversky and Kahneman (1974) introduced the view of human decision-making as a process of minimising uncertainty through the use of three (original) heuristics (or biases). Subsequently, their work has influenced many areas of thinking, but their propositions are particularly salient in the context of ethics in conflict and crisis situations. As such situations are ones in which events are largely unpredictable, the recipient of services is seeking predictability, time is limited and thinking processes are open to influence. The three heuristics which need to be considered are:

- *Anchoring*. This refers to the way in which an individual will tend to base decisions and estimates on previous experience or firm knowledge, which will then be approximated to the current scenario. For example, if asked the likely length of time a hostage-type incident will last the practitioner may well make inferences based on similar experiences they have had, statistics they have referred to and what seems at the time to be reasonable. In reality, the number of variables involved means that the prediction is highly unlikely to be accurate and may indeed mislead the person in charge (thus altering their expectations in turn).
- *Availability*. This refers to the way in which our decision-making can be affected by recent events that we are able to recall more readily and which therefore are seemingly more likely to recur. In other words the availability

of data affects judgment concerning the likelihood of an outcome. The sensitivity of the practitioner may be affected by recent personal experience or exposure to events: if the last three incidents attended occurred on a Monday this does not make Monday a more or less likely day for the next incident, although it may appear to. Similarly, in a televised lottery show managed and overseen by national government (i.e. so that the likelihood of fraud has been minimised), the appearance of any given number in one week has no bearing on the likelihood of its appearance the next.[3] The practitioner needs to be certain that their ethical judgment is not adversely biased by supposition but is based on scientific data.

- *Representativeness.* This refers to assumptions that are made in judgments based on prior stereotypes or societal beliefs about how others will appear, operate, behave or think. In conflict and crisis situations this may refer to judgments about the perpetrator being made on the basis of their appearance leading to inferences about future management. A male of large physical stature at an incident scene may be assumed to be the perpetrator whereas another person, a male of somewhat smaller stature, may be assumed to be the victim. The smaller man, however, has a concealed weapon and is in fact the perpetrator. Making no assumptions about roles is the safest ethical option.

In a conflict or crisis situation the practitioner acting ethically needs to be aware of aspects of their own experiences, biases and judgments which will impact in these general ways on the advice given and actions taken. This should include reflection on cultural considerations, personal health, context and the organisational framework in which they are operating.

> Having considered the presenting situation and reflected on how best to assist all parties in progressing the situation, Tom decides that lowering the tension in the situation, acknowledging Gary's difficulties in managing his emotions and thus minimising the risk to his children would be a constructive approach. Although the situation has now lasted for a lengthy period, it will soon be getting dark and continued negotiation might be helpful in assisting Gary to acknowledge that his protest and unhappiness have been recognised and that as the light fades it might be a natural point to rethink his strategy for making his point. Equally, as his emotions potentially dissipate, his concern for his children may come more to the fore, adding to the likelihood of resolution.

This judgment and advice on Tom's part is based on an analysis of the situation, Gary's individual characteristics, Tom's experience of influencing perpetrators in their behaviour (e.g. using models such as that proposed by Ireland and Vecchi, 2009) and his understanding of providing advice in such situations (see Fisher and Ireland, 2010). He communicates his advice to those talking with Gary. However, the police commander disagrees, feeling that the safety of the children is not being adequately considered, that it is getting late and that negotiations should cease while an intervention plan is considered. Tom asserts his view, but ultimately lacks the overriding authority.

The outcome for ethical considerations in conflict and crisis situations (in particular) can be influenced by the policies and politics of the broader organisational or societal context (Francis, 2009) from time to time. This will impact upon the practitioner's confidence that the 'agency' client has in their practice, and raise concerns about the consequences for their other clients in terms of not only their personal professional reputation, but also the reputation of the profession as a whole. Engaging with an 'agency client' carries such risks and it is a complex issue (beyond the current scope) to unravel the dilemmas arising in this corporate interface, where ultimately members of Tom's client hierarchy may be adversely affected by one member of the hierarchy choosing not to follow the professional and expert advice offered. This outcome reflects the potential for organisational clients to adhere strongly to the *utilitarian* principle referred to in the example of the bus hostage situation earlier.

Outcomes

In the scenario described above, the police commander's intervention leads to one of Gary's children being injured. As such, where does this leave Tom? The Codes of Ethics/Ethical Standards described above (HPC, 2009; BPS, 2009, for example) either strongly recommend or require that the practitioner maintains a written record of their interaction/contact/intervention with the client. The conflict or crisis situation should be no different. The rationale for decisions made, client hierarchy considerations, bases for decision-making and reflections on all options reviewed at each stage constitute an integral part of what a record should consist of (Koocher and Keith-Spiegel, 1998). The need for practitioners to engage in defensible, ethical practice in conflict and crisis situations is highlighted by the scenario described, and although materially different to a clinical consultation, research work or other organisational learning situation, is no different in its ethical principles.

More complex conflicts and crises

Civil conflicts and crises are not necessarily the only situations in which ethical considerations will need to be made. While it is beyond the current scope, there is a need to recognise the increasing complexity of ethical dilemmas for professional practitioners in the areas of military action and strategy, in the field of counter terrorism/extremism and in the broader area of national security. The process of consideration from the standpoint of ethics is similar in terms of process (Koocher and Keith-Spiegel, 1998; Francis, 2009), but the order of complexity is an escalating one. Certainly a variety of interpretations are possible of the appropriate ethical action (see Burton and Kagan, 2007, for an example in the field of national security), but at least the consultation and approach aspects outlined above will be primary considerations.

Conclusions

This chapter has encouraged the reader to systematically reflect on and begin to explore key ethical considerations in conflict and crisis situations. Building on an initial consideration of the principles, codes and practice around professional involvement with conflict and crisis situations, a broad exploration of their application in a number of examples has sought to demonstrate some of the issues which may arise in them, and possible ways of considering ethical decision-making, decision-taking and action, both during and following a conflict and crisis situation.

Conflict and crisis situations can present practitioners with acute difficulties as described above, as well as broader issues in terms of personal accountability, reputation and the standing of the practitioner's profession as a whole.

An important point to note, however, in thinking about the role of ethics in conflict and crisis situations is that, as discussed (Francis, 2009), ethics can never be absolute as such. Rather it is a series of approximations which gradually move towards the best decision and rationale at the time, given the information available and the most objective reflection possible. If the practitioner can reflect on an outcome and assure themselves that this has been achieved then the outcome is likely to have been ethically assured.

However, the practitioner should be aware at all times of the potential for a confirmatory bias towards self-assurance arising from the *anchoring* heuristic (Dawes *et al.*, 1989). While the importance of ethical decision-making in conflict and crisis situations cannot be overemphasised, equally the importance of recognising personal boundaries of capability and how easily recognition can be distorted by circumstances and personal beliefs should not be either. Thoughtfulness is key in making ethical decisions, and ethical decisions in conflict and crisis situations often carry important and weighty consequences.

Notes

1. European Federation of Psychologists Associations.
2. Francis (2009: 81–90) provides a full listing and review of international codes of conduct. Those exampled here reflect the primary codes and statements of principles within which the reader is likely to operate in the UK, the US and Europe.
3. For a fuller discussion of such issues see Taleb (2008) and Loewenstein *et al.* (2001).

References

Andrews, A. (2009) *Medico-Legal Update.* The Annual Bond Solon Expert Witness Conference 2009, Westminster, London, 6 November.

APA (2002) *Ethical Principles of Psychologists and Code of Conduct.* American Psychological Association, online at: http://www.apa.org/ethics/code2002.pdf.

Babad, E. Y. and Salomon, G. (1978) 'Professional dilemmas of the psychologist in an organisational emergency', *American Psychologist*, 33: 840–6.

Beauchamp, T. L. and Childress, J. F. (1979) *Principles of Biomedical Ethics*. Oxford: Oxford University Press.

Borum, R., Fein, R., Vossekuil, B. and Berglund, J. (1999) 'Threat assessment: defining an approach for evaluating risk in targeted violence', *Behavioural Sciences and the Law*, 17: 323–37.

BPS (2006) *Code of Ethics and Conduct*. Leicester: British Psychological Society.

BPS (2009) *Code of Ethics and Conduct*. Leicester: British Psychological Society.

Burton, M. and Kagan, C. (2007) 'Psychologists and national security', *Psychologist*, 20 (12): 723.

Cohen, M. S., Jared, T., Freeman, J. T. and Thompson, B. B. (2009) *Integrated Critical Thinking Training and Decision Support for Tactical Anti-Air Warfare*. Online at: http://www.cog-tech.com/papers/NavyDSS/C2 paper DSS.pdf (accessed 1 December 2009).

Cooper, S. and Fisher, M. J. (2010) 'Ethical considerations in the consultancy and advisory process', in C. A. Ireland and M. J. Fisher (eds), *Consultancy and Advising in Forensic Practice: Empirical and Practical Guidelines*. Chichester: John Wiley & Sons.

Cooper, T. (2007) 'Decision making in a crisis', *Journal of Police Negotiations*, 7 (21): 5–28.

D'Zurilla, T. J. and Goldfried, M. R. (1971) 'Problem solving and behaviour modification', *Journal of Abnormal Psychology*, 78: 107–26.

D'Zurilla, T. J., Nezu, A. M. and Maydeu-Olivares, A. (2004) 'Social problem solving: theory and assessment', in E. G. Chang, T. J. D'Zurilla and L. J. Sanna (eds), *Social Problem Solving: Theory Research and Training*. Washington, DC: APA, pp. 29–45.

Dawes, R. M., Faust, D. and Meehl, P. E. (1989) 'Clinical versus actuarial judgement', *Science*, 243: 1668–74.

DeBono, E. (1995) 'Serious creativity', *Journal for Quality and Participation*, September, pp. 12–18.

EFPA (2005) 'Carta Ethica or Charter of Professional Ethics for Psychologists'. Available at: http://www.efpa.eu/professional-development/carta-ethica-or-charter-of-professional-ethics-for-psychologists (accessed 29 November 2010).

Fisher, M. J. and Ireland, C. A. (2010) 'Acting as the consultant in a crisis situation', in C. A. Ireland and M. J. Fisher (eds), *Consultancy and Advising in Forensic Practice: Empirical and Practical Guidelines*. Chichester: John Wiley & Sons.

Francis, R. D. (2009) *Ethics for Psychologists* (2nd edn). Chichester: John Wiley & Sons.

Greenstone, J. L. (2007) 'The twenty-five most serious errors made by police hostage and crisis negotiators', *Journal of Police Crisis Negotiations*, 7 (2): 107–16.

Home Office (1990) *Prison Disturbances 1990*, Report of an Inquiry by Rt Hon. Lord Justice Woolf and His Hon. Lord Justice Stephen Tumim. London: HMSO.

HPC (2009) *Standards of Proficiency: Practitioner Psychologists*. London: Health Professions Council.

Ireland, C. A. and Vecchi, G. M. (2009) 'The behavioural influence stairway model (BISM): a framework for managing terrorist crisis situations?', *Behavioural Sciences of Terrorism and Political Aggression*, 1 (3): 203–18.

Kohlberg, L. and Lickona, T. (eds) (1976) 'Moral stages and moralization: the cognitive-developmental approach', in *Moral Development and Behavior: Theory, Research and Social Issues*. New York: Holt Rinehart & Winston.

Koocher, G. P. and Keith-Spiegel, P. (1998) *Ethics in Psychology: Professional Standards and Cases* (2nd edn). Oxford: Oxford University Press.

Loewenstein, G. F., Weber, E. U., Hsee, C. K. and Welch, E. S. (2001) 'Risk as feelings', *Psychological Bulletin*, 127: 267–86.

Mason, T. (2000) 'Managing protest behaviour: from coercion to compassion', *Journal of Psychiatric and Mental Health Nursing*, 7: 269–75.

Muir-Gray, J. A. (2001) 'Using systematic reviews for evidence-based policy-making', in M. Egger, G. Davey-Smith and D. Altman (eds), *Systematic Reviews in Health Care*. London: BMJ Books, pp. 410–18.

New South Wales Police (2009a) *Code of Conduct and Ethics*. Online at: http://www.police.nsw.gov.au/_data/assets/file/0015/4326/code_of_conduct_and_ethics.pdf.
New South Wales Police (2009b) *Statement of Values*. Online at: http://\vww.police.nsw.gov.au/_data/pdf-File/0008/83699/statement_of_values.pdf.
New Zealand Police (2009) *Code of Conduct*. Online at: http://www.police.govt.nz/about/code_of_conduct.pdf.
OPSI (Office of Public Sector Information) (2008) *Police Conduct Regulations*. Online at: http://www.opsi.gov.uk/si/si2008/uksi_20082864_en_1.
Pope, K. S. and Brown, L. S. (1996) *Recovered Memories of Abuse: Assessment, Therapy, Forensics*. Washington, DC: APA.
Schafer, J. R. (2002) 'Making ethical decisions', *FBI Law Enforcement Bulletin*, 71 (5): 14–19.
Smith, T. S., McGuire, J. M., Abbott, D. W. and Blau, B. I. (1991) 'Clinical ethical decision making: an investigation of the rationales used to justify doing less than one believes one should', *Professional Psychology: Research and Practice*, 22: 235–9.
Taleb, N. N. (2008) *Fooled by Randomness* (2nd edn). London: Random House.
Tversky, A. and Kahneman, D. (1974) 'Judgment under uncertainty: heuristics and biases', *Science*, 185 (4157): 1124–31.

7

EXPERTISE OF THE NEGOTIATOR IN CONFLICT AND CRISIS COMMUNICATION

Martin J. Fisher

Introduction

Expertise can be described as superior performance that through extended experience and learning leads to an expert level of attainment (Ericsson, 2009). The number of years of experience alone is a poor predictor of the level of expert performance observed (Ericsson, 2006). As such, the application of effective learning experiences and skills practice that is measured is critical to the development of expertise in any field of practice. 'Competence' has been described as referring to the behaviours, performance, knowledge, skills, capability and other qualities and states of the 'competent person' (Short, 1984). Competences are adaptable and as such are transferable across situations and contexts. In the case of negotiators the acquisition of expertise is particularly pertinent given the potential consequences of a crisis or conflict situation being mismanaged or poorly handled (see Marsh, Chapter 8, this volume), and the gaining of competence and sustaining it is equally important given the likely variety of conflict and crisis situations that the negotiator is certain to be involved in. Indeed Van Hasselt *et al.* (2006) cite data from the FBI Hostage Barricade Database System (HOBAS) that 'from 2002-2003, approximately 82% of reported incidents were resolved without death or injury to the subject or victim' (p. 57). The development of expertise and competence generally and more specifically in negotiators is thus critical to both the credibility and the practice of negotiation technique in the resolution of conflict and crisis situations and as such is considered first in this chapter.

Considering the particular role the negotiator plays in incident resolution the second area of discussion is the areas of expertise and competence required of negotiators. Specifically (although other behaviours and actions are involved), the role of effective communication in the skills set of the negotiator is central to how their particular form of expertise might be defined given the prominent role played by 'active listening' in the approach (e.g. Crighton, 1991; HMPS 2009;

Vecchi, 2009a; Vecchi *et al.*, 2005). This chapter therefore focuses on the role that interpersonal communication plays in the development of negotiation skills that influence and invoke change in subject (perpetrator) behaviour, how expertise in this area might be construed psychologically and how the development of such expertise can be promoted through knowledge sharing and training methodologies. It also considers supplementary aspects of negotiator skill such as personal stress management, the selection of potential negotiators and what the most effective training methodologies are in delivering the requisite expertise required.

Developing expertise

Greenstone (2005a, 2005b) suggests that there are few specialist areas within law enforcement that provide law enforcement officers with such a demanding, high-risk and stressful role as that of the hostage/crisis negotiator. Crisis negotiation, observes Charlés (2008), is the law enforcement practice of talking to suicidal individuals, hostage-takers and other barricaded individuals. Police and other negotiators are deployed in a variety of fast-moving, emotionally-charged and life-threatening situations in correctional, situational and public incidents. Each deployment is unique, because individuals are driven, or find themselves driven, to crisis due to a variety of external and internal stimuli. Therefore, any training provision that enhances skills development and expertise must be effective across a wide range of operational incidents: it must deliver competence.

Police negotiators, for example, notes McMains and Mullins (2006), are deployed in incidents ranging from suicide interventions to barricaded sieges. Furthermore, Dolnik and Fitzgerald (2008) suggest that negotiators will be employed in the future in terrorist kidnaps and sieges (also see Ireland and Vecchi, 2009). Therefore the skills, methods and personnel employed must be capable of withstanding extended deployment in demanding and complex incidents. This is a challenging training specification. However, both service administrations and the public expect that the training and the negotiators in deployment as experts are fit for purpose and for use, providing negotiators with the necessary skills to be successful and ultimately minimise loss of life and serious injury. The primary objective for negotiators is the preservation of life and all other facets of the operation such as the arrest or confinement of the subject(s) are of secondary importance.

Negotiation tactics were originally developed for use in public incidents by the New York Police Department (Bolz and Hershey, 1979; Schlossberg, 1979). Increasingly, however, their skills have been utilised to resolve a range of incidents, and they are now an established and effective non-violent tactical option. Hostage negotiation within the policing context evolved from the need to provide a non-tactical alternative to resolve terrorist incidents. Over time these skills and methodologies were increasingly used in other high-risk deployments such as siege and suicide intervention (McMains and Mullins, 2006). Initially originating in the United States, negotiator training programmes have now proliferated around the world.

In gathering the expertise and practice ability required, novice negotiators assimilate knowledge, procedures and skills across a range of subjects such as law, tactics and psychology. Perhaps uniquely within law enforcement, the number of lives saved tangibly measures the effectiveness of the training provision. Hostage negotiation training programmes, observes Hare (1997), are continually evolving, but 'Many agencies continue to use outdated crisis negotiation techniques that are based on principles which more progressive practitioners are continually revising to better account for a more comprehensive range of crisis situations encountered by law enforcement' (p. 151). When discussing training, Poland and McCrystle (1999) comment that: 'Successful training is accomplished by developing negotiator skills that are performed naturally with the minimum of conscious, physical or mental effort' (p. 67). This is a demanding expectation and one that requires negotiator training to be of the highest standard.

Internationally, research (Kennett, 2009) suggests that there is some synergy in training delivery. Within the UK police context there exist a number of one-week regional (basic) courses and a two-week national (advanced) course. A similar programme exists in Canada. In the United States some individual police departments provide bespoke negotiator courses. However, the norm is for 'associations' (regions) to provide the training courses. Furthermore, some of these students progress to the FBI (national) Quantico course. All FBI negotiators only attend the national (Quantico) course. In Australia and Germany longer programmes have been designed.

It appears that internationally courses contain a didactic phase which encompasses law and negotiation techniques and theory. It is noteworthy that scenario role-plays are prevalent internationally. In both the British national and the FBI courses it is known that considerable training time is spent on siege incidents and their resolution. However, as Regini (2002) notes, suicide intervention appears to be the most common deployment faced by negotiators. The current preoccupation with set-piece siege training may therefore be queried in terms of the incident type associated with the majority of deployments; however, the development of adaptive competence and expertise should mean that the process learning gained would supersede any specific content issues. Prior to considering how expertise in negotiation can be specifically developed it is important to understand how expertise more generally can be developed and the broad range of areas in which it has been considered.

Expertise in the field of medical or health knowledge is a relatively commonly studied area (e.g. Elander *et al.*, 2007; Melluish *et al.*, 2007; Boshuizen, 2009; Barrows and Tamblyn, 1980) but common threads of acquiring the superior levels of performance associated with expertise have been found in a number of fields. For example, research on residential burglars suggests that the process of skills acquisition, maintenance and underlying cognitive processes is no different for other, more prosocial pursuits (Garcia-Retamero and Dhami, 2009; Nee and Meenaghan, 2006). Moreover the methodology used for effective knowledge transfer is applicable across a range of areas from the acquisition of therapeutic expertise (Bennett-Levy *et al.*, 2009) to expertise in chess (de Groot, 1946, 1978). Negotiators are no different in terms of the level of expertise required, and in particular the need to develop expertise that facilitates the ability to cognitively manage the complex interplay of changes in perception, categorisation, memory, problem-solving, coordination and skilled action (Palmeri *et al.*, 2004) is a necessity given the contexts in which negotiators are deployed. (The need to manage situational and personal stress is discussed further below,)

The use of problem-based learning (PBL) scenarios has been shown to be effective in providing a learning approach that facilitates the development of expertise (Boshuizen, 2009). This approach requires learners (or novices) to address issues pertaining to their relevant field of expertise through examining scenarios that reflect and are based around authentic situations which have occurred previously. In effect, exposure, alongside knowledge acquisition, to such experiences allows the learner to integrate cognitive and behavioural learning into a composite set of performance outcomes. Evaluation of learning and skills acquisition from such an approach allows effective risk management both from the point of view of the authority and from the learner. In the field of negotiation, as noted above, the stakes are often very high and an approach that mitigates risks will be one that is more readily favoured.

Developments across the field of the study of expertise have led to the evolution of the 'expert-performance approach' (Ericsson, 2009). Over and above initial development of competence, this approach advocates the need for everyday exposure to expertise domain-specific experiences where a judgment, decision or action is required – in effect the development of expertise in a field involves would-be experts continually seeking to refine their learning practice through skills and attitude adjustment (Bransford and Schwartz, 2009) as well as gathering and retaining skills, knowledge and competence in actual practice.

Through such exposure to learning experiences and the amalgamation of new experiences into existing frameworks the development of expertise grows. When examined, the performance differential between the expert and the non-expert becomes measurably significant, be it in the case of residential burglars (Nee and Meenaghan, 2006) or in negotiators (Van Hasselt *et al.*, 2006).

How can expertise be recognised in practice?

Increased practice in a given area of behaviour or thinking style will lead to the generation of a greater level of automaticity in action and thought. Recognition of familiar stimuli will prompt certain responses (Palmeri *et al.*, 2004). This suggestion is proposed to explain behaviour across a range of contexts from aggressive behaviour (Huesmann, 1998) to medical diagnosis (Boshuizen, 2009). In particular, however, the expert will often seek to move beyond performance that is automatic and adequate to a superior level of performance that can be characterised by a heightened level of sensitivity and adaptability to cues in the domain of expertise that have previously been associated with success (Logan,

1988). This approach provides an explanation of why it is that negotiation, and other expertise, develops not only from length of experience, but also as a function of how that experience is integrated into existing levels of knowledge, performance and practice (Ericsson, 2009). Thus, while there will frequently be at least two 'players' in any given interaction, the expert will always have the advantage through their superior ability to respond in a manner that in the past has been successful. Moreover, the level of exposure to authentic scenarios and real life experience will be higher and the learning opportunities will therefore be enhanced, given the expert approach to learning. This maxim has been demonstrated for residential burglars (Nee and Meenaghan, 2006), military decision-making (Cohen *et al.*, 1996) and, most importantly in the current context, negotiation (Van Hasselt *et al*, 2006).

Consider for example the following scenario:

> When John came back to his cell after a visit from his partner, Annie, he seemed to be quite 'down' and depressed. This was surprising as he is due to be released from his five-year sentence for armed robbery in the next month. Later that day, at evening roll call, his landing officer, Sophie, hears crying through his cell door which is ajar; on opening the door to see what is going on, she finds John with one of the knives from his workshop in his hand. He immediately stands up, and states that unless his partner comes to see him during visits the next day he will cut his wrists.
>
> He goes on to state that Annie has said that she doesn't want him to come home when he is released and that she has been seeing Brad, John and Annie's next-door neighbour.
>
> In terms of approach, Sophie is not a trained negotiator, and starts telling John that he should not '*be so stupid*', that she will talk to John's partner and persuade her to come and see him, and that he should give her the knife.
>
> Her response is driven by her perception that the priority is to 'de-escalate' the situation by trying to get John to give her the knife on the basis that if he does so then she will help him solve his problem.
>
> John says '*my life is over – nobody understands how I feel – this will make her come and see me*' before plunging the knife into his own stomach.

If Sophie had been a trained 'expert' negotiator, how might she have handled the situation differently?

> Sophie recognises that John's threat to harm himself is based on the assumption that if his partner finds out what he is doing then this will cause her to rethink their relationship and relent on her decision to leave him and not let him move back into their home. He is thinking emotionally and is using behaviour that has delivered his desired outcomes in the past (threats and aggression), only this time he is threatening himself. He has no history of this so is likely to behave in an unpredictable fashion. Sophie recognises that she needs to try and think unemotionally, remain calm and try to start

> talking to John about the problems he sees himself facing. The problem to tackle is building a rapport with John, so that they can discuss what is going to happen, calmly and in way that draws John to a position where he recognises that threatening to kill himself is unlikely to be an effective way to resolve the issues in his relationship with Annie.
>
> After a long negotiation, in which Sophie involved trained colleagues and slowly worked towards a non-violent resolution, John is moved to the hospital wing where specialist colleagues are able to help him manage his emotional and practical resettlement needs constructively.

The latter approach reflects Sophie's training, experience, learning and previous success at resolving crisis incidents using her expertise in the area of negotiation. At her next training event she takes the scenario back with her and discusses it with other negotiators from other institutions to consider what other approaches she might have considered based on the collective experience of other negotiators.

While this scenario wholly oversimplifies the actual negotiation process, it does exemplify the use of expert knowledge, how it differs from a 'gut' reaction and how each experience is used to develop future performance.

In summary, the development of competence as a negotiator that is adaptable across a range of situational contexts mirrors the development and acquisition of expertise in other areas of professional practice and its status as such should not be undervalued given the stakes of success and failure.

Negotiator selection and competences

Given these expectations of performance and evolving expertise in the domain on the part of negotiators, the selection of the optimal candidates for negotiation training and consequent development of the associated expertise is of paramount importance. McMains and Mullins (2006) suggest that a formal screening process for negotiator selection is required, as the ability of the negotiator to integrate as a part of a team in delivering their knowledge and skills in critical outcome environments needs to be pre-evidenced. In particular the investment of time and money in training and the consequences of poor performance reinforce this. Unfortunately, the international approach to negotiator selection may be best described as 'uneven' and, as Regini (2002) reports, 'Law enforcement agencies strongly believe in the importance of selecting and training well staffed and well equipped tactical teams, but some departments fail to take the same approach with their Crisis Negotiation Teams (CNTs)' (p. 1).

The first stage of any selection procedure is, having recognised that the skills required are trainable, to clearly identify the role specification. Plumbley (1991) advocates the need to analyse the role in depth, understand the position of the role within the organisational structure, funding, the practicalities associated with it and its connections to other functions and departments. Once formulated and prescribed this role specification allows the development of a person/job specification for recruitment/selection purposes. However, perhaps Milner's (2002) observations capture the enormity of the task, when she suggests: 'Attempting to capture the role of negotiator in a concise explanation fails to do justice to the range of skills and abilities required of an effective negotiator. In any event, such skills and abilities are typically addressed in only a few lines at most, within articles and books relating to the broader topic of hostage and crisis negotiation' (p. 7). Regini (2002) and Milner (2002) suggest that negotiators should possess a number; of desirable personality traits. There have been a number of such proposed sets of traits/competences/styles, which subjectively seem to cover the same areas. Examples of published proposals for consideration are briefly reviewed below.

Fuselier (1981: 14–15) proposes the essential traits for a negotiator as described in Figure 7.1. Fuselier's (1981) view is generally supported by McMains and Mullins (2006), Regini (2002) and Slatkin (2005).

Milner (2002: 16) carried out an exploratory study of desired personal characteristics for negotiators and clusters the traits into 12 key areas as shown in Figure 7.2. In considering these findings, it would appear that the subjective nature of these characteristics would make their use in any subsequent selection procedure challenging and in terms of evaluative assessment somewhat difficult to defend. When considering the evaluation of the competences that contribute to effectiveness in negotiators the literature is limited in its scope. As such the use of role play and scenario-based assessment (as a precursor to problem-based learning through the use of authentic scenarios) to evaluate the expertise of negotiators would validate the negotiator characteristics that are prominent in more expert and skilful negotiators. Van Hasselt *et al.* (2005) undertook such a study comparing expert negotiators from the FBI Crisis Negotiations Unit (CNU) and FBI agents with no specific training as negotiators. Figure 7.3 lists the components found within the role-play testing paradigm used that showed a statistically significant difference ($p < 0.001$) in favour of the expert negotiators. While these components all refer to aspects of active listening, they serve to validate the central functional importance of these aspects of negotiator/subject interaction in the negotiated resolution of conflict and crisis situations. As skills

- Emotional maturity
- Good listener
- Able to establish credibility with others easily
- Able to use logical arguments and convince others that their viewpoint is rational
- Able to communicate across socio-economic classes
- Possessing practical intelligence and streetwise common sense
- Willing to accept uncertainty and able to accept responsibility with no authority
- Total commitment
- An understanding that if negotiations are not progressing and lives are threatened he will have to assist in planning an assault to rescue hostages

FIGURE 7.1 Desirable negotiator personality traits (Fuselier, 1981).

• Adaptability	• Dynamic thinking
• Calmness	• Effective communicator
• Caring	• Humility
• Commitment	• Professional integrity
• Detachment	• Resilience
• Discernment	• Self-assuredness

FIGURE 7.2 Desired personality characteristics for negotiators (Milner, 2002).

Paraphrasing	Emotion labelling
Reflecting and mirroring	Total active listening skills[a]
Overall active listening skills[b]	

[a]Observed active listening skills through the trials
[b]Subjective measure made by an independent set of raters

FIGURE 7.3 Components of negotiation skill – areas of significant differences between experts and untrained FBI agents (Van Hasselt *et al.*, 2005).

and knowledge are the deliverable outcome measures of training interventions with novice negotiators rather than aptitude or other features such as 'innate talent' (Ericsson, 2009), then the relevance and face validity of active listening skills is apparent.

McMains (2009) reinforces the focal concern of active listening skills in negotiation and cites four affirmations that should underpin any negotiation that is effectively incorporating active listening: 'There is No place I would rather be; There is Nothing else I would rather do; There is Nobody else I would rather be with: I will remember this well' (p. 179). Such self-statements are reflective of developed expertise which has been described above. Certainly, the use of authentic scenario-based training programmes develops the competences and skills required for a negotiator to be successful in their practice. Van Hasselt *et al.* (2006) were able to demonstrate that through the implementation of such a training programme the components described in Figure 7.3 can be delivered as outcomes in participants in the FBI negotiator training programme. The training programme also includes assisting participants in minimising the use of problem-solving statements and a problem-solving ('quick fix') orientation effectively. This approach can be unhelpful in the negotiation process, particularly in the early stages, and negate the positive effects of the active listening process to build influence in moderating subject behaviour (as in the 'John' scenario above) (Lanceley, 1999; Rogan *et al.* 1997; Ireland and Vecchi, 2009).

In the UK procedures present as equally uneven (Kennett, 2003). In the UK policing context some police forces utilise processes that are multi-faceted, with supervisory comment on a candidate's ability, interviews and role plays. For other police forces, officers are directly approached by existing team members to join the cadre and no formal, measured selection procedure is used. Any selection process, state Tyson and York (2000), should be both reliable and valid. Kennett (2009) suggests that the Ontario Provincial Police selection policy appears to be the most comprehensive of the international selection procedures reviewed. In 1999 a major Royal Canadian Mounted Police review recommended that 'the Task Force should establish selection criteria that are defensible in court for negotiators' (Royal Canadian Mounted Police, 1999: 25). The current Ontario Provincial selection process suggests that this recommendation has been implemented. It both details desirable negotiator traits and clearly delineates a selection policy. The potential candidate's supervisors are required to judge suitability, then there is an interview process and practical assessment phase. Furthermore, the candidate undergoes a 'voluntary' psychological assessment. Subsequently, a selection committee reviews all the data collected on the candidate. The policy then describes a development process for the candidates. Initially they are 'apprenticed', i.e. observing and providing minor non-negotiation assistance. Thereafter, if successful on the basic course, they will undertake non-primary negotiator duties. Eventually, officers are authorised by the negotiator coordinator to undertake a primary/lead role in the field.

This contrasts somewhat with the approach adopted in the selection and training of negotiators in the Prison Service in England and Wales of the UK where the approach reflects that adopted by UK police forces in its substance. All deployed negotiators must successfully complete a prescribed and accredited training programme, with 'refresher' training being completed after a fixed duration (HMPS, 2009). However, in terms of selection procedures for training there is no centrally prescribed methodology which is applied to potential negotiators, although pre-selection activities are in development.

Internationally then, in spite of strong evidence of the benefit of validated selection procedures and strong administrative support towards that end, the policy on proposed beneficial personality and other aptitude and performance characteristics remains uneven. It is likely that this is an area for further research and validation studies to consider, especially given the success of Van Hasselt *et al*, (2005, 2006) in developing the FBI CNU Role Play Test (RPT).

Training provisions for negotiators

The use of authentic scenarios in negotiator training can be traced back to the creation of negotiator training programmes in the 1970s. Their continued use suggests they are still considered to be an effective training medium (Kobetz and Cooper, 1979) and in the context of PBL are validated and endorsed as an effective approach to developing expertise generally (Boshuizen, 2009). Indeed, 'The use of role-play to train crisis and hostage negotiators is universal as there are almost no other ways to do it' (Slatkin. 2001: 74). However, Slatkin (2001) later observes that: 'Apart from a feel-good experience, role-play scenarios may fail to deliver real skills practice' (p. 74). This observation appears to raise fundamental concerns about the validity of international training programmes with their apparent over-reliance on this specific training tool. Kobetz and Cooper (1979) add to these concerns, commenting, 'Out of this need has evolved a unique series of constantly changing field exercises that have, on occasions, surprised their authors nearly as much as those who have participated in them' (p. 24).

Poland and McCrystle (1999) discuss the use of scenarios in the training environment and make two recommendations: first, that the scenarios are based on actual (i.e. authentic) incidents, thereby increasing the validity of the experience; and, second, that they remain controlled and focused. Such control would assist in replication and reliability of the learning experience. 'Challenging, yet real-world scripted, practical exercises' observe Van Hasselt *et al.* (2008), 'not only reinforce negotiation concepts, strategies and techniques, but also significantly enhance the trainees' confidence levels' (p. 261). The reliability of practical scenarios is further discussed by Littlejohn-Shinder (2001). Here is advocated the use of defined learning objectives, planning, realism and, importantly, the careful choice and direction of actors to achieve greater reliability. Both Littlejohn-Shinder (2001) and Slatkin (2005) note that role-players are almost exclusively law enforcement or correctional officers. In Littlejohn-Shinder's (2001) view, police officers, for example, fail to make good actors as 'they have difficulty switching off the police persona' (p. 23). Furthermore, suggests Slatkin (2001), police actors often play roles that are outside their sphere of knowledge (as has been established, criminal conduct in itself reflects the primary facets of expertise in the field) (Nee and Meenaghan, 2006). Therefore characterisations used in scenarios may be based on myth, rumour and perception of subject thinking rather than more genuine behaviour and cognitive style.

The use of structured role plays, suggests Slatkin (2005), would provide students with the opportunity to concentrate on key communication skills, such as rapport building or use of technical equipment. Furthermore, he suggests that these 'micro-skills' could be assessed and student-focused development plans could be created. In Mirabella and Trudeau's (1981) investigation, they discovered that negotiators described the use of role plays as acceptable but not ideal. Furthermore, they noted that many police departments were 'now using tape recording and transcripts of actual incidents to provide highly realistic training for negotiators' (p.46). The use of tape recordings and transcripts in the UK remains the exception rather than the rule, although in the FBI CNU research, tape-recorded scenarios were used to assess training outcome effectively as well as prompting learning during the course of training. Indeed in sensitising negotiators to kidnapping-type incidents, the use of audio-only materials may be beneficial (Dolnik, 2003).

A core outcome of the negotiated resolution is the effect of influencing the subject to change their behaviour and by inference their thinking. The opportunity to practise the use of active listening skills in role-play scenarios is, as stated, validated in the FBI CNU circumstance (Van Hasselt *et al.* 2006, 2008). Active listening is a trainable set of skills as demonstrated by Van Hasselt (2006) as well as in the forensic skills interventions literature (e.g. Goldstein, 1999). More broadly, Bennett-Levy *et al.* (2009) conclude that for enacting learning strategies, role play and self-experiential work, together with reflection and appropriate modelling, were the most effective methods. These recent findings reinforce the efficacy of scenario-based training in building skills across a variety of contexts (e.g. Bellack and Hersen, 1998). Kolb (1984) describes the Experiential Learning Cycle (Figure 7.4) which outlines the assimilation processes that arise in learning. The process is proposed to start with a concrete experience (i.e. authentic scenario). This then leads to the novice making personal observations about that experience which complement and are integrated into prior learning and form enhanced concepts. This builds adaptive competence and facilitates further learning through repeated exposure to experience.

As interactive technology advances on the Internet, interactive training environments online (e.g. Stone, 2001) are likely to become more viable as options for negotiator training in the future. However, as Van Hasselt *et al.* (2008) observe, the need to gain external validity for scenario-based training is a continuing and pressing need in the field. Gredecki (Chapter 2, this volume) identifies the theoretical underpinnings of the negotiated approach and these principles need to be incorporated effectively into scenarios that are contained in training packages in development.

As an illustration of these points, reconsider the scenario presented above involving 'Sophie' and 'John'. It is useful to describe the thinking and actions that an expert negotiator such as the latter presentation of 'Sophie' might engage with in negotiating with 'John'. Critically the foci are active listening, observation of the subject's behaviour and the use of learned expertise in making ongoing adjustments to approach. Opposite is a possible excerpt from early in the negotiation exemplifying the negotiator's expertise.

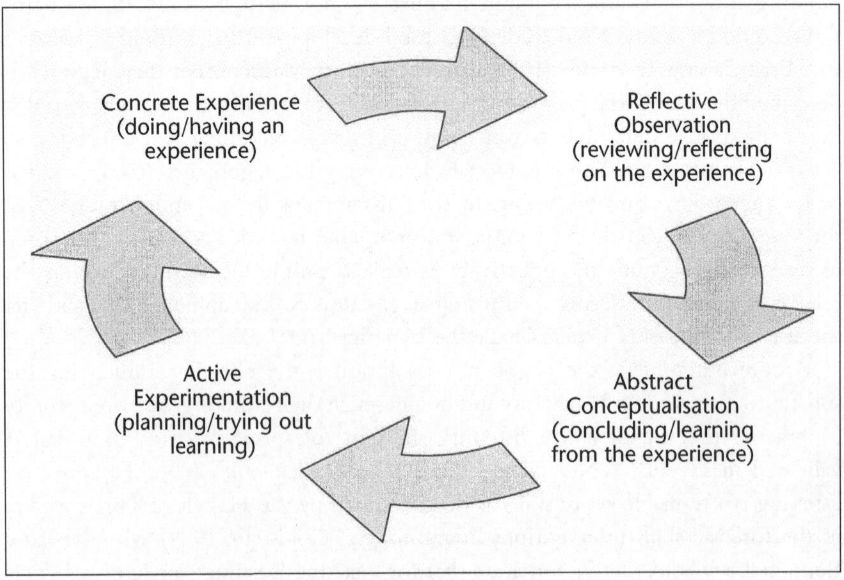

FIGURE 7.4 Kolb's (1984) Experiential Learning Cycle

'Sophie's' situational observations	*Assessment made based on expertise and competence*	*Expert knowledge and principles*	*Actions*
He is stood in his cell with a knife threatening himself – he is stood facing me.	He is staring, trembling and tearful. He is shaking and sweating. I must remain calm and focus on his needs so that I can manage this effectively.	When people present as he does then their behaviour is likely to be unstable. He is frustrated and has high levels of arousal. He is a risk to me and himself.	I need to speak calmly and not move suddenly – I can help to calm him down by acting calmly myself. *'You seem really upset – what's made you feel like this?'*
John angrily says: '*It's just not fucking fair is it?'*			
He is willing to talk to me but he is very agitated. He is focusing on my being here and not the knife in his hand.	He is very emotionally aroused and has been ruminating about something – he is *not* being very clear. I need to help him express his emotions verbally to reduce arousal and continue to distract his attention away from the knife.	People will often follow similar patterns of responding when they are emotionally upset. Some, like this man, will take a 'victim stance' to draw attention to their perceived situation and needs.	Retain calm posture and tone *'Things in life can often seem unfair – I sometimes feel that way. What is it that seems so unfair for you?'*
John angrily says: '*Well it's that bitch of a wife of mine – I'll show her who's in charge, fucking around with my head'*.			
He's lowered the knife completely now and he's pointing at me with his finger. He is shouting and expressing how he feels. The door is fully open and he is at the back of his cell.	He is still trembling and emotionally aroused but he has lowered the knife – his arm is more relaxed. He is willing to share his emotions and feelings of anger. I am still calm and have distracted him from the weapon. He is likely to carry on talking to me – I must be positive and use open questions and an open but cautious posture. I will try and avoid face-to-face posture and keep my distance – remain aware of my space. Remain outside the cell but with the door wide open so other colleagues will see me.	Aggression is directed towards his wife. He is unable to tell her how he feels about her (what has she done?). Aggression is being displaced towards himself and expressed verbally. He can only maintain this level of arousal for a limited period. Expressing his feelings of anger openly will help dissipate the arousal. I can encourage him to be more specific about the issues he has.	Try to continue to be calm in tone and posture and find out what it is about his wife's actions that has upset him so much and made him so angry. I need to have my hands in view, mirror his concern and keep the dialogue going. *'What is it that you think your wife has done that has upset you this much?'* Acknowledge emotion.
John says aggressively: '*'She won't fucking well have me home in three weeks AND she's been seeing the next-door neighbour …'*			

In summary then, the majority of negotiator training internationally uses authentic scenario-based experiential training to enhance the skills, expertise and adaptive competence which negotiators require to deliver the service on which authorities rely to resolve conflict and crisis incidents. Expertise in a skill domain develops in relation to the learning experiences in that the sequences and styles of thought and actions in the domain are reflected in competences that are adaptive across situations.

Stress inoculation and the negotiator

According to Brown and Campbell (1995), policing in general and the role of police negotiators in particular (Bohl, 1997), are highly stressful occupations. Mitchell and Dyregrov (1993) investigated the general personality types of emergency personnel resulting in the personality characteristics listed in Figure 7.5.

As can be seen, some of the traits identified by Mitchell and Dyregrov (1993) appear to contradict those articulated by Milner (2002) above (e.g. calmness and detachment). This raises the question, are law enforcement/correctional officials the right individuals to become negotiators? Furthermore, as described above, international selection procedures tend to be uneven and therefore negotiators and the public may be placed in a position of risk because negotiators undertaking the role may have not been mentally and physically tested prior to selection and training. Also, particularly within the UK, many negotiators are not included within a continuous 'well person' regime. The risks in respect of this are that over a protracted period of time the stresses and strains of deployment may adversely affect negotiators and these deteriorations may not be detected. The reality is that operational deployments are extremely stressful in their own right. Deployments are, in the truest sense of the words, 'a matter of life and death'. The potential mental and physical toll on the negotiator is considerable.

Further sources of stress are associated with the perceived divergent agendas of tactical officers and negotiators, described as 'the hidden conflict of crisis

- Need to be in control
- Obsessive (perfect job)
- Strong need to be needed
- Highly motivated
- Need for immediate gratification
- Need for stimulation
- Easily bored
- Risk taker
- Rescue personality
- Highly dedicated
- Compulsive
- Action orientated

FIGURE 7.5 Personality characteristics of law emergency services personnel (Mitchell and Dyregrov, 1993).

intervention' by Vecchi (2002). This divergence may also adversely affect the negotiator's well-being. Tactical officers train regularly to ensure that their responses are honed and appropriate, and often anecdotally they perceive the negotiator as 'soft' and 'in the way'. The negotiator faces a different set of challenges. Their role is to attempt to create an empathetic relationship with the subject in order to build rapport. Once empathy and rapport have been formed, this allows the negotiator to gain the subject's trust which will allow them to establish influence. This influence is utilised by the negotiator to save the subject/hostage-taker's life or that of other(s) (Vecchi, 2009a).

The negotiator's individual interpersonal skills and their use of effective active listening skills are keys both to the successful resolution of the incident and to the communication process in general. However, the creation of such an empathetic relationship requires the negotiator to invest, at some level, in the subject – active listening contributes to this problem-sharing approach. Arguably, this leaves the negotiator exposed. The action of understanding, being aware of, being sensitive to and vicariously experiencing the feelings, thoughts and experiences of another may cause either immediate or post-incident emotional residue. Gilmartin (2002: 49) discusses the 'hyper-vigilance recovery period' in which he considers the short- and long-term effects of being exposed to stress on a regular basis on a negotiator's personal life. Routine policing exposes officers to an environment that will be likely to adversely affect their home life. This exposure causes many police officers in the negotiator role to become exhausted, detached, isolated and apathetic when they return from duty. It seems reasonable to suggest that negotiators, who are also police/correctional officers, are also exposed not only to routine stressors but also to critical incidents of the highest stress and risk, and this is therefore likely to increase the potential for harmful negative effects. The stress responses of negotiators are discussed by Morgan (2008).

Of particular note is the likely negative effect that they will experience subsequently with any involvement in a deployment that ends in death or serious injury. Furthermore, he suggests a strategy of 'stress inoculation' therefore would seem to present as an effective mitigation for consideration by authorities. This strategy would include selecting potential negotiators who might be prone to excessively emotional responses and who have poor coping mechanisms. Pre-deployment stress-management programmes which include education, stress anticipation, stress management, role playing and team support strategies may further mitigate against unplanned outcomes for the negotiator (Morgan, 2008). Utilising such a regime will result in negotiators being inoculated against the stresses found within the operational environment. However, Morgan (2008) concludes with an acknowledgment that there will be on occasions a need to interpose post-incident contact. Internationally, there is a variety of standard operating procedures for post-incident support. These often involve occupational health, peers and coordinators. However, whatever the process adopted, it must be borne in mind that negotiators are wholly different to tactical officers. They have often invested deeply in the incident and it is likely that the experience will stay with them for some time to come. Authorities must be mindful of these needs and make provision for mitigating negative correlates (see also Tucker and Capelin, Chapter 9, this volume).

In summary, as Brown and Campbell (1995) note, policing today's society is a stressful occupation and arguably the working environment of a negotiator is axiomatically more so. 'We should bear in mind', notes Ainsworth (2002), 'that hostage situations are, by their very nature, tense and dangerous events and all those involved are at risk' (p. 162). Negotiators, observes Bohl (1997), are exposed to both physical and psychological harm. She further describes the potentially debilitating effects of stress on negotiators. However, some stress has a positive effect on individual 'actors' (Bohl, 1997; Rosenbluh, 2005). As Rosenbluh (2005) notes, however, if stress remains uncontrolled, physical and mental problems and 'adaptation' diseases such as drug and alcohol abuse may emerge. Internationally, the use of volunteers in this role appears to be common, as undoubtedly it would be difficult for senior managers to order officers to undertake such a dangerous, demanding and stressful role. Kennett (2009) notes that there is an apparent lack of any policy in the UK requiring mandatory mental health screening prior to appointment or indeed regular checks throughout a negotiator's career. Developments elsewhere may in time spread (Tucker and Capelin, Chapter 9, this volume), but in the meantime training and developmental activities for negotiators should not exclude considerations related to the impact of the negotiator role on the individual.

Summary and conclusions

The expertise of the negotiator in conflict and crisis situations is based on a series of adaptive competences that develop and are enhanced by learning experiences, reflection and practice. Although there is debate in the literature around the nature of the competences, the role of active listening in developing rapport with the subject, empathy with their position and ultimately, the ability to influence their decision-making, are key. In addition to the expertise needed to effect the role successfully, the negotiator also needs to be able to effectively manage their own position in terms of the associated outcomes of their role. This is particularly pertinent in terms of stress management and personal resources. Supplementing training in negotiation skills with other complementary skills is central to the effective maintenance of the expertise and fitness to be deployed.

Training and skills development based on authentic role-play scenarios is effective in delivering the outcomes in expertise that are required (Van Hasselt *et al.*, 2006); however, a greater emphasis on initial selection methods that have construct and ecological validity and that converge in the success of deployments of trained, expert negotiators need to be implemented.

Expert knowledge of the structure of a domain allows more effective and efficient information processing than that found in novices: experts do not think any better than novices; rather they think better things and can remember and elaborate on knowledge more effectively (de Groot, 1946, 1978). In the field of conflict and crisis negotiation where saving lives is the primary goal such ability is critical.

References

Ainsworth, P. B. (2002) *Psychology and Policing*. Cullompton: Willan.

Barrows, H. S. and Tamblyn, R. M. (1980) *Problem-Based Learning: An Approach to Medical Education*. New York: Springer.

Bellack, A. S. and Herson, M. (eds) (1998) *Behavioural Assessment: A Practical Handbook* (3rd edn). Boston, MA: Allyn & Bacon.

Bennet-Levy, J., McManus, F., Westling, B. E. and Fennell, M. (2009) 'Acquiring and refining CBT skills and competencies: which training methods are perceived to be the most effective?', *Behavioural and Cognitive Psychotherapy*, 37: 571–83.

Bohl, N. (1997) 'Post-incident crisis counselling for hostage negotiators', in R. G. Rogan, M. R. Hammer and C. R. Van Zandt (eds), *Dynamic Processes of Crisis Negotiation Theory, Research and Practice.* Westport, CT: Praeger Security International.

Bolz, F. and Hershey, L. (1979) *Hostage Cop*. New York: Rawson Wade.

Boshuizen, H. P. A. (2009) 'Teaching for expertise: problem-based methods in medicine and other professional domains', in K. A. Ericsson (ed.), *Development of Expertise: Toward Measurement of Expert Performance and Design of Optimal Learning Environments.* New York: Cambridge University Press.

Bransford, J. D. and Schwartz, D. L. (2009) 'It takes expertise to make expertise: some thoughts about why and how and reflections on the themes in Chapters 15–18', in K. A. Ericsson (ed.), *Development of Expertise: Toward Measurement of Expert Performance and Design of Optimal Learning Environments*. New York: Cambridge University Press.

Brown, J. and Campbell, E. (1995) *Stress and Policing: Sources and Strategies*. Chichester: John Wiley & Sons.

Charlés, L. L. (2008) *When the Shooting Stopped: Crisis Negotiation at Jefferson High School*. Lanham, MD: Rowman & Littlefield.

Cohen, M. S., Freeman, J. T. and Thompson, B. B. (1996) *Integrated Critical Thinking Training and Decision Support for Tactical Anti-Air Warfare*. Arlington, VA: Cognitive Technologies.

Cooper, T. (2007) 'Decision-making in a crisis', *Journal of Police Negotiations*, 7 (21): 5–28.

Crighton, D. A. (1991) *Psychological Contributions to Hostage Incidents and other Serious Disturbances: A Literature Review*. Conference Paper presented at the Prison Service Psychology Conference, Scarborough, 16–18 October.

de Groot, A. D. (1946) *Het denken van den schaker: Een experimenteel-psychologische studie*. Amsterdam: Noord-Hollandsche Uitgevers Maatschapp.

de Groot, A. D. (1978) *Thought and Choice in Chess*. The Hague: Mouton.

Dolnik, A. (2003) 'Contrasting dynamics of crisis negotiations: barricade versus kidnapping incidents', *International Negotiation*, 8: 495–526.

Dolnik, A. and Fitzgerald, K. (2008) *Negotiating Hostage Crisis with the New Terrorists*. Westport, CT: Praeger Security International.

Elander, J., Towell, T. and Fox, P. (2007) 'Competence-based training and assessment by portfolio: the health psychology model', *Psychology Learning and Teaching*, 6 (2): 73–9.

Ericsson, K. A. (2006) 'The influence of experience and deliberate practice on the development of superior expert performance', in K. A. Ericsson, N. Charness, P. Feltovich and R. R. Hoffman (eds), *The Cambridge Handbook of Expertise and Expert Performance*. Cambridge: Cambridge University Press.

Ericsson, K. A. (2009) 'Enhancing the development of professional performance: implications for the study of deliberate practice', in K. A. Ericsson (ed.), *Development of Expertise: Toward Measurement of Expert Performance and Design of Optimal Learning Environments*. New York: Cambridge University Press.

Ericsson, K. A. (ed.) (2009) *Development of Expertise: Toward Measurement of Expert Performance and Design of Optimal Learning Environments*. New York: Cambridge University Press.

Faure, G. O. (2004) 'Negotiating with terrorists: the hostage case', *International Negotiation*, 8: 489–94.

Fuselier , G. D. (1981) 'A practical overview of hostage negotiations', *FBI Law Enforcement Bulletin*, 50: 5–12.

Garcia-Retamero, R. and Dhami, M. K. (2009) 'Take-the-best in expert-novice decision strategies for residential burglary', *Psychonomic Bulletin and Review*, 16 (1): 163–9.

Gilmartin, K. M. (2002) *Emotional Survival for Law Enforcement: A Guide for Officers and Their Families*. Tucson, AZ: E-S Press.

Goldstein, A. P. (1999) *The Prepare Curriculum: Teaching Prosocial Competences* (rev. edn). Champaign, IL: Research Press.

Greenstone, J. L. (2005a) 'Peer support for police hostage and crisis negotiators: doing what comes naturally', *Journal of Police Crisis Negotiators*, 5 (1): 45–56.

Greenstone, J. L. (2005b) *The Elements of Police Hostage and Crisis Negotiations*. New York: Haworth Press.

Greenstone, J. L. (2007) 'The twenty-five most serious errors made by police hostage and crisis negotiators', *Journal of Police Negotiations*, 7 (2): 107–16.

Hare, A. (1997) 'Training crisis negotiators: updating negotiation techniques and training', in R. G. Rogan, M. R. Hammer and C. R. Van Zandt (eds), *Dynamic Processes of Crisis Negotiation: Theory, Research and Practice*. Westport, CT: Praeger Publishers.

Her Majesty's Prison Service (HMPS) (2009) *Negotiator Training Course*. HR Directorate, HMPS Learning and Development Group, Curriculum Development Department.

Huesmann, L. R. (1998) 'The role of social information processing and cognitive schema in the acquisition and maintenance of habitual aggressive behavior', in R. G. Geen and E. Donnerstein (eds), *Human Aggression: Theories, Research, and Implications for Social Policy*. San Diego, CA: Academic Press, pp. 73–109.

Ireland, C. A. (2007) 'Crisis negotiation with a mentally-disordered offender population: development of a training package in a high secure forensic hospital', BPS, Division of Forensic Psychology, *Forensic Update*, 91: 20–5.

Ireland, C. A. and Vecchi, G. M. (2009) 'The Behavioural Influence Stairway Model (BISM): a framework for managing terrorist crisis situations?', *Behavioural Sciences of Terrorism and Political Aggression*, 1 (3): 203–18.

Kennett, R. J. (2003) *An Evaluation of the Selection and Training of Hostage Negotiators Nationally*. Dissertation submitted in partial fulfilment of MEd (Training and Evaluation), University of Hull, UK.

Kennett, R. J. (2009) 'Implications for the Selection and Training of Hostage Negotiators, Through an Analysis of Hostage Negotiation Data'. Unpublished thesis submitted for the degree of Doctor of Education, University of Hull, UK.

Kobetz, R. and Cooper, H. H. A. (1979) 'Hostage rescue operations: teaching the unteachable', *Police Chief*, 46 (6): 24–7.

Kolb, D. A. (1984) *Experiential Learning Experience as a Source of Learning and Development*. Engelwood Cliffs, NJ: Prentice Hall.

Lanceley, F. J. (1999) *On Scene Guide for Crisis Negotiators*. New York: CRC Press.

Littlejohn-Shinder, D. (2001) 'Maximizing the effectiveness of role-play scenarios training exercises in development of police crisis intervention skills', *Journal of Police Crisis Negotiations*, 1 (2): 19–27.

Logan, R. D. (1988) 'Toward an instance theory of automatization', *Psychological Review*, 95: 492–527.

McMains, M. J. (2009) 'Making negotiations a focal concern: enhancing active listening skills', *Journal of Police Crisis Negotiations*, 9 (2): 176–9.

McMains, M. J. and Mullins, W. C. (2006) *Crisis Negotiations: Managing Critical Incidents and Hostage Situations in Law Enforcement and Corrections* (3rd edn). Cincinnati, OH: Anderson.

Melluish, S., Crossley, J. and Tweed, A. (2007) 'An evaluation of the use of simulated patient role plays in the teaching and assessment of clinical consultation skills in clinical psychologists' training', *Psychology Learning and Teaching*, 6 (2): 104–13.

Milner, C. (2002) 'The Crisis Negotiator: An Exploratory Study of the Skills, Abilities and Personal Characteristics of an Effective Negotiator'. Unpublished thesis submitted in partial fulfilment of MSc in Forensic Psychology, University of Surrey.

Mirabella, R. W. and Trudeau, J. (1981) 'Managing hostage negotiations. An analysis of twenty-nine incidents', *Police Chief*, May, pp. 45–7.

Mitchell, J. T. and Dyregrov, A. (1993) 'Traumatic stress in disaster. Workers and emergency personnel, prevention and intervention', in J. P. Wilson and B. Raphael (eds), *International Handbook of Traumatic Stress Studies*. New York: Plenum Press, pp. 905–14.

Morgan, P. R. (2008) *Critical Issues in Crisis Negotiations*. Hong Kong: PRM Publications.

Nee, C. and Meenaghan, A. (2006) 'Expert decision-making in burglars', *British Journal of Criminology*, 46: 935–49.

Noesner, G. W. (1999) 'Negotiation concepts for commanders', *FBI Law Enforcement Bulletin*, January.

Northcraft, G. B., Neale, M. A. and Barley, P. C. (1994) 'Joint effects of assigned goals and training on negotiator performance', *Human Performance*, 7 (4): 257–72.

Palmeri, T. J., Wong, A. C. and Gauthier, I. (2004) 'Computational approaches to the development of expertise', *Trends in Cognitive Sciences*, 8: 378–86.

Plumbley, P. (1991) *Recruitment and Selection* (5th edn). Worcester: Billing & Sons.

Poland, J. and McCrystle, M. J. (1999) *Practical Tactical and Legal Perspectives of Terrorism and Hostage-Taking*. New York: Edwin Mellen Press.

Regini, C. (2002) 'Crisis Negotiation Teams, selection and training', *FBI Law Enforcement Bulletin*, 71 (11): 1–5.

Rogan, R. G., Hammer, M. R. and Van Zandt, C. R. (1997) *Dynamic Processes of Crisis Negotiation: Theory, Research and Practice*. Westport, CT: Praeger Publishers.

Rosenbluh, E. S. (2005) 'Stress and its consequences', *Journal of Police Crisis Negotiations*, 5 (1): 79–80.

Royal Canadian Mounted Police (1999) *Major Case Management Task Force Report*, Report prepared for Senior Executive Committee of the RCMP.

Schlossberg, H. (1979) 'Police response to hostage situations', in J. T. O'Brien and M. Marcus (eds), *Crime and Justice in America*. New York: Pergamon Press, pp. 87–102.

Schmidt, H. G. and Moust, J. H. C. (2000) 'Towards a taxonomy of problems used in problem-based learning curricula', *Journal of Excellence in College Teaching*, 11 (2): 57–72.

Short, B. C. (1984) 'Competence re-examined', *Educational Theory*, 34: 201–7.

Slatkin, A. A. (2001) 'Structured role play for negotiators', *Law and Order*, March, pp. 74–6.

Slatkin, A. A. (2005) *Communication in Crisis and Hostage Negotiations: Practical Communication Techniques, Stratagems and Strategies for Law Enforcement, Corrections and Emergency Service Personnel in Managing Critical Incidents*. Springfield, IL: Charles C. Thomas.

Stone, R. (2001) 'Virtual reality for interactive training: an industrial practitioner's viewpoint', *International Journal of Human-Computer Studies*, 55 (4): 699–711.

Strentz, T. (2006) *Psychological Aspects of Crisis Negotiation*. Boca Raton, FL: Taylor & Francis.

Tyson, S. and York, A. (2000) *Essentials of Human Resource Management* (4th edn). Oxford: Butterworth Heinmann.

Van Hasselt, V.B., Romano, S. J. and Vecchi, G. (2008) 'Role-playing: applications in hostage and crisis negotiation skills training', Behaviour Modification, 32 (2): 248–63.

Van Hasselt, V. B., Baker, M. T., Romano, S. J., Sellers, A. H., Noesner, G. W. and Smith, S. (2005) 'Development and validation of a role play test for assessing crisis (hostage) negotiation skills', *Criminal Justice and Behaviour*, 32 (3): 56– 69.

Van Hasselt, V. B., Baker, M. T., Romano, S. J., Schlessinger, M. Z., Zucker, M., Dragone, R. and Perera, A. L. (2006) 'Crisis (hostage) negotiation training: a preliminary evaluation of program efficacy', *Criminal Justice and Behaviour*, 33 (1): 56–69.

Vecchi, G. M. (2002) 'Hostage/barricade management: a hidden conflict within law enforcement', *FBI Law Enforcement Bulletin*, 71 (5): 1–7.

Vecchi, G. M. (2009a) 'Conflict and crisis communication: a method for influencing and persuading behavioural change', *Behavioural Sciences*, 34: 34–42.

Vecchi, G. M. (2009b) 'Critical incident response, management, and resolution', *Inside Homeland Security*, 7 (2): 7–16.

Vecchi, G. M., Van Hasselt, V. B. and Romano, S. J. (2005) 'Crisis (hostage) negotiation: current strategies and issues in high-risk conflict resolution', *Aggression and Violent Behavior: A Review Journal*, 10: 533–51.

8

WHEN THE MANAGEMENT OF THE CRITICAL INCIDENT GOES WRONG

Pitfalls and suggested approaches

Debbie Marsh

A critical incident can be defined as 'any incident where the effectiveness of the police response is likely to have a significant impact on the confidence of the victim, their family and/or the community' (Cambridgeshire Police Force (UK), Critical Incident Policy, p. 2). There is a wide variety of potential critical incidents but this chapter focuses on situations which have been created by groups of individuals involving negative interaction with law enforcement agencies.

Historical summary

The existence of critical incidents dates back to pre-Roman times. In relation to hostage-taking it was deemed common practice to take hostages to ensure compliance between nations as guarantees of treaties (Call, 1999). During the Middle Ages, there was an expectation in European nations that people would be held captive to assure compliance by warring nations. It was not just in the arena of international conflict where hostage-taking was common place; merchants were taken captive to guarantee that other merchants of the same nationality would pay their debts (Souchon, 1976). Kidnap (contrary to common law) and false imprisonment have been criminal offences since the 1850s (Offences Against the Person Act 1861, 1982). Yet, it wasn't until 1982 that this common practice of hostage-taking became a criminal offence in the United Kingdom, for example.

Prior to the 1970s, the two resolution options available to crisis and critical incident managers were the 'soft' and 'hard' approaches. The first option consisted of conceding to the 'demands' of the perpetrator in order to achieve a resolution to the incident; this might, for example, include the safe release of hostages. This approach prioritised the safety of human life. However, it also encouraged hostage-takers to increase the frequency of their activities and the weight of their demands. The second option, the 'hard' approach, was one where governing nations or administrative bodies would choose not to comply with the demands of the perpetrator but would utilise tactical resources to resolve the incident by force. McCaffery (1994) noted that until the early 1970s, hostage situations were typically reconciled by means of a massive police presence, often ending in a tactical assault. This method of resolution would often result in people being injured or killed, and mortality rates on occasion reached 80 per cent for those involved when authorities resorted to force (Schlossberg, 1979).

The 'hard' approach was often favoured in the management of internal, national crisis incidents. This was particularly notable in the United States where such an approach was adopted to manage a series of prison riots and advocated complete suppression of anti-establishment behaviour through the use of rapid and overwhelming force to defeat all resistance. Needham (1977) noted that, up until the 1960s, this suppression-based model was utilised when dealing with a succession of prison riots in the United States. However, while force was successful in the sense it ended a particular disturbance, the violent showdowns in the prisons continued to develop in spite of the States' use of force to suppress them (Whyte, 2005).

One of the most notorious prison incidents occurred in the United States of America, at New York's Attica Prison in September 1971. A group of prisoners overpowered staff and broke into the 'Keeplock' area (the office which contained the override system for all the cell doors) (McMains and Mullins, 2001). Within minutes all the prisoners were unlocked and had taken control of the establishment. The prisoners held over 40 prison employees (both correctional officers and civilian workers) hostage while they issued a list of demands. A form of negotiations followed for three days until the New York Commissioner ordered a tactical intervention. The intervention left 39 people dead and 80 wounded. Eleven of the dead and 33 of the wounded were prison personnel (McMains and Mullins, 2001). These domestic disturbances in the United States were followed by the international incident at the Munich Olympics, where, on 5 September 1972, 13 Arab terrorists invaded the Olympic compound that housed the Israeli Olympic athletes and took 11 hostages. The terrorists demanded the release of 200 Arab prisoners being detained in Israel and 'free' transport to Egypt. As they were transported to the airport, the authorities intervened and assaulted the terrorists. In total, 22 were killed; this included hostages, terrorists and police enforcement staff (McMains and Mullins, 2001). It is often stated (Whyte, 2005; McCaffery, 1994; McMains and Mullen, 2001) that both the domestic pressures and the international outcry following the Attica prison riot and the Munich Olympics incident promoted the generation of a third option: that of negotiation. Observers suggest that these events motivated the New York City Police Department to develop the revolutionary negotiation tactics that would lead to the resolution of high-conflict incidents without the loss of life experienced in Munich (McMains and Mullins, 2001; McCaffery, 1994).

The negotiated approach

The Williamsburg incident, on 19 January 1973, provided the opportunity to assess this new approach. The incident involved four armed robbers who entered a sporting goods store in New York City. A silent alarm was triggered which summoned the police who effectively trapped the armed robbers inside the store. In the initial encounter, gunfire was exchanged which resulted in the death of one police officer and injury to a further two police officers. The police force began to negotiate with the perpetrators rather than resorting to the previous method of tactical intervention. The siege, as it became, was successfully negotiated to a conclusion later that same day with no further injuries. In place of the usual tactical approach to an incident in which adrenalin and emotions can be elevated on both sides, the more controlled, referenced, reflective and managed approach proved successful. It was considered a significant change in strategy and tactics for the New York Police Department. This success was developed further in 1973 when the FBI established a hostage negotiation training programme at their Training Academy. This approach has been developed subsequently and is now considered to be the internationally accepted approach to crisis management (McMains and Mullins, 2001). As Noesner (1999) noted, negotiation has consistently proven to be successful in terms of peaceful resolutions. Crisis management teams have a range of options in order to resolve incidents.

It is widely acknowledged negotiation is the starting place for most incident management, though there are times when incident commanders will utilise more than one strategy in order to resolve an incident. For example, at Talledega in the United States, 21 August 1991, Cuban detainees awaiting deportation to Cuba took 26 hostages as they overran a federal correctional institution. A negotiation team was established from both correctional and FBI personnel. As the detainees became more organised, they presented a list of demands which included: press coverage of their plight, medical attention for prisoners and the establishment of a commission of prominent citizens who could plead their case to the general public. It became evident to the incident commander that negotiations were not progressing sufficiently well and that the safety of the hostages was under threat; thus a tactical entry was ordered early on 30 August (nine days later). Fagan and Van Zandt (1993) reported that, even though the incident was resolved tactically, negotiators were a valuable part of the overall operation; they were able to 'support the crisis'.

The range of options, skills and knowledge available to an incident commander should imply that all conflict and crisis situations can be resolved successfully with minimal harm to any involved. However, there have been several incidents in recent history where crisis management approaches have gone seriously wrong, resulting in high mortality rates for the majority involved. The remainder of this chapter will investigate in some detail three examples of when incident management has gone wrong. It will consider the errors made and contemplate alternative management strategies and possible approaches in order to avoid similar difficulties arising in the future before going on to identify the implications for the negotiators involved.

To begin it is useful to provide a brief description of the three incidents used as examples: the 'Waco siege', Texas, USA; the Moscow State Theatre siege, Russia; and the Beslan school siege, Russia.

The 'Waco siege', Texas, USA

> On 28 February 1993, the FBI engaged in a 'standoff' with the Branch Davidians, a religious order outside Waco, Texas. The siege resulted from a failed assault by the Alcohol, Tobacco and Firearms agency to serve a search warrant on the group for illegal weapons. In the course of the siege, 25 people surrendered, 18 of whom were children. As time passed, the FBI used the '10-day rule' which resulted in the electricity being turned off to the compound; the compound was bombarded with loud music and noise; the FBI increased its tactical assaults by using 'flash bangs' on Branch Davidians completing their daily chores. The Branch Davidians did not retaliate against any of these assaults; eventually their leader indicated the group might surrender once a task had been completed which the incident commander perceived to be a stalling tactic. The siege ended on 19 April 1993, when 75 Branch Davidians perished in a raging inferno, 51 days after the start of the siege, and as the FBI utilised tear gas and incendiary devices to assault the compound.
>
> *(Edwards, 2001)*

The Moscow State Theatre siege, Russia

> On 23 October 2002, between 40 and 50 Chechen terrorists seized control of the Moscow State Theatre, taking approximately 980 people hostage. The siege lasted two and half days. During this time over 200 hostages were released and four people were killed, one of whom had entered the theatre once the Chechens had taken control. The siege ended when the Russian Special Forces pumped a chemical agent into the theatre before tactical teams entered. The intervention left all the perpetrators and a large number of hostages dead.
>
> *(Dolnik and Pilch, 2003)*

The Beslan School siege, Russia

> On 1 September 2004, Chechen terrorists took control of School Number One in Beslan, taking over 1,100 people, including over 750 children, hostage. On the third day, Russian Special Forces stormed the building. A series of explosions shook the school and were followed by fire, which engulfed the school, and a chaotic gun battle ensued. This resulted in at

> least 330 hostages being killed, including over 180 children. Hundreds more were wounded or reported missing.
>
> *(Forster, 2006)*

From these brief summaries it is clear that each incident has its own characteristics. There are, however, key themes which run through each of these incidents which impacted on the incident management. These are: the role of the media; a political agenda; the role of objective decision-making; and the use of excessive force.

Role of the media

Critical incidents are major news stories and as such attract enormous amounts of attention from domestic and international media. In the majority of incidents those in charge recognise the role and interest of the media. However, a distance is maintained between the reporters and the incident: this prevents the media becoming involved in the process of negotiation and thus allows the incident commander and their management team to ostensibly retain control of the situation. In the case examples above, incident managers did not adopt this strategy and this decision contributed towards the negative outcomes.

This is most clearly demonstrated in the case of the Moscow incident; the incident management team manipulated the media to gain public support. For example, day 3 saw the release of 15 hostages and a promise to free the remaining foreign nationals. The Russian authorities issued a statement that promised to spare the lives of the perpetrators if all hostages were released unharmed. This public statement angered the perpetrators and prompted a renewed threat to execute the hostages the following morning if their demands were not met (Dolnik and Pilch, 2003). In this climate of increased tension a rumour of a pending assault was circulated between officials and reporters at the scene. This, combined with the perpetrators' awareness that the Russian Special Forces had arrived, caused panic in the theatre. A distressed male hostage launched an attack on a female guard and a bullet was fired. The bullet caused serious injuries to two other hostages sitting nearby. The perpetrators were devastated and called for medical assistance; the recipient of the call did not ask the cause or nature of the injuries. The incident commander believed the perpetrators were starting to action their threats and the command for intervention was given (Dolnik and Pilch, 2003). The news story had enabled the tactical intervention. When the tactical intervention was actioned a hostage rang the local radio station in distress (Dolnik and Pilch, 2003). However, by utilising the media in this way, it further damaged the ability of the authorities to manage the developing incident effectively. Accordingly, the world's media were expecting an intervention when the assault took place. It was watched by the world, and the catastrophic loss of life was public knowledge as events unfolded. The authorities were not provided with any time to manage the situation effectively and to inform the families of victims.

In other incidents, the media have been used to generate public support for authorities in order to endorse a chosen course of action. This can be seen in both the Beslan school (Forster, 2006) and the Waco sieges (Edwards, 2001). First, the media's confrontational tone regarding press releases engineered hostility from the terrorists which undermined the planned negotiation strategy. The terrorists perceived the incident command team as hostile rather than supportive and willing to work towards a peaceful resolution (Forster, 2006). In the Waco scenario, rumour and speculation of child abuse in the besieged compound prompted the incident commander to continually escalate the tactical interventions used throughout the siege. There was no evidence to indicate any form of child abuse had taken place. However, this information added further pressure to an already tense, emotionally-driven situation (Kopel and Blackman, 1997).

The media phenomenon and its influence on the actions of public authorities could be observed as symptomatic of modern society. However, the efficacy of its role in incident management is questionable at best. Incident commanders who attempt to utilise the press to gain support or manipulate the events may cause themselves and their teams further problems as the media are a largely ungoverned, uncontrollable entity which can not be guaranteed to accurately report the facts of a situation (Herman and Chomsky, 1988). Successful incident commanders who regulate and funnel the press releases around serious incidents to factual accounts only, can validate the situation for the perpetrators (unless they have a statement of 'no press involvement'), while minimising any negative impact on those involved, thereby protecting the negotiation process.

Political pressure

Serious incidents are emotive events which can put considerable pressure on governments and other aspects of public administration to reach a resolution in an acceptable manner. An acceptable manner can be difficult to define consistently as public opinion is inclined to vary; thus it is crucial for governmental authorities to be seen to be acting promptly, proportionately and appropriately to resolve the incident in order to retain public confidence. Although serious incidents in their many forms are legislated as crimes and as such warrant punishment or at least sanction, the public are very unlikely to condone the excessive use of forceful violence, especially when this results in the death of those that have been held hostage. A further consideration for a public authority is how their actions are perceived by other potential or actual terrorist groups. There is a slim division in judgment between being seen as weak and being seen as hostile. Any conciliatory action could be perceived as weakness which may encourage further attacks. However, if the management is too aggressive, this can serve to advance hostilities which impacts on both the terrorists' behaviour and the hostages' trust in the authorities to ensure their safety in the event of being taken hostage. Loveday (2000) noted it is often the case that the process by which targets are accomplished can become secondary to the primary goal of achieving them. This reference was made in relation to the UK Crown Prosecution Service, although it is directly relevant to the present discussion. The desire to resolve the situation can override other essential factors involved in the successful management of the current incident and future incidents. Once again public pressure and the need to resolve the incident as soon as possible can narrow the perceptions of the realistic options available to the decision-makers. Thus the only option which would demonstrate their strength and ability to control the situation would be a tactical response.

The Moscow theatre siege provides a good example of how growing public concern can affect decision-making. After several days, the perceived pressures on the incident command team mounted as families and friends of the hostages started demonstrations outside the theatre siege area. This placed significant additional pressure on the authorities to resolve the siege (which by definition had now become both a critical incident and a crisis) as public confidence had begun to wane around the government's ability to manage serious incidents. The government, rather than separating the governance of the incident command and allowing the incident command team to manage the siege according to the demands of the situation, allowed public pressure to influence the incident management. The consequent perceived pressure called for resolution and thus at that time limited the options available to the incident commander to tactical intervention only (Dolnik and Pilch, 2003).

Such effects may also be observed in the Russian government's response to the Beslan school siege which was also influenced by the prevailing political agenda and past events. This impacted on the authorities' desire to negotiate the situation to resolution. Since the Moscow theatre siege the government had not used negotiation as a tactic in incident management. This incident provided the authorities with the opportunity to regain public confidence in their ability to manage critical and crisis incidents effectively. This opportunity in turn impacted on the behaviour of the terrorists who did not believe the authorities were willing to listen and peacefully resolve the incident. They immediately executed 20 hostages to indicate their commitment to their cause. Despite these actions the terrorists did engage in negotiations (Forster, 2006).

A key element of public confidence reflects how citizens believe that they would be treated if they were to be taken hostage, and, moreover, how the authorities might seek to protect them and work towards their safe release. If the governing authority advocates a tactical response which results in a large number of casualties, the public will have no faith in the administration to keep them safe and effect a rescue given public consciousness of outcomes in the past from such approaches. This poses considerable problems for incident management teams as hostages may be prone to either seeking to resolve the incident for themselves, i.e. trying to overpower the perpetrators or taking the 'safer option' which could entail joining forces with the perpetrators as this would increase their chances of survival. Both options will impact on the management of incidents.

Rational decision-making

A key aspect in the successful management of critical and crisis incidents is the ability to develop a strategic approach based on the facts of the incident. The strategy should be regularly appraised to ascertain its validity in the face of both new information and the passage of time. The starting place for this is likely to be past experience which will inform the incident management team as to which options are likely to be efficacious. However, it is crucial for the incident commander to recognise the individual characteristics and/or unusual or idiosyncratic aspects involved in each event. Failure to recognise the defining facts of each incident can lead to errors and mistakes. Reason (2005) makes the distinction between 'errors' and 'mistakes': an *error* is when the plan does not achieve its aim. These tend to occur when completing routine tasks in familiar environments. A *mistake* is when the plan is inadequate and unable to achieve the desired outcome ('not fit for purpose'). Reason (2005) further divides this category into 'rule-based' and 'knowledge-based' mistakes. The former is when an incident commander uses an old solution in the new situation inappropriately. If this mistake occurs, it is likely to cause negative ramifications where an inappropriate resolution is considered or utilised. There is no dispute that experience and prior knowledge are essential tools for incident commanders, and if they consider the use of an existing solution to be applicable to address the current situation, then the application of this prior experience can be both economical and effective. Knowledge-based mistakes arise when incident commanders attempt to understand situations that are unusual, dynamic and unclear. Making sense of this type of situation involves consideration of all facts available, using all specialist advisors and drawing on past experience. Reason (2005) noted that this will be likely to involve a combination of conscious deliberation, rehearsal and creative thinking. Reason (2005) highlights that part of this process is 'mindful' consideration. However, this is underpinned by involuntary and well established ways of assimilating information which is demonstrated in an individual's daily decision-making. It is easy to become over-reliant on these underpinning structures when under pressure and faced with a challenging, unfamiliar situation (Reason, 2005). Successful incident commanders are aware of their thinking biases and can account for them in the decision-making process.

If we now examine the scenarios above, in the Waco incident the incident commander had considerable experience in siege/hostage management and brought this knowledge and experience with them to the Waco siege. However, they failed to recognise that the fundamental difference in the Waco siege was that those involved were not held against their will but free to leave at any time (Edwards, 2001). Therefore employing tactics based on hostage management did not prove successful. An example of this is the so called '10-day rule'. If an incident lasts for 10 days, the incident management team can utilise the option which involves shutting off amenities to the subject property, including electricity, in order to create discomfort for the hostage-takers. However, at the Waco siege, the 10-day rule undermined the negotiation strategy as the incident command team had failed to take account of several points: first, the people in the compound were not hostages; and second, there were several infants and children on the property who required milk – shutting off the electricity supply would have had a significant impact on the food supplies needed in order to sustain their feeding (Edwards, 2001). This would, therefore, have been perceived as an extremely hostile action by the perpetrators. In addition, the command team had not established their intelligence communications correctly as the property had generators which were capable of providing the electricity required. Thus while the children's food was safe, there was a significant impact on the trusting relationship between negotiators and inhabitants. The establishment of trust in the negotiation process is crucial and should be considered the foundation for a successful negotiation strategy. In the absence of this, negotiators will be unable to engage with the perpetrators in a meaningful manner. This then means they will be unable to establish the motivation for the incident and thus be incapable of producing resolution options.

Establishing trust can be undermined by perpetrators seeing negotiators and tactical response teams as having opposite aims (Vecchi, 2002). These perpetrator beliefs can impact on the negotiator's well-being. Tactical officers may equally be seen to perceive that the negotiator is 'soft' and 'in the way'. The negotiator's role is to attempt to generate rapport with the subject through the use of empathy (cognitive and emotional). These facets of a dialogue allow the negotiator to establish a degree of trust with the perpetrator which will subsequently affect the ability to influence the perpetrator's thinking and therefore actions (Vecchi, 2009a). Also, the negotiator seeks to 'buy time' in order to allow the incident/subject to stabilise and allow the actors/protagonists to become more rational in their thinking. Finally, intelligence gathering and motivation formulation can provide tactical resources with insights (Kennett, 2009). The negotiator's own interpersonal skills and their use of effective listening skills are key to both the successful resolution of the incident and to the communication process in general (Fisher, Chapter 7, this volume). Such an empathic relationship inevitably places demands on the negotiator's personal resources given the context in which the relationship has developed. The negotiator thus may be exposed vicariously to the experiences that the subject is experiencing, and consequent sensitivities, feelings and thoughts may become more apparent. This is evidenced in both the WACO and Moscow siege examples covered here.

Each of the tactical interventions would have damaged the negotiation process and would have placed the negotiators under additional stress to maintain dialogue and rapport. It has to be borne in mind that, while negotiator teams and tactical teams clearly have different roles and responsibilities, they have an overarching responsibility to support the incident commander. This can be achieved by establishing working boundaries and clear lines of communication. If this is achieved, negotiators should be able to inform any intervention and be fully briefed regarding any tactical intervention, which will minimise any negative impact on their relationship with the perpetrators.

As situations progress and events unfold, issues arising in the situation can become clouded by emotion and physical exhaustion, both of which can influence perceptions of the effectiveness of a strategy in terms of its suitability and future management options. Perhaps an optimal way to separate the physical and emotive aspects of incident management is to provide an objective assessment and to critically evaluate the evidence and intelligence arising from the incident. This involves considering the initial intelligence and any updates in information, and then examining the negotiation process to highlight any markers of progress: release of hostages, reduced demands, open communication between parties, for example, in addition to consideration of any markers of deterioration (i.e. violence towards hostages, refusal to engage). Such markers will provide evidence to either support the maintenance of the current negotiation strategy or signal that change is required. This impartial approach allows the command team to make objective decisions based on the characteristics of the incident and those involved. This process did not happen at Waco, Moscow or Beslan. As all three subject incidents progressed, there is evidence to suggest the command teams were gathering the dynamic intelligence to support a decision for intervention rather than examining the information as it presented and utilising it to re-evaluate and then inform the strategy (Edwards, 2001; Forster, 2006). This form of crisis management stifles innovation and the ability to approach difficult situations in novel ways, which is likely to guarantee that incident commanders will tend to rely on tried and tested methods irrespective of previous consequences.

In the Waco siege, for example, there are several key points which highlight this approach. The negotiation team believed they were negotiating with a 'prophecyopath', an individual who truly believes (s)he is a prophet of God (Edwards, 2001). This perception resulted in the team holding the belief that they would be unable to negotiate the incident to a resolution. Thus they did not believe negotiation could work and this affected their ability to evaluate any progress made. Over the course of the siege, the team negotiated the surrender of 25 people and had gained a commitment from the leader that once a piece of work was completed they would all surrender. This should have been seen as a significant marker of progress. However, it was at this point the incident commander sought permission for intervention.

A further example can be seen in the lack of evaluation regarding tactical techniques in the siege. Following the initial conflict which resulted in the siege, the Branch Davidians did not act aggressively towards the authorities, and no later acts of violence were seen. The authorities, however, utilised several tactical measures over the duration of the incident. These included, as stated above, shutting off the electricity supply, bombarding the site with loud music and firing 'flash bang' devices at Branch Davidians who were carrying out daily chores; none of these reactions served any function other than to impede negotiations by damaging the trusting relationship between negotiators and perpetrators (Edwards, 2001). The command team should have identified potential outcomes when discussing the use of the intervention, both positive and negative, and then assessed which outcomes were achieved following the intervention. By using this method the team would have been able to identify the value, if any, of using further tactical techniques.

The perpetrators involved in the Moscow theatre incident made it clear they had no issue with any foreign national captives and offered to release anyone with a foreign passport; this offer was not actioned (Dolnik and Pilch, 2003). However, the perpetrators responded and released 150–200 children, pregnant women, people with health needs and some foreign national captives within hours of the initial assault on the theatre (Dolnik and Pilch, 2003). A further 25 hostages were released on the second day, and the perpetrators restated their offer to release all foreign national hostages. Again, this offer was not actioned but the terrorists released 50 Russian hostages (Dolnik and Pilch, 2003). The third day saw the terrorists offer to release 75 foreign national hostages. Then the terrorists released 15 more hostages throughout the day with no conditions or demands. Also, medical teams and the Red Cross were allowed to enter the theatre, and took in medical supplies, food and warm clothes. Once outside the theatre, they reported the perpetrators were not beating or threatening the captives and that the majority of the hostages were calm. That night saw four more hostages released, with the promise of all the children being released in the morning (Dolnik and Pilch, 2003). When considering the presenting intelligence and evidence, the negotiated approach had secured the release of over 200 hostages in two and half days, and delivered assurances of further releases in the morning. This would and should have been considered a successful strategy; however, it was at this point a tactical intervention was ordered.

There are conflicting accounts as to why the intervention was ordered at this point; the authorities cite the fact the terrorists had started to carry out their threats to shoot the hostages (Dolnik and Pilch, 2003). There are two points to consider in relation to this argument; four people had been killed by the terrorists in the course of the siege and these deaths did not trigger an intervention, raising the question why suspected violence would trigger the assault when actual violence did not. Also, this justification is undermined by the fact that a hostage called the local radio station while the chemical agent was being pumped into the theatre to call for a stop to the tactical intervention (Dolnik and Pilch, 2003). The command team had neglected to account for the success of the negotiation team in securing the release of significant numbers of hostages over the course of the incident.

The intervention plans were agreed by the command team and higher governmental authorities prior to the intervention taking place. However, there does not seem to have been any consideration for the potential outcomes – there were no contingency plans to manage casualties, for example. This is reflected in the deficiency in emergency services available at the scene. This can only lead to the conclusion being drawn that the command team did not foresee the casualties or extent of casualties caused by the intervention and thus did not arrange for fire and medical emergency services to be at the scene. The Moscow theatre incident would indicate this point. The tactical intervention was initiated by the release of a chemical agent into the theatre, but due to the secretive nature of the assault it meant that the authorities did not discuss this with the medical staff, which meant medical officials did not have the necessary medicines to treat those suffering the effects of the gas after the resolution of the siege (Dolnik and Pilch, 2003). Thus more people died or suffered serious injury. In the Beslan siege, there were limited emergency services at the scene of the siege when the intervention was authorised and caused a fire that spread throughout the school. The limited resources available were unable to control the fire which resulted in a significant number of hostages being seriously injured or killed (Forster, 2006). This concept is called 'imaginability' by Tversky and Kahneman (1974), and it relates to how incident commanders generate contingency plans for any chosen course of action, e.g. if *x* is a chosen course of action what else could also happen, i.e. *a*, *b*, *c* or *d*? In this form of scenario planning, there is also the consideration of the likelihood of any of the identified potential consequences (*a*, *b*, *c* or *d*) happening. This process can assist incident commanders in considering all the potential outcomes and planning accordingly, or can negatively impact either by creating too many possible outcomes so the risk becomes grossly overestimated or by underestimating the alternatives. Because of this, realistic prospective dangers are not planned for and mitigated as necessary. There was a clear lack of consequential thinking in the incident command team, specifically in relation to the intervention plans.

It is worth considering how, when we are faced with new experiences, unusual situations are analysed and managed. As human beings we will often resort to previous experience to shape and guide how we manage the novel situation. This is combined with immediate influences (colleagues, the political agenda and the media) and resilience factors (emotional state and tiredness).

Reason (2005) noted the most common thinking bias is 'confirmation bias'. This means that, when a decision has been reached, the team then only seek to gather and acknowledge information which supports that decision, discarding any contrary evidence. This bias can result in decisions being made on selected information and can cause a number of negative consequences. These can include overconfidence in the team's ability to manage the situation and underestimation of the abilities of the 'opposition'.

Fraser, MacKenzie and Dror (2009) refer to this process as 'selective exposure', where people select the evidence that supports already established beliefs and opinions. This process is often discussed in literature on cognitive dissonance (Festinger, 1957, 1964). Once a choice is made 'a negative affect is experienced as a result of the negative aspects of the choice [being highlighted] and the positive aspects of the alternatives [being shown]' (Fraser MacKenzie and Dror, 2009: 307). Thus the decision-maker uses selective exposure to support their decision to avoid the negative affect (Tversky and Kahneman, 1974).

The combination of overconfidence, in the sense that several similar situations have been resolved, gives an underestimation of the opposition's ability to create a number of problems for the incident management team. This position can influence the incident commander's ability to evaluate information as insignificant or not relevant if it indicates a change of tactic or plan is necessary (Granot, 1998; Needs, 2010). The misplaced confidence is underpinned by an unconditional belief in the ability to succeed; this in turn blocks the incident commander's ability to consider other management options (Needs, 2010). This can be seen in the Beslan school siege where it is suggested that negotiation was never considered a serious option, although the execution of 20 hostages should reasonably have prompted an intervention. This was not actioned at the time due to the lack of critical decision-makers present at the incident; moreover, there were insufficient tactical personnel to mount an intervention (Forster, 2006). Thus the opportunity passed and negotiation channels were opened which lasted for only two days before the intervention was ordered (Forster, 2006).

To conclude this section, it is worth noting how a number of issues can impact on rational decision-making: overconfidence, selective exposure and confirmation bias, all of which can interact. Tversky and Kahneman (1974) highlight that even if the probabilities of any one possible happening are low, the combined probability of one of the negative outcomes occurring is higher, and the probability of the plan being unsuccessful is consequently high. The combined probabilities affect the overall success of the chosen intervention. This is demonstrated in all three examples referred to. For incident commanders, therefore, it is important to consider the range of possible outcomes and the probability of any of these outcomes happening along with the overall success rate.

Excessive force

In all three examples the use of force utilised to resolve the siege was excessive. The level of tactical response replicated that of armed forces entering battle zones against enemies who would be heavily armed. A key issue to recall in all the examples cited is that the perpetrators had firearms and in some cases explosive devices, and all had fired weapons during the course of the incident. However, the choice to use incendiary rocket propelled grenades (RPG) and tanks in the Waco and Beslan incidents and the chemical agent in the Moscow siege ensured military effectiveness in terms of eradicating the terrorists' presence in the structure, but did little to minimise collateral casualties among the victims: the weapons used in these incidents were capable of high lethality and had no mechanism to differentiate between victims and hostage-takers which ultimately resulted in considerable casualties. Tactical intervention was a disproportionate response to the incidents, especially as the negotiated approach was reaping rewards.

The above factors effectively created an environment which would not support the negotiation process, as the negotiation team were effectively sabotaged by the media, a variety of agendas and subjective command team decision-making. The repercussions of these incidents are considerable. In the case of the Waco siege incident, there has been the creation of the Critical Incident Response Group (CIRG), the FBI's rapid response unit designed to manage critical incidents.

This unit consists of specialists in all areas of crisis management which enable the incident commander to make informed objective decisions concerning the appropriate strategy to adopt (Vecchi, 2009).

Unlike the Waco siege, the management of the sieges in Russia have not been subject to review or change. In November 2002, three Russian citizens began proceedings to litigate against the authority in its management of the Moscow theatre siege. This action provoked a further 58 complaints, resulting in a total of 61 litigants seeking damages of over $60 million (Javeline, 2006). The basis of the action cites the number of failures of the authority which caused the death or injury of the complainants or their relatives. These failures included: not evacuating the theatre; failure to provide adequate medical attention; failure to transport injured parties to hospitals in a timely fashion; and lack of medical supplies (Javeline, 2006).

When incident management goes wrong, the costs are highly visible and are often measured in terms of loss of life. This often results in compensation claims from families of those who have died. Other consequences can be seen in terms of public confidence in governments. The FBI has highlighted an alternative approach which they adopted after the Waco siege: an independent unit which responds to critical events. This unit is formed of specialists who can advise incident commanders as to the individual characteristics and issues of the events which need to be considered, in addition to the expertise and experience they bring to any situation with them. This allows incident commanders the opportunity to utilise past experience while not ignoring the unique elements of the current situations.

All critical incidents should operate a 'negotiation first' strategy, which would mean empowering the negotiation team to make connections and begin talking before considering intervention. This is not ignoring the option of tactical response or the skills they bring to incident command, rather to work along the lines of evidenced decision-making and reasonable force. Thus any critical or crisis incident command should be able to reason that they have worked towards resolution using the lowest level of force and subsequently justify any increase in tactical response as a reaction to violence initiated by the perpetrators. This strategy would regularly require evaluations that should consider the situation, any markers of progress and/or deterioration, what options were considered with the positive and negative reasons associated, and finally which strategy was adopted with full reasoning. The team should identify time frames or circumstances which would promote a review of the strategy, for example violence towards a hostage, release of hostages and so forth. All strategies should consider the potential consequences if implemented. For example, if intervention was to be authorised what could be the likely outcomes – fire, casualties, further crises and other negative events? This allows command teams to ensure emergency service provision is readily available as the intervention is actioned which will serve to minimise the number of casualties.

A further identified issue is the need to restrict and regulate the media involvement. Incident commanders should have an awareness of the media and what options they have available to them in the course of an incident in order to manage media interest.

Staw (1997) concludes that decisions are not made in sterile isolation; there are a number of factors which affect the decision-making process, and organisational culture is identified as a key influence. Thus decisions can be seen as socially determined and influenced by the public's perception, the political agenda, the experience of incident commanders, the desired image the authority wishes to project and the political and social relationship between the authorities and perpetrators, all of which need to be taken into account when managing an incident. The key aspect is to be aware of all these factors and the context in relation to the offence. Incident commanders should be aware of all the factors mentioned and their implications regarding the incident, and establish a monitoring system which allows them ongoing evaluation of their influence. Only with this information can managers decide on the appropriate course of action.

In summary, the management of incidents is a complex process that is reliant on an objective evidence approach. This involves specialist input to develop a management strategy for the incident commander. This chapter has discussed the implications when this approach is not adhered to and the implications for all those involved.

References

Ainsworth, P. B. (2002) *Psychology and Policing.* Cullompton: Willan.

Asch, S. E. (1946) 'Forming impressions of personality', *Journal of Abnormal and Social Psychology*, 41: 1230–40.

Bohl, N. (1997) 'Post-incident crisis counseling for hostage negotiators', in R. Rogan, M. R. Hammer and C. R. Van Zandt (eds), *Dynamic Processes of Crisis Negotiation: Theory, Research and Practice*, Westport, CT: Praeger Publishers.

Brown, J. and Campbell, E. (1995) *Stress and Policing: Sources and Strategies.* Chichester: John Wiley & Sons.

Call, J. A. (1999) 'The hostage triad: takers, victims and negotiators', in H. V. Hall (ed.), *Lethal Violence: A Sourcebook on Fatal Domestic, Acquaintance and Stranger Violence.* Boca Raton, FL: CRC Press.

Charlés, L. L. (2008) *When the Shooting Stopped: Crisis Negotiation at Jefferson High School.* Lanham, MD: Rowman & Littlefield.

Chermak, S. M., Freilich, J. D. and Shemtob, Z. (2009) 'Law enforcement training and domestic far right', *Criminal Justice and Behaviour*, 36 (12): 1305–22.

Cooper, T. (2007) 'Decision making in a crisis', *Journal of Police Negotiations*, 7 (2): 5–28.

Cristal, M. (2003) 'Negotiating under the cross: the story of the forty-day siege of the Church of Nativity', *International Negotiation*, 8: 549–76.

Dolnik, A. and Pilch, R. (2003) 'The Moscow theatre crisis: the perpetrators, their tactics, and the Russian response', *International Negotiation*, 8: 577–611.

Edwards, J. C. (2001) 'Self-fulfilling prophecy and escalating commitment: fuel for the WACO fire', *Journal of Applied Behavioural Science*, 37 (3): 343–60.

Fagan, T. J. and Van Zandt, C. R. (1993) 'Lessons from Talladega: even in "non-negotiable" situations, negotiations play an important role', *Corrections Today*, 55 (2): 12, 134 and continuing.

Faure, G. O. (2004) 'Negotiating with terrorists: the hostage case', *International Negotiation*, 8: 489–94.

Forster, P. K. (2006) 'Beslan: counter-terrorism incident command: lessons learned', *Homeland Security Affairs*, II (3) (October).

Fraser MacKenzie, P. A. F. and Dror, I. E. (2009) 'Selective information sampling: cognitive coherence in evaluation of a novel item', *Judgement and Decision Making*, 4: 307–16.

Gilmartin, K. M. (2002) *Emotional Survival for Law Enforcement: A Guide for Officers and Their Families.* Tucson, AZ: E-S Press.

Granot, H. (1998) 'The human factor in industrial disaster', *Disaster Prevention and Management*, 7 (2): 92–102.

Greenstone, J. L. (2005a) 'Peer support for police hostage and crisis negotiators: doing what comes naturally', *Journal of Police Crisis Negotiators*, 5 (1): 45–56.

Greenstone, J. L. (2005b) *The Elements of Police Hostage and Crisis Negotiations.* New York: Haworth Press.

Greenstone, J. L. (2007) The twenty-five most serious errors made by police hostage and crisis negotiations', *Journal of Police Negotiations*, 7 (2): 107–316.

Hare, A. (1997) 'Training crisis negotiators: updating negotiation techniques and training', in R. Rogan, M. R. Hammer and C. R. Van Zandt (eds), *Dynamic Processes of Crisis Negotiation: Theory, Research and Practice.* Westport, CT: Praeger Publishers.

Herman, E. S. and Chomsky, N. (1988) *Manufacturing Consent: The Political Economy of the Mass Media.* New York: Pantheon Books.

Javeline, D. and Baird, V. A. (2006) 'Who sues government? Evidence from Moscow theatre hostage case', *Comparative Political Studies*, 40 (7): 858–85.

Kennett, R. J. (2003) 'An Evaluation of the Selection and Training of Hostage Negotiators Nationally'. Unpublished Masters thesis, University of Hull, UK.

Kennett, R. J. (2009) 'Implications for the Selection and Training of Hostage Negotiators, Through an Analysis of Hostage Negotiation Data'. Unpublished doctoral thesis, University of Hull, UK.

Kobetz, R. and Cooper, H. H. A. (1979) 'Hostage rescue operations – teaching the un-teachable', *Police Chief*, 46 (6): 24–7.

Kopel, D. B. and Blackman, P. H. (1997) *No More Wacos.* New York: Prometheus Books.

Littlejohn-Shinder, D. (2001) 'Maximizing the effectiveness of role-play scenarios training exercises in development of police crisis intervention skills', *Journal of Police Crisis Negotiations*, 1 (2): 19–27.

Loveday, B. (1999) 'The impact of performance culture on criminal justice agencies in England and Wales', *International Journal of the Sociology of Law*, 27: 351–77.

Loveday, B. (2000) 'Measuring performance in criminal justice: an initial evaluation of the application of the New Public Management to criminal justice agencies in England and Wales', in M. Fabri and Ph. M. Langroek (eds), *The Challenge of Change for Judicial Systems.* Washington, DC: IOS Press.

McCaffery, K. (1994) 'Effective response to hostage incidents', *HMCP Gazette*, 56 (5).

McMains, M. J. and Mullins, W. C. (2001) *Crisis Negotiations: Managing Critical Incidents and Hostage Situations in Law Enforcement and Corrections* (2nd edn). Cincinnati, OH: Anderson.

Milner, C. (2002) 'The Crisis Negotiator: An Exploratory Study of the Skills, Abilities and Personal Characteristics of an Effective Negotiator'. Unpublished Masters thesis, University of Surrey, UK.

Mirabella, R. W. and Trudeau, J. (1981) 'Managing hostage negotiations: an analysis of twenty-nine incidents', *Police Chief*, May, pp. 45–7.

Morgan, P. R. (2008) *Critical Issues in Crisis Negotiations.* Hong Kong: PRM Publications.

Needham, J. P. (1977) *Neutralization of Prison Hostage Situations – A Model*, Sam Houston State University Criminal Justice Monograph 8(1). Thesis presented to the Faculty of the Institute of Contemporary Corrections and the Behavioural Sciences, SAM Houston State University.

Needs, A. (2010) 'Systemic failure and human error', in C. A. Ireland and M. J. Fisher (eds), *Consultancy and Advising in Forensic Practice.* Chichester: Wiley/BPS Blackwell.

Noesner, G.W. (1999) 'Negotiation concepts for incident commanders', *FBI Law Enforcement Bulletin*, January.

Plumbley, P. (1991) *Recruitment and Selection* (5th edn). Worcester: Billing & Sons.

Poland, J. and McCrystle, M. J. (1999) *Practical, Tactical and Legal Perspectives of Terrorism and Hostage-Taking.* New York: Edwin Mellen Press.

Reason, J. (2005) 'Safety in the operating theatre – Part 2: Human error and organisation failure', *Quality and Safety in Health Care*, 14: 56–60.

Regini, C. (2002) 'Crisis negotiation teams, selection and training', *FBI Law Enforcement Bulletin*, 71 (11): 1–5.

Rosenbluh, E. S. (2005) 'Stress and its consequences', *Journal of Police Crisis Negotiations*, 5 (1): 79–80.

Rosenthal, R. and Rubin, D. B. (1978) 'Interpersonal expectancy effects: the first 345 studies', *Behavioural and Brain Sciences*, 3: 377–86.

Schlossberg, H. (1979) 'Police response to hostage situations', in J. T. O'Brien and M. Marcus (eds), *Crime and Justice in America.* New York: Pergamon Press, pp. 87–102.

Slatkin, A. A. (2001) 'Structured role-play for negotiators', *Law and Order*, March, pp. 74–6.

Slatkin, A. A. (2005) *Communication in Crisis and Hostage Negotiations: Practical Communication Techniques, Stratagems and Strategies for Law Enforcement, Corrections and Emergency Service Personnel in Managing Critical Incidents.* Springfield, IL: Charles C. Thomas.

Souchon, H. (1976) 'Hostage-taking: its evolution and significance', *International Criminal Police Review*, 299: 168–73.

Staw, B. M. (1997) 'The escalation of commitment: an update and appraisal. Organizational decision making', in Z. Shapira (ed.), *Organizational Decision Making*, Cambridge Series on Judgment and Decision Making. New York: Cambridge University Press, Vol. X, pp. 191–215.

Strentz, T. (2006) *Psychological Aspects of Crisis Negotiation.* Boca Raton, FL: Taylor & Francis.

St Yves, M. (2006) 'The psychology of rapport: five basic rules', in T. Williamson (ed.), *Investigative Interviewing: Rights, Research, Regulation.* Cullompton: Willan, pp. 87–106.

Tversky, A. and Kahneman, D. (1974) 'Judgement under uncertainty: heuristic and biases', *Science*, New Series, 185 (4157): 1124–31.

Van Hasselt, V., Romano, S. J. and Vecchi, G. (2008) 'Role-playing: applications in hostage and crisis negotiation skills training', *Journal of Behaviour Modification*, 32 (2): 248–63.

Vecchi, G. M. (2002) 'Hostage/barricade management: a hidden conflict within law enforcement', *FBI Law Enforcement Bulletin*, May.

Vecchi, G. M. (2009) 'Critical incident response, management, and resolution', *Inside Homeland Security*, Spring.

Whyte, P. D. (2005) *Negotiation and Hostage Taking: The 1996 Japanese Experience in Lima, Peru.* Faculty of Law, University of British Columbia.

9

POST-CRITICAL INCIDENT
Considerations

Abigail S. Tucker and Joanna Capelin

The impact of traumatic events on individuals has been widely established (National Institute of Mental Health, 2002; National Institute for Health and Clinical Excellence, 2004). The motivation to respond as mental health professionals can arguably be described as human and at times heroic, but is nonetheless an important area for research and intervention. One particular area of burgeoning research and controversy has been in the area of post-critical incident outcomes. This chapter aims to provide a critical evaluation of current and historical literature around a wide range of critical incidents. This will include practical illustrations and current best practices for consideration as the controversy, research and implementation in this area evolves.

In order to thoroughly examine this issue there must be provision of clear definitions to establish a consistent framework for analysis and discussion. A 'critical incident' has been defined as a stressful event that is so consuming it overwhelms existing coping skills (Kureczka, 1996) and can include events such as hostage-taking, barricades and other crisis/conflict events. Another definition describes a critical incident as an event that has the potential to interfere with a person's normal management of everyday stress (Malcolm *et al.*, 2005). The response to a critical incident has been variously labelled (e.g. crisis response or critical incident stress) but ultimately refers to physiological, psychological and behavioural responses to the critical incident. A crisis response has been defined as the actual presentation of an individual whose coping resources have been overwhelmed and there is evidence of impairment (Caplan, 1963). Similarly, critical incident stress has been defined as the physiological, affective and cognitive response experienced after exposure to a critical incident (Carlier *et al.*, 2000). Common examples of critical incidents in the field of law enforcement are outlined in Figure 9.1.

- Line of duty death or police suicide
- Officer involved shooting
- Multiple fatalities or death of a child
- Barricade suspect/hostage situation
- Highly profiled media event

FIGURE 9.1 Common examples of critical incidents in law enforcement.

For the purpose of this chapter post-critical incident will refer to the key period of time following any given disaster, critical incident or trauma where the critical incident itself has resolved and those impacted may or may not be presenting with a crisis response. This definition will refer to post-critical incident as the time frame from critical incident resolution up to 30 days thereafter. This is of course not to communicate that post-critical incident responses do not include management systems for how to respond beyond 30 days of the incident, but instead is offered as a functional definition for this discussion. Table 9.1 delineates some of the styles and definitions of post-critical incident debriefing responses. Throughout the course of this chapter responses to a critical incident will be reviewed and examined. The subject matter of critical incidents and possible responses includes history, theory, international research, application and vast opportunity for discussion; for the purpose of this chapter only salient points will be reviewed.

TABLE 9.1 Definitions of post-critical incident debriefing responses

Debriefing	Any face-to-face interaction provided post-critical incident with the intention of recovery and support. This can range from individual, group single session, by peers or by mental health professionals.
Critical Incident Stress Debriefing (CISD)	Often referred to as the 'Mitchell model'. This is a formalised seven-phase group discussion pertaining to a critical incident, disaster or traumatic experience (Everly *et al.*, 2000).
Critical Incident Stress Management (CISM)	'A comprehensive, integrated, multi-component crisis intervention system' (Mitchell and Everly, 2011) (see Table 9.2 for further definition).
Process debriefing	Atle Dyregrov adapted Mitchell's critical incident stress debriefing model with a focus on group process, group characteristics and leadership (Dyregrov, 1989, 1997). Developed within Europe where there is an emphasis on group support (e.g. the importance of group members in normalising reactions).
Psychological first aid	Goals of meeting both physical and psychological needs, providing support and necessary referrals if needed – aim for the acceleration and promotion of recovery.

History, background and theory: post-critical incident

High-impact events such as the Oklahoma City Bombing, the 1993 World Trade Center bombing, the Pan Am disaster and the September 11, 2001 attacks on the Twin Towers in America tax the resources of civilians and emergency responders alike (National Institute of Mental Health, 2002; Malcolm *et al.*, 2005). The recognition that post-incident responses were real and important events appears to begin in history with the labelling of those responses. Following American war times, including the American Civil War in 1865, the adverse psychological and sometimes physiological responses of soldiers impacted by battle experience were dubbed 'shell shock', 'combat fatigue' or 'combat stress' reactions (MacDonald, 2003). This phenomenon would continue to evolve in our collective consciousness. In the first World War Charles Myers, a consultant psychologist to the British Expeditionary Force conducting research between 1915 and 1916, hypothesised that many of the medical complaints of shell shock (i.e. brain injury and shrapnel injuries) overlapped with psychological symptoms (Shepard, 2000). Of equal relevance more recently is the aftermath of the Cocoanut Grove fire in Boston, Massachusetts in 1943 in which Erich Lindermann studied the process of grieving (Lindermann, 1979). The Cocoanut Grove was a nightclub which in 1942 burned down killing 492 people. Lindermann, a psychiatrist, studied survivors and their relatives. His publication, *Symptomatology and Management of Acute Grief*, has been frequently cited as foundational in this area of study (Lindermann, 1944).

In the 1960s Gerald Caplan began formulating his primary prevention model which has shaped modern crisis intervention theory (Caplan and Caplan, 2000). In the last two decades there have been multiple and diverse applications of crisis intervention. Psychological first aid and trauma-focused psychological interventions have typically been designed to target civilians (Castellano and Plionis, 2006; Roberts *et al.*, 2009). Emerging in the 1970s the field of disaster mental health has more recently been designed to target first responders (e.g. paramedics, police, etc.) (Castellano and Plionis, 2006). However, it was during the 1980s that disaster mental health took shape divergent from broad-spectrum post-incident response towards emergency mental health with the evolution of Critical Incident Stress Management (CISM).

In more recent research experts have focused on evidenced-informed practice, the clarification of terminology (e.g. debriefing versus Critical Incident Stress Debriefing) and the integration of theories and organisations to reach the supra-ordinate goal of providing consistent, evidenced-based post-critical incident services to any and all who may be impacted (National Institute of Mental Health, 2002). The following contributing theories and concepts will be reviewed for background and perspective:

- Gerald Caplan's Crisis Theory;
- the Early Psychological Intervention Subcommittee (EPI) of the National Volunteer Organizations Active in Disaster (NVOAD);

- Incident Command;
- Process Debriefing;
- Crisis in Context Theory; and
- the Johns Hopkins' paradigm for disaster mental health services.

Gerald Caplan's Crisis Theory

Gerald Caplan's 40-year plus contribution to the field of primary prevention of psycho-social disorders is often referenced in the discussion of crisis theory (Caplan, 1963, 1972, 1986). The premise of Caplan and Caplan's work (2000) toward primary prevention is based on a public health model and calls for 'organized programs for reducing the incidence of a disorder in a defined population' (p. 131). Caplan and Caplan (2000) refer to responses to crisis by the mental health field as 'preventive intervention,' and describe the potential development of psychopathology in relation to crisis as a vulnerable possibility. One of Caplan's more recent insights has been to call for controlled applications of preventative interaction (i.e. empirically based applications founded on solid research) and specified limitations designed to respect the rights, privacy and autonomy of the populations served (2000).

Early Psychological Intervention Subcommittee of NVOAD

In 2004, the Early Psychological Intervention Subcommittee (EPI) of the National Volunteer Organizations Active in Disaster (NVOAD) was initiated and includes four founding members: NVOAD, the Salvation Army, the American Red Cross Disaster Mental Health programme and the international Critical Incident Stress Foundation (ICISF). While the founding members of NVOAD are all US entities, their current members, responses and goals are international. NVOAD was founded in 1970 after multiple disaster organisations attempted to respond to Hurricane Camille in the Gulf Coast of the United States. Despite their good intentions, the overlapping responses of unorganised disaster response agencies resulted in duplication of services, deficits in the services being provided, poor communication and frustration from volunteers and those who needed services. NVOAD now responds to disasters across the country with the goal to prepare, respond, recover and mitigate the negative effects of disasters. NVOAD is the primary point of contact for voluntary organisations in the National Response Coordination Center and is a signatory to the National Response Plan.

The Salvation Army's Emotional and Spiritual Care (ESC) team uses chaplains and mental health professionals to provide emotional and spiritual support in response to individuals, families and communities affected by disaster. The Salvation Army's ESC team primarily utilises psychological first aid provided on a continuum of care that includes training, education, screening, triage, support, psychological first aid and referrals (http://www.salvationarmyusa.org). Similarly, the American Red Cross created the American Red Cross Disaster Mental Health programme (Everly *et al.*, 1989) in response to the aftermath of Hurricane Hugo in 1989. The American Red Cross aligned with the American Psychological Association (APA) and each Disaster Response Network is led and coordinated by an APA psychologist and American Red Cross volunteers.

The final member of NVOAD to be outlined is the International Critical Incident Stress Foundation. Jeffery T. Mitchell (1983) began applying the theory of critical incident stress debriefing in the 1970s to help emergency responders quickly recover from a traumatic incident. Critical Incident Stress Debriefing (i.e. the 'Mitchell model') is a formalised seven-phase group discussion pertaining to a critical incident, disaster or traumatic experience. Later, Mitchell collaborated with George S. Everly, Jr and developed Critical Incident Stress Management, namely 'a comprehensive, integrated multi-component crisis intervention system' (Mitchell and Everly, 2001). Critical Incident Stress Management represents an effective, strategic continuum of care approach to crisis intervention – see Table 9.2 below (Roberts *et al.* 2005; Sheehan *et al.*, 2004). Emergency mental health emerged as a theoretical framework and speciality from the founding work of Jeffery T. Mitchell (1983). As Critical Incident Stress Management developed during the 1990s, over 350 crisis response teams were created forming the International Critical Incident Stress Foundation (ICISF). ICISF members are trained to understand the basic physiology and psychology of stress, stress management and traumatic stress. Critical Incident Stress Management continues to expand by incorporating new research and strategies from the fields of emergency mental health, psychology, faith interventions, military procedures and individual Critical Incident Stress Management team experience (Everly, 2003; Everly and Langlieb, 2003; Malcolm *et al.*, 2005). The comprehensive, multi-faceted, integrated nature of Critical Incident Stress Management was designed for the needs of emergency responders, their families and their organisations (Everly and Mitchell, 1999; Malcolm *et al.*, 2005). Critical Incident Stress Management was not developed to replace psychotherapy or to interfere with the natural recovery of human resiliency. Rather, it was designed to facilitate a triage-like process for a non-psychiatric population in the face of a critical incident as a means of returning the individual and/or the organisation to levels of prior functioning (Everly and Mitchell, 1999; Malcolm *et al.*, 2005).

Incident Command System

An Incident Command System (ICS) is a standardised incident management concept designed to allow responders to adopt an integrated organisational structure equal to the complexity and demands of any incident without being hindered by jurisdictional boundaries (OHSA, 2009). Incident command systems have been widely adapted and can be found applied to national disasters, barricade/hostage situations and historically in response to multiple jurisdiction fire management. In 2004, for example, the US Department of Homeland Security issued the National Incident Management System (NIMS) to provide a consistent

TABLE 9.2 Core components of Critical Incident Stress Management

Intervention	*Timing*	*Activation*	*Goal*	*Format*
1. Strategic planning	Pre-crisis phase	Crisis anticipation	Set expectations Improving coping Stress inoculation	Groups, teams, organisations
2. Demobilisations and staff consultations	Shift disengagement	Event driven	Inform, consult and stress management	Large groups/organisations
3. Assessment of need	Anytime post-crisis	Event driven	Inform, consult and stress management	Large groups/organisations
4. Defusing	Post-crisis (within 12 hours)	Symptom driven	Symptom mitigation Triage	Small groups
5. Critical Incident Stress Debriefing (CISD)	Post-crisis (1–10 days or 3–4 weeks for mass disasters	Symptom driven or event driven	Facilitate psychological closure Triage Symptom mitigation	Small groups
6. Individual crisis intervention	Anytime, anywhere	Symptom driven	Symptom mitigation Return to functioning Referral is needed	Individual
7. Family Critical Incident Stress Management	Anytime	Symptom or event driven	Foster support and communications Symptom mitigation Referral is needed	Families/organisations
8. Community and organisational consultation	Anytime	Symptom driven	Foster support and communications Symptom mitigation Referral is needed	Families/organisations
9. Pastoral crisis intervention	Anytime	Symptom driven	Mitigate 'crisis of faith' Assist in recovery	Individuals, families, group
10. Follow-up referral	Anytime		Assess mental status Assess needed care	Individual/amilies

Adapted from Everly and Mitchell (1999) and Everly and Langlieb (2003).

nationwide template of incident command for all government, non-government and private sector agencies to collaboratively prevent, respond to and recover from the effects of critical incidents (NIMS, 2008). Most national agencies and organisations have incorporated NIMS into their systems of response (e.g. ICISF, American Red Cross), and it seems only likely that it will become a requirement of any responder at any level of command to integrate NIMS into their training and response planning.

Process Debriefing

Atle Dyregrov, a psychologist in Norway, adapted Mitchell's Critical Incident Stress Debriefing model with a focus on group process variables and group characteristics and an emphasis on leadership (Dyregrov, 1989, 1997). His adaptation is named Process Debriefing and has been most commonly used and known in Europe and most notably researched with British soldiers (Deahl *et al.*, 1994; Deahl *et al.*, 2000). Although Process Debriefing is not psychotherapy or counselling, the focus on group process is a delineation between Process Debriefing and Critical Incident Stress Management (Regel, 2007). A joint aspect of Critical Incident Stress Debriefing and Process Debriefing is the need for clear definitions and presentation of the theories as they are both founded in crisis intervention and not counselling; this is frequently incorrectly represented and misunderstood (Regel, 2007).

Crisis in Context Theory

Myer and Moore (2006) argue that crisis intervention theories have been more influenced by practices and interventions in the field than principles of theory. They propose a theoretical model – Crisis in Context Theory (CCT) – which is designed to include not only the individual and individual crisis interventions but also the ecological context and consideration for the systems involved. This theory is congruent with multi-component approaches to post-incident care (e.g. Critical Incident Stress Management: Mitchell and Everly, 2001) or Soldier Peer Mentoring Care and Support (Keller *et al.*, 2005) as it integrates the culture of the community, the multiple systems an individual is a part of, and how the interactions between these contexts directly impact the post-incident response and recovery (Myer and Moore, 2006).

Johns Hopkins' outcome driven paradigm: disaster mental health services

The 'Johns Hopkins' outcome driven paradigm' for disaster mental health services strives to inform disaster mental health services with evidenced-informed theory. This model frames disaster mental health services with structure and psychological concepts including resistance, resilience and recovery (Kaminsky *et al.*, 2006). The mirror to the Crisis in Context Theory is the focus on integrative theories to foster integrative approaches. The Johns Hopkins' paradigm focuses on empirical evidence to support building and rebuilding resistance and resilience, as well as to enhance the recovery process (Kaminsky *et al.*, 2006). The recovery process is defined by the authors as the ability to effectively recover the ability to function adaptively (Kaminsky *et al.*, 2006). This model for disaster mental health services had been predicated by expert opinion which defined the following core competencies for disaster mental health: assessment, skill in one-on-one crisis intervention, skill in small-group crisis intervention, skill in large-group crisis/risk communication, and ability to plan and apply an integrated and multi-component strategy that functions within an Incident Command System (NIMH, 2004).

Differentiation by definition and practice: post-critical incident responses

The research in this area would seem to support a vast array of applications of theory and emerging forms of post-critical incident response. Recent calls for new terminology referenced to post-critical incident responses from the National Institute of Mental Health (2002) have highlighted an ongoing and disruptive challenge in review, research and implementation. The authors respectfully agree that there is a lack of consistent terminology and therefore have organised post-critical incident responses into the following subsets: (1) military applications; (2) psychological first aid; and (3) occupational specialised responses (including emergency response mental health). The authors are conscious that categorising in a field of study that remains controversial may be perceived as premature. However, these categories are developed to provide a consistent framework for learning and discussion (for the reader). To avoid over-incorporation, the role of psychotherapy in response to crisis is not discussed. Regardless it is important to note that psychotherapy has widely received empirical support (specifically cognitive behavioural therapy theories and interventions) in the mitigation of post-traumatic stress disorder symptoms and other anxiety or mood disorders (NICE, 2004; Schnurr *et al.*, 2007).

(1) Military applications

The military has been documenting and examining the role of post-trauma stress for decades and has endured an evolution of terminology from shell shock and combat fatigue to combat stress reaction (Solomon, 2001). Historically, one of the first documented interventions designed to combat stress reactions in military members was developed by Brigadier General Marshall during the Second World War (Marshall, 1947). General Marshall's historical group debriefings were designed to be enacted post-incident, in group format, and with the focus of intent on reconstruction of the event (incident) without judgment (Shalev *et al.*, 1998). The military has long utilised the basic concepts of proximity, immediacy and expectancy, with the goal of mitigating post-traumatic stress disorder and increasing the rate of soldiers' return to duty (Artiss, 1963). In addition the military provides built-in support systems including the chain of command, chaplains and family support systems. The military has also employed the Mitchell model of debriefings (Critical Incident Stress Debriefing) and Dyregrov's Process Debriefing (Deahl *et al.*, 1994; Deahl *et al.*, 2000). Another frequent application of Process Debriefing exists within UK public sector organisations (Regel, 2007). In recent years the military has started evaluating the potential of specialised post-incident response teams that focus on peer mentoring and early triage of trauma-stress symptoms (Keller *et al.*, 2005).

(2) Psychological first aid

The concept of psychological first aid in response to disasters and critical incidents has been in clinical and empirical discussion since at least the 1950s (APA, 1954), and includes contributors from mental health (Raphael, 1986), non-government disaster response agencies such as the American Red Cross (Gard and Ruzek, 2006), the Institute of Medicine (2003) and the field of public health (Everly and Flynn, 2005). Litz (2008) describes his conceptualisation of psychological first aid as different from other forms of post-incident responses in that psychological first aid has the capacity and expectation to use clinical judgment. Another distinction between when to provide psychological first aid rather than other forms of post-critical incident response comes from the literature on group psychological first aid. It suggests that, if physical first aid is provided, psychological first aid should also be considered (Everly *et al.*, 2006). Despite increasing research and attention regarding psychological first aid much of the literature is still grappling with confirming the definition of psychological first aid (Institute of Medicine, 2003), validating its core principles (Ruzek *et al.*, 2007; Gard and Ruzek, 2006) and publishing evidence-based training competencies for professionals (Parker *et al.*, 2006). To date there are two forms of psychological first aid that have been researched and applied: individual and group.

The Institute of Medicine (IOM) (2003) defines individual psychological first aid as a group of skills that are to be provided by trained psychological first aid responders to individuals affected by disasters. These trained skills include education, active listening, support, resource referrals and other active measures of meeting both psychological and physical demands. The consensus goals for individual psychological first aid are to meet both physical and psychological needs, to provide support and necessary referrals if needed, and to aim for the acceleration and promotion of recovery (Raphael, 1986; Everly and Flynn, 2005). Other authors have subdivided individual psychological first aid into eight core actions (listed in Figure 9.2) that aim toward the same goals previously discussed, but offer a more objective and measurable procedure (Gard and Ruzek, 2006; Ruzek *et al.*, 2007).

- Contact and engagement
- Safety and comfort
- Stabilisation
- Information gathering
- Practice assistance
- Connection with social supports
- Information on coping support
- Linkage with collaborative services

FIGURE 9.2 Eight core actions in psychological first aid.

There has been less empirical focus on group psychological first aid. However, given the support individual psychological first aid has received, public health agencies and disaster response organisations alike are enquiring as to how its group counterpart can also be used and assessed (Everly *et al.*, 2006). In their article, Everly *et al.* (2006) highlight in fact that group psychological first aid may be highly applicable to populations that are founded in and function on group cohesion such as the police, the military and other emergency responders. Everly *et al.* (2006) propose that it can be practised within a multi-component system of disaster response, follow evidenced-informed practices, facilitate the use of co-leaders and utilise their suggested six stages of group psychological first aid.

(3) Occupational specialised responses

As was discussed earlier, Critical Incident Stress Management was originally designed for first responders (i.e. police, paramedics) (Everly and Mitchell, 1999) and has expanded over the years to include outlier first responders such as FBI agents (Sheehan, 1999) or missionaries (Jensma, 1999). Another specialised application of group 'Mitchell model' debriefings has been the Assaulted Staff Action Program (Flannery, 1999). In response to the concern regarding patient assaults on staff in psychiatric facilities in America, Dr Raymond B. Flannery developed the Assaulted Staff Action Program (ASAP: Flannery, 1999). Flannery (1999) described this as a voluntary, peer-based crisis intervention programme offered on a voluntary basis to assist staff victims of patient assaults.

Research considerations

While controversy in the field of post-incident responses is noted, one positive consequence of this is that it stimulates empirical research. The role of research with regard to post-critical incidents can generally be broken down into three considerations: (1) examination of research by category and study type; (2) current trends and practices in the research; and (3) implications for the future evident from the research. There are five main areas of research category and study: randomised control trials, controlled studies, meta-analysis, literature reviews and case studies. There is current debate on how post-critical incident responses/crisis interventions are to be empirically examined. There are authors who support adherence to true randomised controlled studies (i.e. randomised control trials, controlled studies and meta-analysis that extrapolates randomised control trials or controlled studies) (Litz *et al.*, 2002) and others (Seligman, 1995; Flannery and Everly, 2004) who support both strict scientific standards and non-randomised experimental designs due to the nature of critical incidents and the ethics in provision of crisis intervention.

In 2001 the Cochrane Review[1] on the effectiveness of psychological debriefings in the mitigation of crisis responses and post-traumatic stress disorder symptoms published their third study of single-session debriefings (Rose *et al.*, 2001). The study focused on randomised control trials and the results indicated that single-session debriefings were not effective in the prevention of post-traumatic stress disorder following a trauma. Against this, Mitchell (2004) summarises the history of Critical Incident Stress Management, reviews its current position and examines research from all five main areas of study as they pertain to Critical Incident Stress Management approaches. In summary, Mitchell (2004) argues that all the negative outcome studies have inherent flaws either in definition, design or application of Critical Incident Stress Debriefing. He further asserts that there are no studies indicating that harm has been done by any Critical Incident Stress Management service if personnel are properly trained and providers adhere to well published and internationally accepted standards of its appropriate practice (Mitchell, 2004).

Similarly, in response to the Cochrane Reviews and other forums (namely the UK's National Institute for Health and Clinical Excellence (NICE) review with the BPS (2005) of post-traumatic stress disorder and its treatment), Regel (2007) asserted that many of those same studies highlighted negative research outcomes on the use of Process Debriefings. Regel (2007) indicated that, due to the NICE guideline recommendations that systematic, brief, single-session debriefings should not be administered following a trauma, many organisations in the UK modified their post-critical incident responses. The NICE guidelines also focused on randomised control trials and found that single-session debriefings were not effective in preventing post-traumatic stress disorder (NICE, 2005). However, they did accurately point out that none of the studies they reviewed were consistent in their 'debriefing' modality. For example, their review of the Critical Incident Stress Management modality did not include any studies that followed the prescribed 'Mitchell model', as it was developed for emergency responders to be administered in a system of integrated care. Regal (2007) wisely raises the issue that single-track empirical scrutiny should not be the basis on which to cease any and all psychological debriefing or Critical Incident Stress Management applications, but should instead renew focus on current research trends and implementation within evidenced-informed models.

Current trends in the research include, but are not limited to, examination of one-session versus multi-component models of post-incident response, and call for consistent terminology and variables that affect research outcomes. One of the issues frequently raised is the demand for definition between one-session debriefing versus post-critical incident response as part of a multi-component model. As previously noted, many studies have highlighted the inefficacy of single-session debriefings (e.g. Bisson *et al.*, 2000; Bisson *et al.*, 2001; Van Emmerik *et al.*, 2002; Marchand *et al.*, 2006). Against this, there has been research identifying that multiple-session early intervention did not demonstrate significant difference compared to no intervention or single sessions (Roberts *et al.*, 2009). Similarly there are research articles making the case that Critical Incident Stress Management and other multi-components be examined separately from studies focusing only on stand-alone debriefings (Richards, 2001; Flannery and Everly, 2004).

Finally, much of the research in existence on post-critical incident responses collectively refers to any application of a debriefing without clarifying the cultural context of the subject population. Mitchell's model of Critical Incident Stress Management (CISM) was founded on the concept of peer support, and has frequently been cited as effective for law enforcement populations (Sheehan, 1999; Chamberlain, 2000; Freeman, 2002; Greenstone, 2000). There are also countless applications of Critical Incident Stress Debriefing models used with mortuary workers, missionaries and culturally diverse populations such as First Nation/Natives (Jensma, 1999; Peterson, 2002; Hughes, 2006). To that end it seems appropriate to request that future research in this field take into consideration not only terminology and methodology, but also the culture of the proposed/subjected population.

A review of research considerations also requires an examination of the variables frequently analysed in post-critical incident applications. Although the framework of the current chapter does not allow for an in-depth review of relevant research there are three common considerations found throughout the extant literature: participant variables, variables related to the critical incident and debriefer/provider variables. Carlier *et al.* (2000) highlighted these three common variables in their research and subsequent article on debriefing (defined in the article as the Mitchell model of Critical Incident Stress Debriefing), studying the impact on post-traumatic stress in police officers exposed to a traumatic event. These are summarised in Table 9.3.

TABLE 9.3 Relevant research variables from Carlier *et al.* (2002)

Variable	*Considerations*	*Outcome*
Participant	Occupational stress, perceived support, past or present illness, neuroticism, introversion, dissociation, etc.	No significant differences
Critical incident	Duration, mortal danger, weapon use, child as victim, etc.	No significant differences
Debriefer/provider	Gender, age, amount of previous experience	No significant differences

In reviewing the lessons learned from research, areas have emerged as consistently imperative for consideration. Table 9.4 outlines the research considerations highlighted in the current chapter. Finally, it is important to highlight the innovation that research brings to application. With this in mind, the chapter will close with an actual research proposal.

Research proposal

Following the NICE findings that suggested Critical Incident Stress Management is not effective (NICE, 2005), the Employee Support Department of Her Majesty's Prison Service (HMPS) in the UK requested ethical approval from their National Research Committee to review current practices within HMPS. Specifically they are reviewing the efficacy of the Mitchell model of Critical Incident Stress Debriefing routinely offered to HMPS staff following a critical incident.

Methodology

Prior to Critical Incident Stress Debriefing, attending staff are asked to complete the Impact of Events Scale: Extended Version (IESE: Tehrani, 2002) and the Generalised Anxiety and Depression Scale (GAD: Goldberg *et al.*, 1988). One month post-Critical Incident Stress Debriefing, those who attended and completed the initial assessments are asked to complete the same measures again. The control groups are those identified as having been involved in the incident who for whatever reason did not attend the Critical Incident Stress Debriefing. The control group are assessed one month post-Critical Incident Stress Debriefing via phone and are asked to complete the IESE and GAD.

TABLE 9.4 A review of research considerations: post-critical incident

Terminology	• Clear and precise definitions of the method of post-incident response • Operational definitions • Language that is consistent and practical
Longitudinal data	Provision of long-term data for many of the ongoing controversies will define the future of practice and expectations for post-critical incident responses
Study replication	With the exception of Flannery's study of the Assaulted Staff Action Plan model (2006) study replication has been a weakness in the literature and ideally will become the new standard for post-incident response research
Diversification of research	• Randomised control trials • Controlled studies • Meta-analysis • Literature reviews • Case studies

Current progress

Prisons from all over the UK are participating. Incidents have included deaths in custody, concerted indiscipline, self-harm and one death in service (i.e. staff). At the time of writing data is being collected and analysed.

Case scenarios of post-critical incident response

Practical examples of post-critical incident responses are rich with opportunities to learn. In an effort to enhance the reader's opportunity to learn from application, the following case scenarios are offered as anonymous conglomerates of the authors' experiences. Fictitious names have been used, as have any identifiable details. These scenarios are both based in a prison setting as an example; they utilise Critical Incident Stress Debriefing referred to throughout as 'debrief' and follow the Mitchell model: (1) Introduction; (2) Facts; (3) Thoughts; (4) Reactions; (5) Symptoms; (6) Teaching; (7) Re-entry.

> **Case scenario 1: Completed suicide of a prisoner**
> Officer Powell (a fictitious name to be used for this scenario) was doing customary cell checks and found a prisoner dead by hanging. He raised the alarm, supported the prisoner's weight until another Officer arrived to cut the ligature and then commenced with cardiopulmonary resuscitation (CPR) until being relieved by nursing staff. Emergency services arrived and the prisoner was taken to an outside hospital where he was pronounced dead. Two weeks later Officer Powell attended the agency-provided debriefing with others who were also on duty that day. Officer Powell expressed how alone he had felt at the time, how he had suffered from feelings of guilt and the difficulties he had had returning to work. He verbalised fear (i.e. re-experiencing symptoms) that every time he looked into a cell he would find someone hanging. He had noticed an increase in his alcohol consumption, triggered by a need to take away the taste in his mouth from the CPR, and also expressed problems in sleeping. He also reported feeling reassured by similar experiences and feelings shared by others, particularly when these came from nursing staff whom he had assumed would be able to deal with death easily. By the end of the debriefing the group had established ongoing support plans.

On occasions the Critical Incident Stress Debriefing model does not appear to fit the circumstances with precision, which raises procedural and ethical questions. For example, there are ethical issues around direct victims of incidents wanting to attend a debrief. Here there can be potential consequences to allowing them to participate and to turning them away, and it should be considered whether there are ever circumstances in which someone not directly involved should be permitted to attend the debrief. There can be further consideration as to the management of a participant's anger at those they feel were responsible for the incident.

The second case scenario raises awareness of the importance of liaising with the establishment prior to the debrief to clarify who will be attending in order to avoid any potential difficulties. It also raises questions about how to assess both individual and group need when providing debriefs, the importance of establishing a relationship and a multi-component system of post-incident response, and finally what support or post-incident response should be appropriate for the prisoners, in this case, who may have also been victimised by or witness to the incident.

Case scenario 2: Concerted indiscipline and rioting within a prison

The critical incident was an act of concerted indiscipline in a high security men's prison in which prisoners took control of one of the prison wings. They barricaded the exits and smashed through doors into staff offices where they proceeded to cause ongoing destruction. Just prior to the incident in the wing that was taken by the prisoners Officer David (a fictitious name for this scenario) was speaking to a prisoner in an interview room. During the prisoner takeover of the wing she found herself trapped. Minutes later, two of her colleagues returned to the wing to retrieve her and removed her to a safe place. The incident proved impossible to resolve through negotiation and was ultimately resolved through tactical intervention. Immediately following resolution of the incident, an operational debrief was conducted, police statements were requested, the Care Team was deployed (peers trained to provide basic listening and counselling skills to staff) and the staff were informed that there would be a critical incident debriefing for those directly involved. The debrief was held approximately three weeks later. Attendees included Officer David, the two colleagues who had rescued her, several other staff involved in the incident and a member of the Independent Monitoring Board (IMB). The debrief commenced with introductions, an explanation of the roles and the format of the debrief, a review of ground rules and the establishment of who was in attendance. It quickly became apparent that the IMB member had come to the meeting as an observer and had not played any part in the incident itself. The customary practice of IMB is to have oversight of custodial procedures and ensure fair treatment of staff and prisoners. In this case, the debriefers explained that it would be inappropriate for the IMB member to observe. He was politely asked to leave, which he did. The second surprise for the debriefers was the presence of Officer David; they had been informed that she was not going to attend as she had not returned to work since the incident. The awareness that Officer David had in effect been captive on the wing during the incident called into question whether it would be appropriate for her attend the debrief. The debriefers discreetly offered Officer David a different type of support and voiced concerns about whether the debrief would be helpful or detrimental to her. However, she was clear that she had attended specifically for the debrief. Her request was acquiesced to and she participated. It proved useful for both Officer David and her colleagues that she was part of the process. She had been feeling angry for what she perceived as a failure to protect her. The debriefers overcame this by explaining that this was not a forum for blame and emphasising that other operational processes were in place to explore the operational side of the incident. Another attendee expressed his own insecurities and anxieties about what happened and in doing so enabled Officer David to realise that her colleagues had been genuinely concerned for her well-being. This brought the group closer together as a team and allowed Officer David to openly communicate with her managers about a phased return to work. The group was then encouraged to explore what further support was needed. They identified the Care Team, and were informed that formal counselling was also available, either from in-service (specially trained peer counsellors) or through external providers. This was important to reassure participants that the debrief was only one part of a multi-component support process.

Ethical considerations

It is important to make clear that there are few empirical articles on the role of ethics and cultural considerations related to post-incident response. This is despite the importance of these issues and is likely due to the inherent ethical difficulties in researching this subject (Everly *et al.*, 2000). Ideally empirical research would compare those who have received a post-critical incident response (e.g. Critical Incident Stress Management, psychological first aid, etc.) with a control group containing someone who has been through an equally traumatic incident, but did not receive any form of post-incident response. However, not offering support to those who may have been traumatised would generally be considered unethical. As Everly *et al.* (2000) point out, 'Traumatic events cannot be timed and planned in advance, and the nature of these critical incidents requires an immediate focus on assistance, not research' (p. 28). In a presentation to HM Prison Service, Tehrani (2006) evaluated how organisational trauma programmes may respond to negative evaluations of post-critical incident responses (i.e. the NICE guidelines, 2005) and either fail to act or act with little or no experience in the field.

Mental health workers may be involved in delivering post-critical incident responses, although it is worth pointing out that often those with no mental health background may also be trained for this role (i.e. Critical Incident Stress Management utilises a peer-based model). Mental health professionals are bound by their own professional codes of conduct. As such they should be fully conversant with and trained in the complex balance between their role as a mental health professional and their role in post-critical incident responses. One important component for providers is to maintain their professional development by remaining abreast of current research. Properly applied techniques by mental health workers trained as competent will also be an important issue for research, increasing internal validity and reliability of post-critical incident responses (Malcolm *et al.*, 2005).

In a discussion of ethics, it is important to briefly raise the issue of children and adolescents in post-incident responses. The NICE guidelines (2005) include a chapter on children and young people with post-traumatic stress disorder, with children referred as aged two to twelve years and adolescents aged thirteen to eighteen years. The NICE guidelines (2005) reviewed studies of interventions with children exposed to traumatic events, but only one of these studies looked at a post-critical incident response. In the article, this is referred to as 'debriefing' (Stallard *et al.*, 2005). Single-session debriefings were compared with a generally 'supportive talk' to children who had been involved in road traffic accidents. There was no clinical difference found between the two groups. The difficulty with this study is the lack of a defined theory or evidence-informed application (e.g. psychological first aid) of the debriefing analysed. The important issue here is the lack of research from which to draw conclusions about the efficacy of any form of post-critical incident response. Future empirical research should consistently draw on established theories. A greater research base will be able to inform theory, policy and practice and ensure that the best application can be implemented with young people subject to traumatic incidents.

Another area of ethical consideration is agency standards and practices. In the UK, organisations have a legal duty of care under the Health and Safety at Work Act 1974, which aims to secure 'the health, safety and welfare of persons at work' (preliminary para. 1.1). In the USA, the Occupational Safety & Health Administration of 1970 (OSHA) has two similar principal functions: (1) to set standards, and (2) to conduct workplace inspections to ensure compliance with these standards. There is a general duty clause (section 5(a)(1)) which mandates that every employer 'shall furnish … a place of employment which is free from hazards that are causing or likely to cause death or serious harm to his employees'. Thus, when a post-critical incident response is offered, staff may feel that this is being done because it is the employer's duty or because the employer wants them to return to work, not because they are genuinely concerned about their well-being. Similarly, when evaluating the effectiveness of any intervention or response, it might be that the individual's return to work or not filing for an industrial accident claim are more measurable than psychological indicators such as the presence of intrusive thoughts (Everly *et al.*, 2000).

Final considerations

To review the current chapter on post-critical incident outcomes and responses, there are three emerging themes: (1) challenges, (2) controversy and (3) best practices. Theoretical challenges include the incorporation of international perspectives as well as drawing from the diverse foundations of post-critical incident responses (e.g. mental health, first responders and military). From these theoretical challenges and resultant controversy, best practices have emerged, including multidisciplinary perspectives (e.g. psychological first aid) and international organisations (e.g. ICISF). There are also challenges regarding the application of post-critical incident responses as practitioners have begun to apply evidence-based practices in the field. The resultant controversy includes debates regarding ethical and cultural considerations, the best practices developed including pre-incident inoculation, clear definitions of post-critical incident response and multi-systemic approaches. Finally, challenges relevant to research emerged including varying terminology, lack of longitudinal data and the need for study replication. The empirical controversy that evolved resulted in best practices including diversification of research to encompass both randomised and controlled studies as well as case studies.

The human response to help others following a difficult event continues to be the foundation of post-critical incident responses. The expanding fields of crisis intervention, disaster response and emergency mental health have educated and enriched our collective perspective and we now face a responsibility to move forward in meeting challenges, managing controversy and developing current best practices. The authors of the current chapter recognise that in the history, research and application of post-critical incident responses, the undeniable enthusiasm, bravery and integrity of those who have been willing to listen to their peers, their colleagues and their communities have paved the way to provide ongoing research, outcomes, challenges and discussion for this evolving area of considerations in post-critical incidents.

Note

1 The Cochrane Library is an international collection of databases in medicine and other healthcare specialities provided by the Cochrane Collaboration and other organisations. At its core is the collection of Cochrane Reviews, a database of systematic reviews and meta-analyses which summarises and interprets the results of high-quality medical research. The Cochrane Library aims to make the results of well-conducted controlled trials readily available and is a key resource in evidence-based medicine.

References

American Psychiatric Association (1954) *Psychological First Aid in Community Disasters*, Washington, DC: APA, pp. 4–9.

American Psychiatric Association (2000) *Diagnostic and Statistical Manual of Mental Disorders* (4th edn, Text Revision). Washington, DC: APA.

Artiss, K. (1963) 'Human behavior under stress: from combat to social psychiatry', *Military Medicine*, 128: 1011–15.

Bisson, J. I., McFarlane, A. and Rose, S. (2000) *Psychological Debriefing*, International Society for Traumatic Stress Studies. Retrieved 21 October 2009 from: http://www.istss.org/TGdebrief.pdf.

Caplan, G. (1963) *Principles of Preventive Psychiatry*. New York: Basic Books.

Caplan, G. (1972) *Helping the Helpers to Help: Mental Health Consultation to Aid Clergymen in Pastoral Work*. New York: Seabury Press.

Caplan, G. (1986) 'Recent developments in crisis intervention and in the promotion of support services', in M. Kessler and S. F. Goldston (eds), *A Decade of Progress in Primary Prevention*. Hanover, NH: University Press of New England, pp. 235–60.

Caplan, G. and Caplan, R. B. (2000) 'The future of primary prevention', *Journal of Primary Prevention*, 27 (2): 131–6.

Carlier, I. V. E., Voerman, A. E. and Gersons, B. P. R. (2000) 'The influence of occupational debriefing on post-traumatic stress symptomatology in traumatized police officers', *British Journal of Medical Psychology*, 73: 87–98.

Castellano, C. and Plionis, E. (2006) 'Comparative analysis of three crisis intervention models applied to law enforcement first responders during 9/11 and Hurricane Katrina', *Brief Treatment and Crisis Intervention*, 6: 326–36.

Chamberlain, J. (2000) 'Cops trust cops, even one with a PhD', *APA Monitor*, 31: 1.

Crane, P. A. and Clements, P. T. (2005) 'Psychological response to disasters: focus on adolescents', *Journal of Psychosocial Nursing and Mental Health Services*, 43 (8): 31–9.

Deahl, M., Gillham, A., Thomas, J., Scarle, M. and Srinivasan, M. (1994) 'Psychological sequelae following the Gulf War: factors associated with subsequent morbidity and the effectiveness of psychological debriefing', *British Journal of Psychiatry*, 165: 60–5.

Deahl, M., Srinivasan, M., Jones, N., Thomas, J., Neblett, C. and Jolly, A. (2000) 'Preventing psychological trauma in soldiers: the role of operational stress training and psychological debriefing', *British Journal of Psychiatry*, 73: 77–85.

Drayer, C. S., Cameron, D. C., Woodward, W. D. and Glass, A. J. (1954) 'Psychological first aid in community disasters prepared by the American Psychiatric Association Committee on Civil Defense', *American Medical Association*, 156 (1): 36–41.

Dyregrov, A. (1989) 'Caring for helpers in disaster situations: psychological debriefing', *Disaster Management*, 2: 25–30.

Dyregrov, A. (1997) 'The process in psychological debriefings', *Journal of Traumatic Stress*, 10: 589–605.

Everly, G. S. Jr (2003) 'Pastoral crisis intervention in response to terrorism', *International Journal of Emergency Mental Health*, 5 (1): 1–2.

Everly, G. S. Jr and Flynn, B. W. (2005) 'Principles and practice of acute psychological first aid after disasters', in G. S. Everly Jr and C. L. Parker (eds), *Mental Health Aspects of Disasters: Public Health Preparedness and Response* (revised edn). Baltimore, MD: Johns Hopkins Center for Public Health Preparedness, pp. 79–89.

Everly, G. S. Jr and Langlieb, A. (2003) 'The evolving nature of disaster mental health services', *International Journal of Emergency Mental Health*, (5) 3: 113–19.

Everly, G. S. Jr and Mitchell, J. T. (1999) *Critical Incident Stress Management*. Ellicott City, MD: Chevron Publishing.

Everly, G. S., Flannery, R. B. and Eyler, V. A. (2002) 'Critical Incident Stress Management (CISM): a statistical review of the literature', *Psychiatric Quarterly*, 73 (3): 171–82.

Everly, G. S., Flannery, R. B. and Mitchell, J. T. (2000) 'Critical Incident Stress management (CISM): a review of the literature', *Aggression and Violent Behavior*, 5 (1): 23–40.

Everly, G. S., Hamilton, S. E., Tyiska, C. G. and Ellers, D. (2008) 'Mental health response to disaster: consensus recommendations: Early Psychological Intervention Subcommittee (EPI), National Volunteer Organizations Active in Disaster (NVOAD)', *Aggression and Violent Behavior*, 13: 407–12.

Everly, G. S., Phillips, S. B., Kane, D. and Feldman, D. (2006) 'Introduction to and overview of group psychological first aid', *Brief Treatment and Crisis Intervention*, 6: 130–6.

Flannery, R. B. (1999) 'Critical incident stress management and the Assaulted Staff Action Program', *International Journal of Emergency Mental Health*, 2: 103–8.

Flannery, R. B. and Everly, G. S. Jr (2004) 'Critical Incident Stress Management (CISM): updated review of findings, 1998–2002', *Aggression and Violent Behavior*, 9: 319–29.

Flannery, R. B., Juliano, J., Cronin, S. and Walker, A. P. (2006) 'Characteristics of Assaultive psychiatric patients: fifteen-year analysis of the Assaulted Staff Action Program (ASAP)', *Psychiatric Quarterly*, 77: 239–49.

Freeman, G. (2002) '9/11 one year later. ACFE members reflect: what have we learned?', *Forensic Examiner*, 77 (9–10): 10–15.
Gard, B. A. and Ruzek, J. I. (2006) 'Community mental health response to crisis', *Journal of Clinical Psychology*, 62: 1029–41.
Goldberg, D., Bridges, K., Duncan-Jones, P. and Grayson, D. (1988) 'Detecting anxiety and depression in general medical settings', *British Medical Journal*, 297 (8): 897–99.
Greenstone, J. L. (2000) 'Peer support in municipal police department', *Forensic Examiner*, 9 (3–4): 33–6.
Hughes, M. L. (2006) 'Critical incident stress debriefing as a trauma intervention in First Nation communities', *Canadian Journal of Counseling*, 40 (2): 82–95.
Institute of Medicine (2003) *Preparing for the Psychological Consequences of Terrorism*. Washington, DC: National Academic Press.
Jensma, J. L. (1999) 'Critical incident intervention with missionaries: a comprehensive approach', *Journal of Psychology and Theology*, 27 (2): 130–8.
Jones, E. and Wessely, S. (2003) '"Forward psychiatry" in the military: its origins and effectiveness', *Journal of Trauma Stress*, 16: 411–19.
Kaminsky, M., McCabe, O. L., Langlieb, A. M. and Everly, G. S. (2006) 'An evidence-informed model of human resistance, resilience, and recovery: the Johns Hopkins' outcome-drive paradigm for disaster mental health services', *Brief Treatment and Crisis Intervention*, 7 (1): 1–11.
Keller, R. T., Greenberg, N., Bobo, W. V., Roberts, P., Jones, N. and Orman, D. T. (2005) 'Soldier peer mentoring care and support: bringing psychological awareness to the front', *Military Medicine*, 170 (5): 355–61.
Kureczka, A. W. (1996) 'Critical incident stress in law enforcement', *FBI Law Enforcement Bulletin*, 10–16.
Lindermann, E. (1944) 'Symptomatology and management of acute grief', *American Journal of Psychiatry*, 101: 141–8.
Lindermann, E. (1979) *Beyond Grief: Studies in Crisis Intervention*. New York: Aronson.
Litz, B. T. (2008) 'Early intervention for trauma: where are we and where do we need to go? A commentary', *Journal of Traumatic Stress*, 12 (6): 503–6.
Litz, B. T., Gray, M. J., Bryant, R. and Adler, A. B. (2002) 'Early intervention for trauma: current status and future directions', *Clinical Psychology: Science and Practice*, 9: 112–34.
MacDonald, C. M. (2003) 'Evaluation of stress debriefing interventions with military populations', *Military Medicine*, 168 (12): 961–8.
Malcolm, A. S., Seaton, J., Perera, A., Sheehan, D. C. and Van Hasselt, V. B. (2005) 'Critical incident stress debriefing and law enforcement: an evaluative review', *Brief Treatment and Crisis Intervention*, 5: 261–78.
Marchand, A., Guay, S., Boyer, R., Iucci, S., Martin, A. and St Hilaire, M. (2006) 'A randomized control trial of an adapted form of individual critical incident stress debriefing for victims of armed robbery', *Brief Treatment and Crisis Intervention*, 6: 122–9.
Marcus, E. H. (2000) 'Disaster mental health services', *Internet Journal of Rescue and Disaster Medicine*, 1 (2). Retrieved 14 October 2009 on http://www.ispub.com/journal
Marshall, S. L. A. (1947) *Men Against Fire*. New York: William Morrow.
Mitchell, J. T. (1983) 'When disaster strikes ...', *Journal of Emergency Medical Services*, 8: 36–9.
Mitchell, J. T. (2004) 'Crisis Intervention and Critical Incident Stress Management: A Defense of the Field'. Retrieved 21October 2009 from: http://www.icisf.org/articles/Acrobat%20Documents/CISM_Defense_of_Field.pdf.
Mitchell, J. T. and Everly, G. S. Jr (2001) *Critical Incident Stress Debriefing: An Operations Manual for CISD, Defusing, and Other Group Crisis Intervention Services.* Ellicott City, MD: Chevron Publishing.
Myer, R. A. and Moore, H. B. (2006) 'Crisis in context theory: an ecological model', *Journal of Counseling and Development*, 84 (2): 139–47.
National Institute for Health and Clinical Excellence (NICE) (2004) *Anxiety: Management of Anxiety (Panic Disorder, with or without Agoraphobia, and Generalized Anxiety Disorder) in*

Adults in Primary, Secondary and Community Care, Clinical Guidelines CG22, issued 2004. London: NICE.
National Institute for Health and Clinical Excellence (NICE) (2005) *Post Traumatic Stress Disorder: The Management of PTSD in Children and Adults in Primary and Secondary Care.* London: Royal College of Psychiatrists and British Psychological Society.
National Institute of Mental Health (2002) *Mental Health and Mass Disasters: Evidence-Based Early Psychological Intervention for Victims/Survivors of Mass Violence*, NIMH Publication No. 02-5138. Washington, DC: US Government Printing Office.
Occupational Health and Safety Administration (2009) 'About Incident Command System (ICS) and Unified Command and the National Response System'. Retrieved 11 November 2009 from: http://www.osha.gov/SLTC/etools/ics/about.html.
Parker, C. I., Everly, G. S. Jr, Barnett, D. and Links, J. (2006) 'Establishing evidence-informed core intervention competencies in psychological first aid for public health personnel', *International Journal of Emergency Mental Health*, 8 (2): 83–92.
Pearn, J. (2000) 'Traumatic stress disorders: a classification with implications for prevention and management', *Military Medicine*, 165 (6): 434–40.
Peterson, A. L. (2002) 'Psychological intervention with mortuary workers after the September 11 attack: the Dover Behavioral Health Consultant model', *Military Medicine*, 167 (9): 83–6.
Raphael, B. (1986) *When Disaster Strikes: A Handbook for Caring Professionals.* London: Hutchinson.
Raphael, B. and Wilson, J. P. (eds) (2000) *Psychological Debriefing: Theory, Practice and Evidence.* Cambridge: Cambridge University Press.
Regel, S. (2007) 'Post-trauma support in the workplace: the current status and practice of critical incident stress management (CISM) and psychological debriefing (PD) within organizations in the UK', *Occupational Medicine*, 57: 411–16.
Richards, D. (2001) 'A field study of critical incident stress debriefing versus critical incident stress management', *Journal of Mental Health*, 70 (3): 351–62.
Roberts, A. R., Everly, G. S. and Camasso, M. J. (2005) *Meta-Analysis of 36 Crisis Intervention Studies: Plenary Address.* Paper presented at the 8th World Congress on Stress, Trauma, and Coping, Baltimore, Maryland, February.
Roberts, N. P., Kitchiner, N. J., Kenardy, J. and Bisson, J. I. (2009) 'Systematic review and meta-analysis of multiple-session early interventions following traumatic events', *American Journal of Psychiatry*, 166 (3): 293–301.
Rose, S. C., Bisson J., Churchill, R. and Wessely, S. (2001) 'Psychological debriefing for preventing post traumatic stress disorder (PTSD)', *Cochrane Database of Systematic Reviews*, Issue 4.
Rose, S., Bisson, J. and Wessely, S. (2003) 'A systematic review of single-session psychological interventions ('debriefing') following trauma', *Psychotherapy and Psychosomatics*, 72 (4): 176–85.
Ruzek, J. I., Brymer, M. J., Jacobs, A. K., Layne, C. M. *et al.* (2007) 'Psychological first aid', *Journal of Mental Health Counseling*, 29 (1): 17–49.
Salvation Army (n.d.) *Our Role in Disaster Services.* Retrieved 13 December 2009 http://www.salvationarmyusa.org
Schnurr, P., Friedman, M. J., Engel, C. C., Foa, E. B., Shea, M. T., Chow, B. K., Resick, P. A., Thurston, V., Orsillo, S. M., Haug, R., Turner, C. and Bernardy, N. (2007) 'Cognitive behavioral therapy for post-traumatic stress disorder in women: a randomized controlled trial', *Journal of the American Medical Association*, 297 (8): 820–30.
Seligman, M. E. P. (1995) 'The effectiveness of psychotherapy: the consumer reports study', *American Psychologist*, 50 (12): 965–74.
Shalev, A., Peri, T., Rogel-Fuchs, Y., Ursano, R. and Marlowe, D. (1998) 'Historical group debriefing after combat exposure', *Military Medicine*, 163: 494–502.
Sheehan, D. C. (1999) 'Stress management in the Federal Bureau of Investigation: principles for program development', *International Journal of Emergency Mental Health*, 1 (1): 39–42.

Sheehan, D. C., Everly, G. S. Jr and Langlieb, A. (2004) 'Current best practices: coping with major critical incidents', *FBI Law Enforcement Bulletin*, 73 (9): 1–13.
Shepard, B. (2000) *A War of Nerves*. London: Jonathan Cape.
Solomon, Z. (2001) 'The impact of post-traumatic stress disorder in military situations', *Journal of Clinical Psychiatry*, 62 (1): 1–5.
Stallard, P., Vellerman, R., Salter, E. *et al.* (2005) 'A randomized controlled trial to determine the effectiveness of an early psychological intervention with children involved in road traffic accidents', *Journal of Child Psychology and Psychiatry*, 47: 127–34.
Summerfield, D. (1999) 'A critique of seven assumptions behind psychological trauma programmes in war-affected areas', *Social Science and Medicine*, 48: 1449–62.
Tehrani, N. (2006) 'Has Debriefing Been NICE-ly Killed Off?', Workshop and Presentation to Delegates at the Critical Incident Debriefers' Development Meeting, Prison Service College, Newbold Revel, Warwickshire, England, 13 October.
United States Department of Homeland Security (2008) 'National Incident Management System'. Retrieved 1 October 2009 from: http:www.fema.gov.
Van Emmerik, A. A., Kampphuis, J. H., Hulsbosch, A. M. and Emmelkamp, P. M. G. (2002) 'Single session debriefing after psychological trauma: a meta-analysis', *Lancet*, 360: 766–71.

10

HELD AGAINST THEIR WILL

Behaviour, considerations and implications for the captive

Carol A. Ireland and Gregory M. Vecchi

> The militants took me downstairs and out the front door. I was very relieved to get out of that gas and smoke. It was rainy and cold. It was good to be in the fresh air. I was feeling relieved to be alive. At that point, I remember thinking, being alive was a pretty good thing.
>
> *(John Limbert, captive from the US Embassy where staff were held for 444 days in captivity, cited in Wells, 1985: 1)*

There is a range of considerations when an individual has been held against their will by another or others, both for the individual/s themselves as well as the professionals who are managing the incident. The behaviour of the individual held against their will (the captive) can form a key part of any management plan when considering successful and peaceful resolution of the incident. This chapter will consider the potential behaviours of the captive, alongside the possible implications of this for themselves and others. This will further include considerations at the start of a conflict and/or crisis incident and how these may affect the potential management of the situation.

There can be confusion in the literature as to what is meant by the term 'hostage', as it has been used interchangeably across a variety of both conflict and crisis situations (Vecchi, 2009e). Some literature refers to 'barricaded hostage situations' where an individual or individuals are held by their captors for instrumental reasons and where there are clear goals (Vecchi *et al.*, 2005; Ireland and Vecchi, 2009; Vecchi, 2009e) such as attempting to escape from a robbery where they have been caught. In contrast, the literature can further refer to 'barricaded crisis situations' where there is also an individual taken hostage, but more likely for expressive and emotional reasons (Booth *et al.*, 2010; Booth *et al.*, 2009; Vecchi, 2009a, 2009b, 2009c, 2009d). For example, their captor is more likely to have no clear plan as to why they have taken a hostage and so the taking of a hostage may have been unplanned. The situation here may focus more on the individual in crisis being emotionally overwhelmed by a set of circumstances, and where they have exceeded their ability to cope effectively with this, transforming it into crisis (Vecchi, 2009a, 2009b). In these circumstances, the individual held against their will is often referred to as the 'victim', and not 'hostage' (Daniels *et al.*, 2007). Yet ultimately, whether an individual or individuals have been held against their will by another for instrumental or more expressive reasons, or even a combination, they would still fall within the notion of 'captive-taking' (Daniels *et al.*, 2007). Clearly the negotiation strategy will differ depending upon the type of situation, be it conflict and/or crisis. This has been covered in earlier chapters. This chapter will cover the role of the individual held captive in these circumstances, namely 'held against their will, covering both conflict and crisis situations.

Case studies indicate that an individual held captive can, in most cases, have the greatest chance of being unharmed. Jenkins (1976) examined 77 hostage incidents from January 1968 to June 1975, including kidnappings, attempted kidnappings, barricade and hostage incidents. Of these incidents, 348 individuals were held captive. Jenkins (1976) noted that 53 of these were killed; one was seriously wounded and released; 27 were wounded or injured during assaults; one suffered a heart attack after lengthy captivity and was released; 15 were subjected to a lengthy captivity and released; and one remained in captivity. The remaining 250 were released unharmed. This indicated that 72 per cent of all captives taken were released unharmed. He further noted that in nine of the 77 incidents examined (14 per cent) the captives were deliberately killed by their captors without provocation of entry by a tactical team (Jenkins, 1976). Of the 348 captives, 3 per cent were executed 'in cold blood', whereas the remainder died during assaults by the tactical teams (Jenkins, 1976). He argued that the average length of days of captivity in regard to kidnapping was 12, compared to two days for international barricade and hostage situations (Jenkins, 1976), with the two days being reduced to around 33 hours once a particularly long incident was removed.

Start of the conflict/crisis incident

It is noted that, early on in a situation, there may be a greater likelihood of a captive escaping, contingent upon the circumstances. Daniels *et al.* (2007) examined 19 school hostage situations in the United States between February 1998 and May 2007. They noted that most escapes by those held captive appeared to take place in the early confusing moments of the event, followed by some others escaping when the police arrived or during the chaos of a tactical assault. Yet, they argue in some cases the details were unclear as to how captives escaped (Daniels *et al.*, 2007). Nonetheless, they state that 63 per cent of captives escaped across the 19 incidents they examined.

The start of an incident can often bring with it chaos and panic. Following the taking over of the US Embassy in Iran on 4 November 1979, captives noted the initial chaos and panic, when the captors were taking control of the Embassy and its residents. One captive recalls:

> As they were leading me down the stairs, these two guys were saying 'Don't be afraid. Don't be scared. We won't hurt you … They led me out the front door, and that's when the picture was taken, the one that appeared on the cover of *Newsweek*. I can recall the thoughts I had at that moment. I wasn't really frightened. I guess I was more caught up with the excitement of events. But I do remember thinking they might shoot me. I thought, 'My God, if they are going to get rid of me, then I'll die with my head up … I thought 'To hell with them! I'm not going to let them think they have me at an advantage', so I stood straight and tall.
>
> *(Bill Belk, cited in Wells, 1985: 3)*

Jenkins (1976) interviewed a number of individuals who had been held captive. It is argued that the first few hours of captivity can bring with them the greatest anxiety, arguably a result of the captive being removed from their normal environment into the unknown, and where verbal and/or physical aggression is used. Such anxiety can remain high for several hours, and then appears to decline once the captive realises that they are not about to be killed, at least not immediately. Further, such anxiety and hyper-arousal can bring with it a blocked or diminished pain perception (Fletcher, 1996), with Hillman (1981) noting, 'Hostage A, a prison officer, was kicked in the head, back, ribs and testicles, but although he could "see" what was happening he could not feel it, or if he felt it, it did not hurt.'

Considerations during the incident

A captive may find it difficult to comprehend the reality of their situation; they may lose their sense of time, as well as lack an awareness of the need for sleep or food (Fletcher, 1996). Further, in a study of 28 individuals held captive, Siegel (1984) reported that 25 per cent noted visual or auditory hallucinations associated with conditions of isolation, visual deprivation, restricted movements, physical abuse and threats of death. The hallucinations reported were complex, with captives reporting 'out of body' experiences, where they were floating out of their bodies or travelling down tunnels (Siegel, 1984). Further, and early on in the situation, captives may experience uncontrollable trembling, fainting/falling asleep, loss of appetite and sleeplessness (Fletcher, 1996).

A captive may explore a number of considerations when held against their will, even in the smallest of detail, including a judgment as to a risk of harm. One consideration during an incident can be for the captive, if they feel their captors may be capable of killing them, to interpret seemingly innocuous situations with such a notion at the forefront. For example, during the taking over of the US Embassy in Iran, one of the captives noted how 'there was always the feeling that they might be capable of killing us'. They noted that, following being blindfolded, 'you tend to imagine things going on around you – and it's easy for your imagination to get the best of you' (John Limbert, captive, cited in Wells, 1985: 5). He noted how he could hear the rustling of paper, which was frightening, as he felt his captors might be writing something down; in much the same way individuals who had been executed could be found with handwritten notes on them, stating the crimes they were supposed to have committed. He noted 'that rustling paper frightened me. I was able to sneak a look out from underneath my blindfold, and saw it was just a student [captor] reading a newspaper' (John Limbert, captive, cited in Wells, 1985: 5).

Furthermore, captives may look for additional signs when considering if their life may be taken. Wells (1985) noted that some of the captives remarked that they were allowed to eat, two at a time. From this, they concluded it was less likely they would be killed, one noting that 'I remember thinking that if they were going to shoot us, they wouldn't bother to feed us' (John Limbert, captive, cited in Wells, 1985: 6). Another noted that, during an interrogation, they were threatened and physically assaulted, yet their captors failed to follow through any threats of permanent physical injury, such as cutting off his arm. The captive noted this as an important signal, seeing this as crucial, remarking 'when they failed to follow through on some of their threats, it was my first indication that they weren't going to do anything that would put a permanent scare on me, which gave me an immediate edge. I knew I still had a chance of getting out of there alive' (Colonel Charles Scott, captive, cited in Wells, 1985: 10). This would certainly concur with the work of Dolnik (2004), who argues that the deadlines regarding threats are an important consideration, where the captor can carry out the threat or fail to do so. To carry out a threat of substantial physical harm may trigger a forceful resolution, yet if the captor fails to carry out their threat it begins to weaken their negotiating position. A failure to carry out the threat can send a clear message that they are reluctant to harm the captive, despite their threats to do so.

It is argued that, as time progresses and the captive realises that they are not going to be killed immediately, then 'a certain routine sets in', noting that anxiety levels may increase again just prior to release (Jenkins, 1976). It is felt this is more likely a result of the 'routine of captivity' being interrupted, and a renewed uncertainty as to what might happen. Jenkins (1976) further argues that a captive's depressed or low mood may steadily worsen as captivity continues and further identifies the sense of humiliation. In their interviews with ex-captives, they noted that most felt humiliated by their captivity. Jenkins (1976) emphasises that this is a normal reaction, as it can be regarded as humiliating for an adult to feel so helpless, to be under constant guard, and to be placed in a position where they have to seek permission for the most basic of needs, including being compelled to undertake normally private functions under the watchful eyes of their captors. Yet despite such humiliation, it is noted that the captive can be very adaptive and resilient, and can manage their situation 'surprisingly quickly' (Jenkins, 1976).

Captive behaviour

Most individuals have no prior experiences of being a hostage, and as such may behave in response to how they think things will happen, and which may appear to others as irrational behaviour (Sime, 1990). People's behaviour may further be influenced by what they see in the media, which may or may not be correct (Sime, 1990). They may simply respond to a novel situation using normal social rules, such as customers caught in a fire in a shop still queuing to pay (Wood, 1990). Wilson (2003) argues that there are a number of responses that a captive can demonstrate. First, they may be compliant, where they do what is requested of them by their captors. They may demonstrate passive-resistance. This may include non-compliance, such as refusing to engage in a request or not completing a request in its fullest requirement, such as binding another captive when asked, but only lightly binding them. There may also be deception. This can be a risky form of passive-resistance, but the captive may attempt to deceive their captor in some way. A captive may alternatively demonstrate active-resistance. This may include efforts to persuade the captor, attempt to overpower them or escape. A captive's behaviour can vary depending on a range of circumstances as well as the experiences the captive brings to the situation. Wilson and Smith (1999) argue that people can typically behave in such situations how they *think* a captive should behave. This may include, for example, the view that captives should be passive and obedient, and captors should be aggressive and in control, and where the authorities negotiate. Daniels *et al.* (2007) explored the behaviour of captives who were held in a school. They note one captive, a teacher, describing how they remained calm and would comply with the demands of the perpetrator when they entered the classroom with a gun. They note that when the perpetrator demanded that they move to the back of the classroom the teacher stated 'I just said "okay" and, um, so we just went and sat in the corner and we all just sat there quietly' (p. 66). Daniels *et al.* (2007) further argue the importance of this calm and complying approach in leading to a successful resolution, in agreement with the work of Wilson and Smith (1999). However, Wilson and Smith (1999) argue that if captives deviate from these typically expected roles, then the risk to them can increase, such as a disobedient captive being at a heightened risk of injury, and actually frustrating other captives.

Other decisions, such as these and where the captive has deviated from this expected role, have met with tragedy. For example, during the Moscow theatre siege in 2002 where Chechen rebels took a large number of people hostage, it is suggested that the rescue operation was triggered by a breakdown in communication that first began with the behaviour of one of the hostages (also see Marsh, Chapter 8, this volume). Dolnik and Pilch (2003) emphasise the difficulties in gaining an accurate picture of the theatre siege, yet they note that the Chechen rebels somehow became aware an elite counterterrorism force was planning on raiding the theatre. This caused anxiety for both the captors and their captives, as two of the rebels, including their leader, reportedly rushed into the main hall of the theatre where captives were present, shouting that an assault was about to take place. Both the rebels and the captives waited for this assault. After approximately 20 minutes a distressed male hostage reportedly jumped to his feet, and ran toward the female captor who was guarding the main explosive, 'throwing a bottle at her in his stride' (Dolnik and Pilch, 2004). She reportedly fired her gun in the air and told him to sit down, but he did not. Another rebel then reportedly fired at the man, but missed, hitting another male captive in the eye, with the same bullet piercing the chest of a female captive behind. It is documented that the captors were distraught, and asked their captives to phone the Red Cross. Due to a breakdown in communication, it is reported that the commanders of the incident wrongfully believed the rebels had begun their threats of execution. Subsequently, 128 captives were killed, as a result of a controversial rescue operation (Dolnik and Pilch, 2004). Of these 128, 126 died as a result of gas poisoning used by the counterterrorism force (Dolnik and Pilch, 2004), although the exact figures are unclear.

Another important consideration is what beliefs and values a captive brings to the situation, which can potentially impact upon the situation itself. Wilson (2003) argues that a security guard on a hijacked flight may attempt to overpower the potential captor as the protection of others is ultimately their role. Further, during the taking over of the US Embassy in Iran, one of the captives, Corporal William Gallegos, noted how their beliefs strongly influenced their behaviour at that time. He noted that, despite being threatened, assaulted and having a gun placed to his head and the trigger pulled on an empty chamber, he refused to tell them anything. He noted:

> It was more like they were trying to intimidate me. Still, I wouldn't say anything. I mean nothing … I wouldn't talk to them. I didn't say anything to anybody … They could do whatever they wanted to me, and I wasn't going to give them the satisfaction of doing anything for them. That was my job. I was a Marine … I just sat there and didn't say anything.
>
> *(Wells, 1985: 8)*

Stockholm Syndrome

While Stockholm Syndrome has been regularly referred to in the literature, its actual presence in incidents is less clear. If it does exist, it is arguably not a syndrome, but a potentially natural reaction to a traumatic event. As a result of its wide reporting in the literature, it is important to include it here. This is where broadly positive feelings develop between the captive and their captor. The term originated following a hostage incident in Stockholm, Sweden in 1973 (Ochberg, 1983; Fuselier, 1988; De Fabrique *et al.*, 2007; De Fabrique *et al.*, 2007; Vecchi, 2009c). It is noted that four bank employees were held for five days in a bank vault, with explosives strapped to them. The captives are reported to have developed intense positive feelings toward the hostage-takers, and have come to view the hostage-takers as 'protectors', feeling that the police were the real threat to the safety of the group (Ochberg, 1983; Fuselier, 1988; De Fabrique, Romano *et al.*, 2007; De Fabrique, Van Hasselt *et al.*, 2007; Vecchi, 2009c). The captives reported fearing the police more than their captors, with one hostage later setting up a 'defence fund' for their captors. The syndrome was initially felt to appear quite frequently in hostage situations (Fuselier, 1988), although this has now been refuted. De Fabrique, Van Hasselt *et al.* (2007) note that, from 4,700 incidents examined, 73 per cent of captives showed no evidence of Stockholm Syndrome, with the remaining 27 per cent showing only partial signs.

One of the biggest challenges is the actual definition of what Stockholm Syndrome is, and if it therefore actually exists in its promoted form. Arguably, it may have been the result of assumption and speculation as opposed to being evidenced systematically and through research. It is mostly regarded as an automatic, often unconscious, emotional response to the trauma of victimisation, and is not something which becomes a 'rational choice' for the captive (Strentz, 2006). While there has been much controversy around the factors which account for its existence, there is the general idea that three factors at least should be present for the syndrome to occur. These include (De Fabrique, Romano *et al.*, 2007; De Fabrique, Van Hasselt, *et al.*, 2007; Vecchi, 2009c):

- The individual must be held captive for a significant period of time.
- The captive and their captor/s must maintain ongoing personal contact (e.g. the captive must not be hooded or isolated in a separate room from the captors).
- The captors must treat the captive/s kindly, or at the very least not physically or verbally threaten them.

Importantly, three further components have been considered to occur separately or in some combination with one another (Fuselier, 1999; De Fabrique, Romano *et al.*, 2007; De Fabrique, Van Hasselt *et al.*, 2007; Vecchi, 2009c). These are:

- negative feelings on the part of the captive toward authorities;
- positive feelings by the captive toward the captor; and
- positive feelings by the captor toward the captive.

Although these descriptors may initially appear quite straightforward, these components have not been clearly evidenced in the literature. De Fabrique *et al.* (2007) argue that, after reviewing the literature, there are a number of conditions that appear to meet the greatest consensus for the syndrome, or certainly a derivative of it, to take place. These include:

- The person held in captivity cannot escape and depends on the captor for life. The captor becomes the person in control of their basic needs for survival and their life itself.

- The captive endures isolation from other people, and has only the captor's perspective available. As such, captors may prevent the captive from knowing the response of the 'outside world' to the situation – keeping the captive entirely dependent on them.
- The captor may threaten to kill the captive, giving the perception they have the ability to do so. In such a case, the captive may choose to endure the situation and comply with demands rather than risk injury or death.
- The captive notes their captor as demonstrating some degree of kindness toward them or others. This is considered a key aspect, and even the absence of aggression may be regarded as an act of kindness by the captive.

There can be a number of challenges when identifying if the syndrome exists, which as noted may be a result of a lack of detailed research in the area. Firstly, there can be uncertainty as to what is considered a sufficient length of time in order for the syndrome to be facilitated. There can be the assumption that if the captive is physically harmed, they are not able to develop positive feelings toward their captor. This is not always the case, and further omits the definition of assault: what one person considers an assault, another may not. Furthermore, there is the assumption that a significant element of Stockholm Syndrome is the close proximity of the captive to their captor. There may be something potentially protective for the captive in their relationship with their captor; however, without further research, it is not clear as to the exact nature of this relationship and the factors that would develop such a positive interaction.

Perhaps one of the more helpful understandings of the relationship between the captive and their captor is that of transference; it may be issues of transference that have been noted, as opposed to the elusive understanding of Stockholm Syndrome. Here, transference is viewed as a function of shared experiences, where there is dependency, proximity and the tension of the crisis situation (Whyte, 2005). This can include positive transference, which can act as a protective factor for the captive, minimising a risk of harm. Here the captor develops an attachment to their captive(s), and by doing so, makes it difficult to harm them. Alternatively, the captive may align themselves with the cause of the captor and begin to suspect the authorities' motivation in ending the siege (Whyte, 2005). Alternatively, there can be negative transference. This is where the captive does not develop an attachment to their captor, and may be argumentative and more challenging for the captor to deal with. Such a situation can place the captive at an increased risk of injury or death (Whyte, 2005).

Jenkins (1976) argues that the captive may indeed develop positive attitudes toward their captor/s, and notes that many of the captives interviewed identified this. Jenkins (1976) argues that this may take place as the captive and captor share similar interests, in that both would like to see the demands of the captor met. The captive further notes the importance of not antagonising the captor into action, including the demonstration of violence toward them. Jenkins (1976) argues that there can be an instinctive drive for the captive, where they make efforts to develop a human bond with the captor, in the hope that they will be regarded as a human being, as opposed to a commodity with which to be bargained and towards whom violence may be easily demonstrated. Jenkins (1976) argues that the captive may instinctively attempt to talk to their captor in an effort to establish rapport. By doing so, it would then be no surprise if the captive began to appreciate, or even sympathise with, the dedication and resolve of the captor (Jenkins, 1976). Jenkins (1976) further argues that the captive is often helpless in the situation, becoming totally reliant on the captor, including whether they live or die. Jenkins (1976) argues that it is through this realisation that the captive may initially depend upon and then identify with their captor, developing a bond between them which may be further reciprocated by the captor.

Effective course of action for a captive

It can be difficult to prescribe for a captive what the best course of action may be during an incident; one incident may vary from the next, along with the motivations and intentions of the captor. Jenkins (1976) argues against the provision of any specific guidelines for a captive, arguing that the circumstances of the capture, its conditions, the motivations of the captors and their personalities may vary too much to make such summaries helpful. Wilson and Smith (1999) argue the importance of compliance as a captive to be the best course of action, and that it is important for the captive not to destabilise the situation.

It has been argued that individuals who may be considered at risk of being held captive, such as state officials, would do well to consider how they may evade any risk of attempts to hold them captive. Jenkins (1976) argues that this may include considering scenarios and formulating plans to evade capture, with the assumption that doing so will heighten awareness and an ability to generate options more quickly should a situation arise. Jenkins (1976) also emphasises the importance for the captive to 'think positively', and to consider that only a small number of captives have been executed in similar situations. From interviews with ex-captives, of note was the importance of maintaining a sense of humour and using this in an effort to manage any anxiety and relieve any tension, both on the part of the captive and captor. Yet such humour should be carefully considered. Importantly, Jenkins (1976) argues the value of the captive focusing on their own survival. Key aspects to this include the maintenance of a routine as much as possible, such as regular sleeping and eating, and undertaking a level of physical exercise if possible.

While incidents can vary greatly, the importance of an individual psychologically protecting themselves is considered helpful. Kentsmith (1982) and Wilson (2003) argue that a strong sense of identity in the captive can be important, and can help to preserve a sense of self-worth during the situation. They further argue that a strong sense of purpose and meaning in life can appear to act as a protective factor during the incident. They emphasise that, while incidents can vary, there can be a need for the captive to humanise themselves. This may include talking of family and friends, but only when it is safe to do so, and not if this antagonises the captor(s). What may be helpful for a captive is to consider that there is a team of staff working to get them out, and that they are a priority, even though sometimes it may not appear to be the case. For example, some negotiations may specifically aim not to raise the profile of the captive, yet this does not mean they are not important. It can also be helpful to consider that ending a situation safely and peacefully can take time, and successful negotiation cannot be rushed. Importantly, if there are negotiators involved, it can be helpful to allow the negotiators to deal with the situation and to await action by the authorities.

Psychological impact

The psychological impact of being held captive can vary, with some captives appearing psychologically intact and others experiencing a range of difficulties. Allodi (1994) notes a response pattern to a crisis situation, in which the individual may initially deny or avoid the recalling of the experience, then move toward acceptance of what took place along with the grief and depression attached to this, then finally achieving recovery and integration. Ochberg (1980) noted a range of possible symptoms, which would fit with a diagnosis of post-traumatic stress disorder (PTSD), which is an extreme psychological reaction to an experienced trauma. Ochberg (1980) notes the following possible symptoms following an incident where an individual has been held captive. These include:

- anxiety;
- nightmares;
- startle reactions;
- phobias;
- self-medication through drugs and alcohol;
- psychophysiological reactions;
- delayed-onset depression (particularly once the media and general attention from others has calmed down);
- paranoid reactions;
- obsessions.

Notably, such symptoms can continue for some time (Wilson, 2003), although usually they dissipate within a matter of weeks or months. Van der Ploeg and Kleijn (1989) examined the psychological impact on captives in the Netherlands. During the 1970s, the Netherlands experienced eight large-scale hijackings, where nearly 500 people were held captive. In 1985, the long-term after-effects (up to nine years) on these captives were studied. It was found that approximately one third of the ex-captives suffered negative effects resulting from the hostage-taking, mentioning symptoms related to PTSD and generalised anxiety disorder as well as a variety of medical symptoms. Twelve per cent were found to be still in need of aftercare and help. This was despite nearly all of them having had several contacts with professional healthcare workers in the period following their captivity. Yet, in the study, there were also some positive outcomes noted. For example, almost 50 per cent of the hostages and their families were able to identify positives from the situation, such as valuing life and their families more than before, as well as having a generally more positive outlook. Speckhard *et al.* (2005) argue that being held captive can shake the very world assumptions that an individual makes, causing them to rethink their priorities after and to redefine themselves as individuals. They noted, for example, how one hostage explained that she realised how much she valued her family and friends afterwards, reporting: 'I was 12 when I lost my mother. I have three children ... When I returned home I told everyone how much I love them' (p. 14). This same captive noted how she became less influenced by the views of others after the event, reporting: 'Earlier, before this happened, I was making decisions with others in mind, thinking of how they would react, but now I live for myself. Now, I understand that life is fantastic and I must take care of myself, not fearing what other people think' (p. 14). Ochberg (1980) noted that those captives that responded in positive terms to the event felt an opportunity for mastery, reassessment of values, renegotiation of critical relationships with others and felt a new lease of life.

The potential impact of PTSD has been considered in a variety of life-threatening scenarios. Delahanty (2007) reports that research into the psychological consequences of the terrorist attack on the World Trade Center in New York led to relatively high rates of PTSD in those directly affected; 37 per cent of survivors reported such symptoms. Notably, and as indicated in other research, the reporting of such symptoms rapidly declined. Fifteen per cent of those directly affected and 5 per cent of those not directly affected were likely to have met the criteria for PTSD one month later. This decreased to even lower percentages some six months later (Delahanty, 2007). When applied to population sizes, Delahanty (2007) predicted that 91,000 New Yorkers may have met the diagnostic criteria for PTSD, and 322,000 probably met a sub-threshold of this during the months following the attack. Importantly, Delahanty (2007) notes the remarkable recovery and resiliency of such individuals. This is not to disregard those that struggle to deal with the distress they experience, but to emphasise that individuals can generally show a great resilience and hardiness in their recovery from a traumatic incident. Arguably, if there is more than one individual involved in the trauma, there may be the benefit of support, and their reactions may be more normalised and hence dealt with more effectively. For example, Giebels *et al.* (2005) noted that in situations where there were multiple captives, there could be a sense of social support in that they are 'not alone in this'.

The level and frequency of impact can vary depending upon the circumstances. For example, Saab *et al.* (2003) examined the psychological distress in Lebanese captives of war. They noted that, in their sample of 118 hostages, individuals were detained for an average period of 3.4 years, with 86 per cent being tortured. They noted psychological distress in their sample of 42.1 per cent. This was in comparison to psychological distress in 27.8 per cent of a control group from the same community as the captives but who had not experienced any period of detention. They noted that, even two years after release, more than one-third of the Lebanese captives released from Khiam prison were found to show psychological distress. Importantly, public reaction and social support can be important protective factors against psychological distress, with Allodi (1998) observing a positive impact on the mental health of victims of torture when the public's attitude toward the victim was a positive one and where a network of social support was in place.

In Saab *et al.*'s (2003) study, they noted that the most frequently reported symptoms were a loss of concentration and insomnia, followed by difficulty in enjoying day-to-day activities. There were no gender or age differences in the level of distress, although captives who were married were noted to be more distressed than those who were not. Interestingly they noted that those who were most distressed had fewer years of education (Saab *et al.*, 2003), but an explanation for this finding is less clear.

In exploring different types of captives, Vila *et al.* (1999) conducted an 18-month longitudinal study examining the impact on 26 children (aged 6–9 years) who had been held captive in their school. Specifically, this event took place on the 3 December 1995 when a class of 29 children and their school teacher at a public elementary school in a suburb near Paris, France, were taken and held captive for two hours by a man armed with a gun. The teacher and a number of the children were verbally abused and threatened. It is noted that all captives were fearful of being killed and that the captor appeared to have mental health issues. After negotiation, he was arrested peacefully by the police. Vila *et al.* (1999) noted symptoms of acute stress in 96 per cent of the children directly involved in the event. After two months, 18 of the children developed disorders: seven cases of PTSD and 11 cases of sub-threshold PTSD. There were three cases of separation anxiety, one case of a specific phobia and two cases of major depressive disorder. They further noted that levels of anxiety decreased rapidly over time. Avoidance decreased more gradually, followed by symptoms of intrusion. It was further noted that children who were not directly involved in the event experienced some manifestation of symptoms, with two cases of PTSD and six cases where PTSD was sub-threshold. It was observed that, with such individuals, their symptoms of intrusion did decrease more markedly over time in comparison to those children directly involved in the incident. Interestingly, they noted that psychological debriefings did not prevent the occurrence of symptoms but children who received no debriefings had the worst outcomes (Vila *et al.*, 1999). Moreover, the duration of captivity does not necessarily impact on the psychological symptoms experienced, in that even a short event where children were not directly involved can still lead to the development of PTSD symptoms. Therefore following an event where an individual/s is held captive, one cannot assume that a short event will lead to reduced symptoms, and further, there cannot be the assumption that the only individual affected will be the individual/s held captive.

There has been further detailed research into the potential impact of the captive. Rahe *et al.* (1990) conducted a range of tests on 52 Americans who were held for 444 days in Iran in November 1979. It is important to note the background of this hostage situation. The hostage-taking was felt to be of little surprise to those working at the Embassy, as there had been an earlier attempt in February 1979. In fact, it was felt that the Embassy was unprotected, despite the earlier attempt. Because of this, many of the captives felt being held captive was unnecessary, and could even have been prevented if their government had been more proactive (Rahe *et al.*, 1990). Upon their release, each captive saw a psychiatrist for one to two hours per day, as well as daily group meetings in order to discuss their experiences and to agree on statements that were to be released to the press (Rahe *et al.*, 1990). Psychological testing, including the Minnesota Multiphasic Personality Inventory (MMPI), the 16 Personality Factor Questionnaire (16-PF) (Rahe *et al.*, 1990), as well as measures of stress management abilities, indicated that the captives appeared to have successfully managed their ordeal immediately after their release. This would offer some support to the notion that individuals can be resilient in such events (Jenkins, 1976). Yet the MMPI and 16-PF focus more on personality issues and not necessarily on psychological states. There was also a reliance on self-reporting measures, which the authors note offers no indication as to what the scores may have been prior to captivity and hence no base-rate. In contrast, the plasma, saliva cortisol, urinary catecholamines and saliva testosterone were seen to be highly elevated in these individuals. Such physiological measures seem to indicate distress, anxiety and elation (Rahe *et al.*, 1990). Yet it is not clear if this was a result of being held captive or of being released. Furthermore, 13 Americans had been released some 14 days after being held hostage, and these individuals were returned to their homes quite quickly. Most of these individuals reported to having felt they would have preferred to have stayed two to three days more in hospital 'before facing the stresses of homecoming' (Rahe *et al.*, 1990).

Interestingly, both the military and civilian personnel who had been held for 444 days put their 'best foot forward' in that they emphasised how well they had dealt with the ordeal. Yet, despite their efforts, they demonstrated feelings of resentment and alienation as well as minimising their problems (Rahe *et al.*, 1990). This may suggest that self-report measures of captive psychological well-being may not be reliable.

Following the Moscow theatre siege in 2002, some captives, following their release, noted a range of psychological challenges. One noted difficulty in entering large gatherings as a result of post-traumatic arousal, even four months after the event. Yet this captive identified the value of support in overcoming this by attaching herself to close colleagues in an effort to calm herself. She notes that 'At first it was very difficult for me to go to the auditorium of the Ministry of Health. I went with my chief doctor and took her hand' (Speckhard *et al.*, 2005: 7). Another explained that the intrusive thoughts did not take place until some months after the event, noting that as time progressed, the reality of what had happened was acknowledged. They noted 'the first months [following captivity] were better than now. At first I was so happy to be alive, but now the (intrusive) memories start' (Speckhard *et al.*, 2005: 7). This would certainly fit with Allodi's (1994) observation of the response pattern to a crisis situation, where the individual can initially deny or avoid the recalling of the experience and then move toward acceptance of what took place with aspects of grief and depression present. There was evidence of avoidance, with one captive avoiding public transport for four months after the event, at great consequence to their daily life, which corresponds with the model proposed by Allodi (1994). Other avoidances were more innocuous, with one captive reporting that she felt no longer able to look at chocolate, as it reminded her of her captors giving out chocolates from the snack bar during the siege. She further noted with amusement the support she received from loved ones, reporting: 'The first two weeks lots of people came, and they came to see me in the hospital and they all brought chocolates!' (Speckhard *et al.*, 2005: 7). Arguably, such avoidance and isolation can be helpful in the short term, providing it does not have a negative impact on an individual's life. Speckhard *et al.* (2005) argues that a decision to avoid non-family members can be a result of wishing to avoid voyeurism and their own feeling of inner alienation, with one captive noting 'I feel better sometimes but I feel I must avoid people' (Speckhard *et al.*, 2005: 8). It was also noted that it was not just the captives themselves who had psychological challenges, but also those who had not been taken captive, such as family members, which echoes the work of Vila *et al.* (1999). One captive noted how her son had become hypervigilant following the event, reporting:

> My son is more like me, sensitive. Now my son is always watching me. He doesn't leave me alone and he always wants to know where we are going. He's a big boy but he still sits on his father's lap and says 'Papa I really, really love you'. If we move through our home in the middle of the night, to go to the bathroom for instance, our children wake up and ask, 'How do you feel?'
>
> *(Speckhard* et al., *2005: 9)*

This chapter has offered an overview of the considerations of the captive during and following captivity. The behaviour of a captive may vary and can be dependent not only on the assessment of the risk they perceive in the situation, but also their own values and beliefs. There is a range of considerations for the captive; however, there is no guaranteed manner of engagement to bring a peaceful resolution for them, only suggestions of engagement that have the highest chances of success. Most importantly, captivity can have a range of implications for the captive, some challenging and some even positive, such as the reassessment of their values and life itself. Yet it can also have an impact on those around them, and the potential impact on both the captive and their loved ones cannot be ignored.

References

Allodi, F. A. (1994) 'Post-traumatic stress disorder in hostages and victims of torture', *Psychiatric Clinics of North America*, 17: 279–88.

Booth, B., Vecchi, G. M., Finney, E. J., Van Hasselt, V. B. and Romano, S. J. (2009) 'Captive-taking in the context of workplace violence: descriptive analysis and case examples', *Victims and Offenders*, 4: 76–92.

Booth, B., Vecchi, G. M., Angleman, A. J., Finney, E. J., Marker, C., Romano, S. J. and Van Hasselt, V. B. (2010) 'Captive-taking in the context of domestic violence: a descriptive analysis', *Victims and Offenders*, 5: 183–98.

Daniels, J. A., Royster, T. E. and Vecchi, G. M. (2007) 'Barricaded hostage and crisis situations in schools: a review of recent incidents', Proceedings of Persistently Safe Schools: The 2007 National Conference on Safe Schools. Washington, DC: Hamilton Fish Institute.

De Fabrique, N., Romano, S. J., Vecchi, G. M. and Van Hasselt, V. B. (2007) 'Understanding Stockholm Syndrome', *FBI Law Enforcement Bulletin*, 76 (7): 10–15.

De Fabrique, N., Van Hasselt, V. B., Vecchi, G. M. and Romano, S. J. (2007) 'Common variables associated with the development of Stockholm Syndrome: some case examples', *Victims and Offenders*, 2 (1): 91–98.

Delahanty, D. L. (2007) 'Are we prepared to handle the mental health consequences of terrorism?', *American Journal of Psychiatry*, 164 (2): 189–91.

Dolnik, A. (2004) 'Contrasting dynamics of crisis negotiations: barricade versus kidnapping incidents', *International Negotiation*, 8: 495–526.

Dolnik, A. and Pilch, R. (2003) 'The Moscow theater hostage crisis: the perpetrators, their tactics, and the Russian response', *International Negotiation*, 8 (3): 577–611.

Fletcher, K. (1996) 'The management of released hostages', *Advanced in Psychiatric Treatment*, 2: 232–40.

Fuselier, G. D. (1988) 'Hostage negotiation consultant – emerging role for the clinical psychologist', *Professional Psychology: Research and Practice*, 19 (2): 175–9.

Giebels, E., Noelanders, S. and Vervaeke, G. (2005) 'The hostage experience: implications for negotiation strategies', *Clinical Psychology and Psychotherapy*, 12 (3): 241–53.

Hillman, R. G. (1981) 'The psychopathology of being held hostage', *American Journal of Psychiatry*, 138: 1193–7.

Ireland, C. A. and Vecchi, G. M. (2009) 'The behavioral influence stairway model (BISM): a framework for managing terrorist crisis situations?', *Behavioral Sciences of Terrorism and Political Aggression*, 7 (3): 203–8.

Jenkins, B. M. (1976) *Hostage Survival: Some Preliminary Observations*, Rand Paper Series, Rand Corporation, online at: http://www.rand.org/pubs/papers/P5627/.

Kentsmith, D. K. (1982) 'Hostages and other prisoners of war', *Military Medicine*, 147 (11): 969–72.

Ochberg, P. M. (1980) 'Victims of terrorism', *Journal of Clinical Psychiatry*, 41 (3): 73–4.

Ochberg, P. M. (1983) 'Hostage victims', in B. Eichelman, D. A. Soskis and W. Reid (eds), *Terrorism: Interdisciplinary Perspectives*. Washington, DC: American Psychiatric Association, pp. 83–8.

Rahe, R. H., Karson, S., Howard, N. S., Rubin, T. T. and Poland, R. E. (1990) 'Psychological and physiological assessments on American hostages freed from captivity in Iran', *Psychosomatic Medicine*, 52: 1–16.

Saab, R. B., Chaaya, M., Doumit, M. and Farhood, L. (2003) 'Predictors of psychological distress in Lebanese hostages of war', *Social Science and Medicine*, 57: 1249–57.

Sime, J. (1990) 'Escape behaviour in fires and evacuations', in D. Canter (ed.), *Fires and Human Behaviour* (2nd edn). London: David Fulton.

Speckhard, A., Tarabrina, N., Krasnov, V. and Mufel, N. (2005) 'Posttraumatic and acute stress responses in hostages held by suicide terrorists in the takeover of a Moscow theater', *Traumotology*, 11 (1): 3–21.

Strentz, T. (2006) *Psychological Aspects of Crisis Negotiation*. Boca Raton, FL: CRC Press.

Van der Ploeg, H. M. and Kleijn, W. C. (1989) 'Being held hostage in The Netherlands: a study of long-term after effects', *Journal of Traumatic Stress*, 2: 153–69.

Vecchi, G. M. (2009a) 'Conflict and crisis communication: a methodology for influencing and persuading behavioral change', *Annals of American Psychotherapy*, 12 (1): 34–42.

Vecchi, G. M. (2009b) 'Conflict and crisis communication: the behavioral influence stairway model and suicide intervention', *Annals of American Psychotherapy*, 12 (2): 32–9.

Vecchi, G. M. (2009c) 'Conflict and crisis communication: workplace and school violence, Stockholm Syndrome, and abnormal psychology', *Annals of American Psychotherapy*, 12 (3): 30–9.

Vecchi, G. M. (2009d) 'Conflict and crisis communication: methods of crisis intervention and stress management', *Annals of American Psychotherapy*, 12 (4): 54–63.

Vecchi, G. M. (2009e) 'Critical incident response, management, and resolution: structure and interaction in barricaded hostage, barricaded crisis, and kidnapping situations', *Inside Homeland Security*, 7 (2): 7–16.

Vecchi, G. M., Van Hasselt, V. B. and Romano, S. J. (2005) 'Crisis (hostage) negotiation: current strategies and issues in high-conflict resolution', *Aggression and Violent Behavior*, 70: 533–51.

Vila, G., Porche, L. M and Mouren-Simeoni, M. C. (1999) 'An 18-month longitudinal study of posttraumatic disorders in children who were taken hostage in their school', *Psychosomatic Medicine*, 61: 746–54.

Wells, T. (ed.) (1985) *444 Days: The Hostages Remember*. San Diego, CA: Harcourt Brace Jovanovich.

Whyte, P. D. (2005) 'Negotiation and Hostage Taking: The 1996 Japanese Experience in Lima, Peru'. Unpublished paper, Faculty of Law, University of British Columbia. Online at: http://cfcj-fcjc.org/clearinghouse/drpapers/2005-dra/whyte.pdf.

Wilson, M. A. (2003) 'Hostage behaviour in aircraft hijacking: a script-based analysis of resistance strategies', in R. Bor (ed.), *Passenger Behaviour*. Aldershot: Ashgate.

Wilson, M. A. and Smith, A. (1999) 'Roles and rules in terrorist hostage taking', in D. Canter and L. Alison (eds), *The Social Psychology of Crime: Groups, Teams, and Networks*. Aldershot: Dartmouth.

Wood, P. G. (1990) 'Survey of behaviour in fires', in D. Canter (ed.), *Fires and Human Behaviour* (2nd edn). London: David Fulton.

Note: The views expressed in this chapter do not necessarily represent the views of the FBI.

INDEX

Added to a page number 'f' denotes a figure, 't' denotes a table and 'n' denotes a note.